Hiking Lysefjord and Beyond:
day trips in the Stavanger Region

Ute Koninx and Rosslyn Nicholson

Copyright © 2016, 2020, 2023 by Ute Koninx and Rosslyn Nicholson

All photos and illustrations © by Ute Koninx and Rosslyn Nicholson
Map data: Kartverket, Geovekst and kommunes

ISBN: 978-1-8380218-1-8

First published in 2016 as "From Beaches to Mountains: 38 walks and hikes in the Stavanger Region".

Second edition (with new title and additional hikes): May 2023
Second printing, with minor updates and corrections, September 2023

All rights reserved. No part of this publication may be reproduced in any form, or by any means electronic, mechanical, recording, or otherwise, without written permission from the authors, except for brief quotations used in reviews.
This book is sold subject to the condition that it shall not, by way of trade or otherwise, be lent, resold, hired out or otherwise circulated without the authors' prior consent in any form of binding, or cover other than that in which it is published and without a similar condition, including this condition, being imposed on the subsequent purchaser.

Disclaimer: Although effort has been made to ensure that the information in this book is correct at the time of publishing, the authors make no warranty about accuracy of its content and cannot accept responsibility for any consequences arising from the use of this book. You are responsible for your own safety while hiking or otherwise enjoying the outdoors. Just because a trail is described in this book, it does not mean that it will necessarily be safe for you. Be aware that trail conditions may change over time and according to the weather, and make allowances for the limits of your party.

Foreword

With stunning scenery, magical light, and easy access, the Western Fjords of Norway are a magnet for outdoor enthusiasts. Here, within a small area, you will find a kaleidoscope of nature's drama and beauty. Rough mountains, deep-cut fjords, delightful islands and windswept coasts can all be experienced on a day's adventure.

Some of Norway's most iconic hikes are located on Stavanger's doorstep, but there are many, many less well-known but equally wonderful walks, hikes, and treks in the area. Norwegian culture and heritage incorporates this marvellous resource: here it is normal to go for a walk every day (or perhaps more often than that). The STF (Stavanger Hiking/Trekking Association) maintains an extensive network of trails and cabins in Rogaland county. Combine this with easy access by means of an international airport, and excellent ferry, road and rail connections, and it becomes natural that visitors are discovering the region.

We are very pleased to present this significantly expanded and newly revised edition of our English language hiking guide to the Lysefjord and Stavanger Region. We have updated the directions and hiking information throughout the book, and included new exciting hikes and walks in all of the chapters. We have also introduced a section dedicated to the amazing Lysefjord, allowing the hiker to explore many more hikes around this iconic fjord. We are particularly pleased that more hikes are now accessible by public transport. Invariably, a couple of other hikes are no longer featured, as we feel that they no longer meet our expectations due to recent building activity or other changes.

We hope to entice those that came to the Western Fjords to explore the world-famous hikes to discover that there is so much more here! We hope those new to the Stavanger Region or new to hiking feel equipped to start exploring this fantastic region on foot and find out for themselves why hiking is such a big part of Norwegian culture. There is no better way to feel like a local!

The hikes we present are suitable for many, be it a family wanting to go on an adventure, a group of friends exploring or just you and your daypack. Equally they can be as easy or as challenging as you wish. We believe there is something for everybody here.

Happy Hiking!

Ute Koninx and Rosslyn Nicholson, April 2023

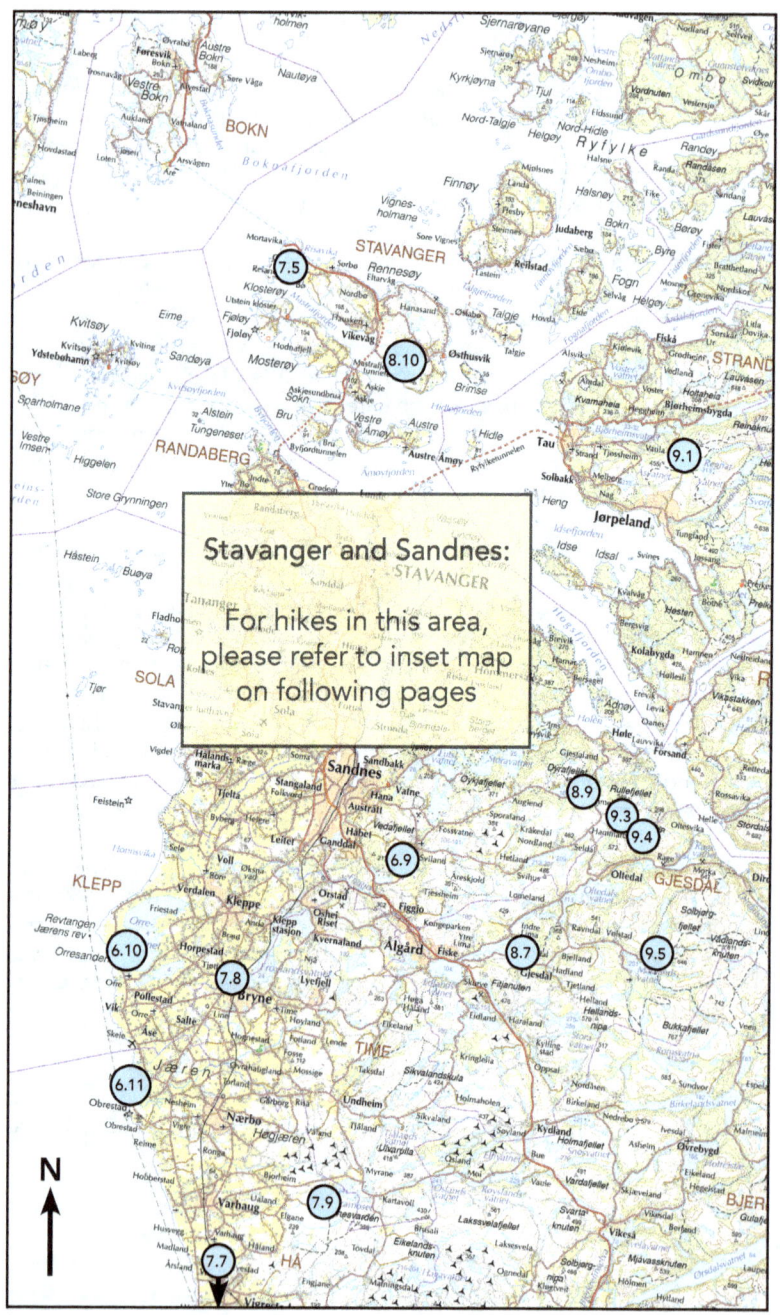

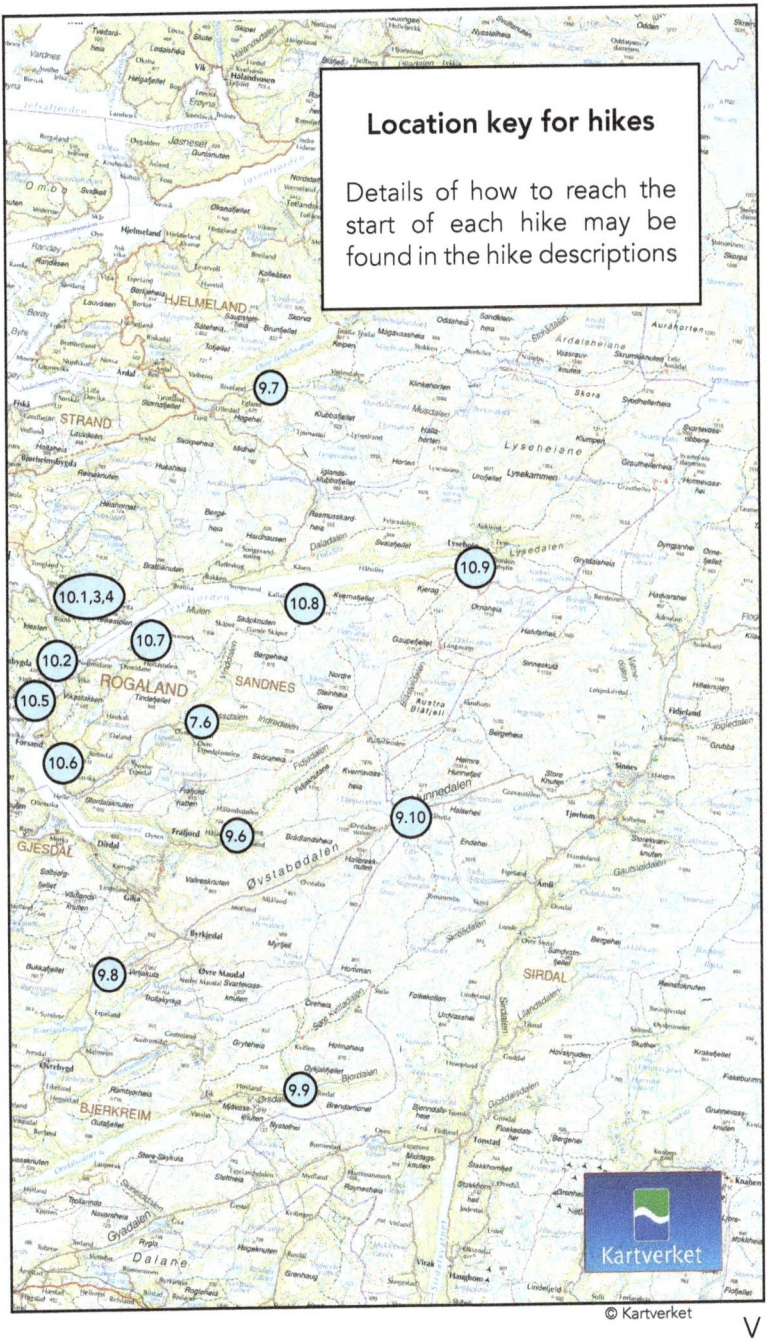

Location key for hikes

Details of how to reach the start of each hike may be found in the hike descriptions

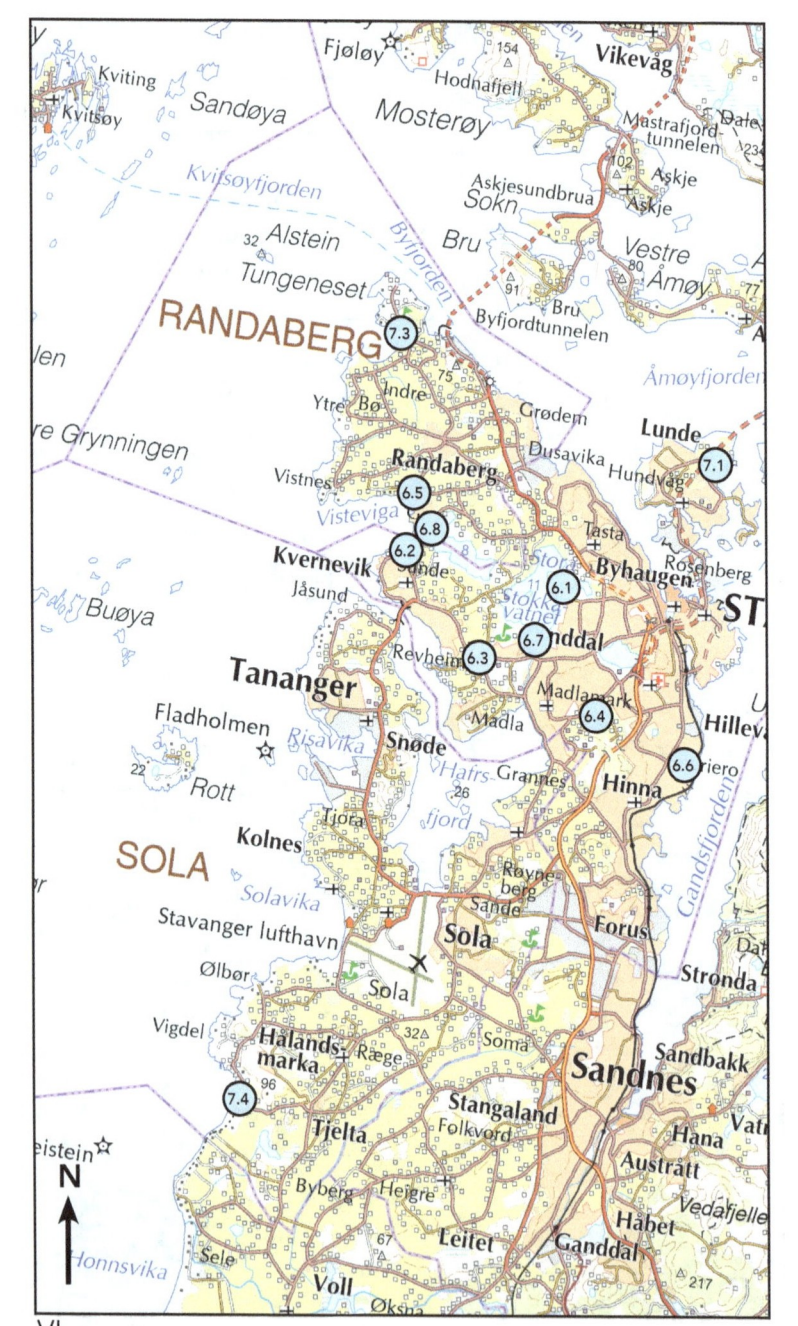

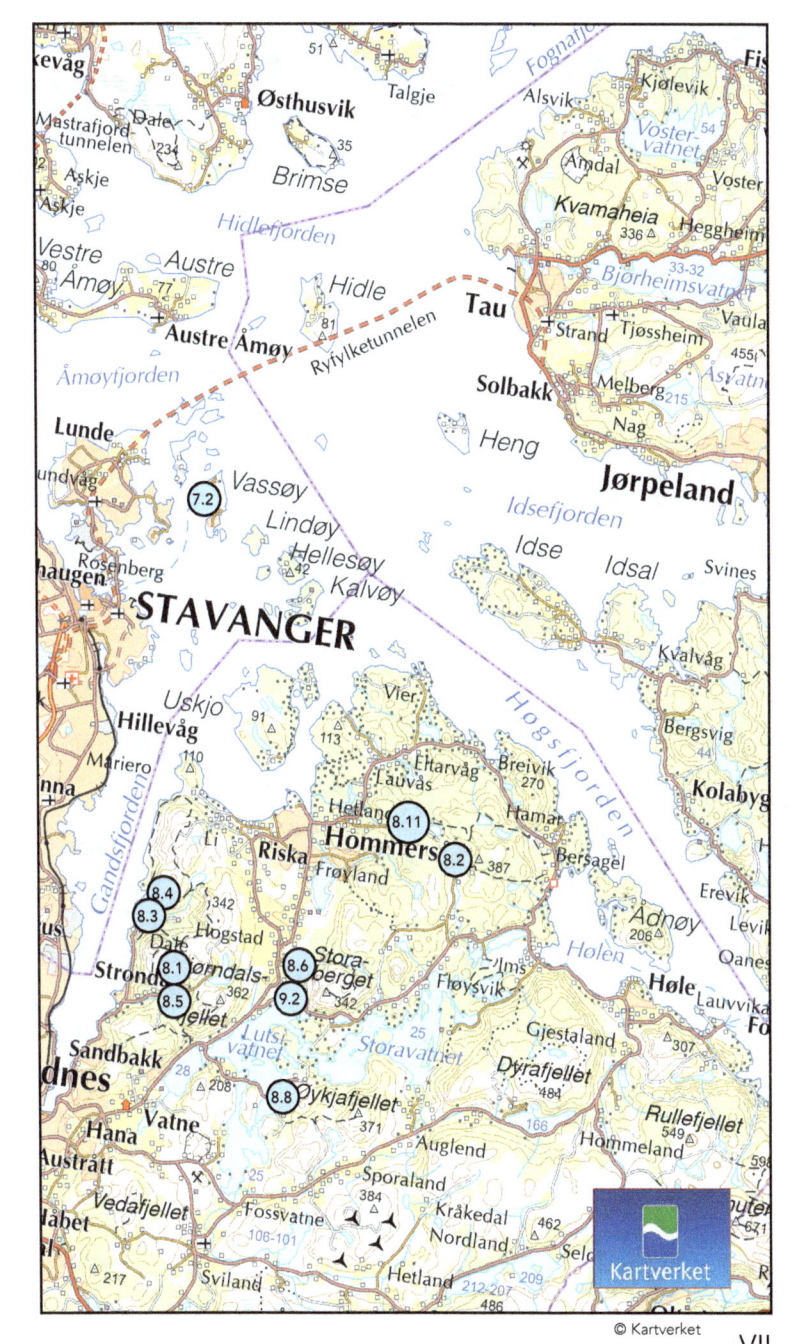

Contents

Introduction..1
Chapter 1: Making the Most of the Weather in Rogaland 3
Chapter 2: Finding the Way (GPS Not Necessary) 11
Chapter 3: Equipment Matters 29
Chapter 4: Easy Ways to Eat Well on the Trail 39
Chapter 5: Enticing Reluctant Kids, Teenagers (and possibly dogs) 47
Chapter 6: Urban Fresh Air and Sunday Waffles 53
    Hike 6.1:   Lille Stokkavatn and Byhaug Cafe 55
    Hike 6.2:   The Kvernevik Coast 59
    Hike 6.3:   Madlasandnes...63
    Hike 6.4:   Sørmarka and Ullandhaug Tarn 67
    Hike 6.5:   The Viste Coastline 71
    Hike 6.6:   Mariero to Jåttå...75
    Hike 6.7:   Store Stokkavatn 79
    Hike 6.8:   Hålandsvatnet..83
    Hike 6.9:   The Arboretum and Steinfjellet 87
    Hike 6.10: Orre Friluftshuset and Beach 91
    Hike 6.11: Hå Gamle Prestegard to Obrestad Havn 95
Chapter 7: Shorter Hikes, Stunning Scenery 99
    Hike 7.1:   The Lundesnes Tour 101
    Hike 7.2:   Around Vassøy 105
    Hike 7.3:   The Tungenes Peninsula...109
    Hike 7.4:   Hellestø...113
    Hike 7.5:   Reianes 117
    Hike 7.6:   Røssdalen 121
    Hike 7.7:   Ogna to Brusand 123
    Hike 7.8:   Frøylandsvatnet... 127
    Hike 7.9:   Synesvarden.. 131
Chapter 8: The Way to the Top: Local Hills and Fantastic Views 135
    Hike 8.1:   Dalsnuten 137
    Hike 8.2:   Vårlivarden 141
    Hike 8.3:   Skjørestadfjellet and Resasteinen 145
    Hike 8.4:   Lifjell 149
    Hike 8.5:   Bjørndalsfjellet 153
    Hike 8.6:   Storaberget 157
    Hike 8.7:   Eikefjellet 161
    Hike 8.8:   Øykjafjellet 165
    Hike 8.9:   Undeknuten 169
    Hike 8.10: Rennesøy Hodet... 173
    Hike 8.11: Vårlivarden (longer route)..................................... 177

Chapter 9: Longer Days and Overnight Adventures.......................... 181
- Hike 9.1: Reinaknuten..183
- Hike 9.2: Storaberget (longer route)...187
- Hike 9.3: Bynuten..191
- Hike 9.4: Selvigstakken..195
- Hike 9.5: Vådlandsknuten 199
- Hike 9.6: Månafossen and Månedalen................................. 203
- Hike 9.7: Viglesdalen...207
- Hike 9.8: Vinjakula...211
- Hike 9.9: Kvitlen..215
- Hike 9.10: Tomannsbu..219

Chapter 10: Around the Lysefjord 223
- Hike 10.1: Preikestolen..225
- Hike 10.2: Fantapytten..229
- Hike 10.3: Moslifjellet...233
- Hike 10.4: Gryteknuten...237
- Hike 10.5: Sokkaknuten..241
- Hike 10.6: Uburen...245
- Hike 10.7: Sollifjellet...249
- Hike 10.8: The Flørli Steps 253
- Hike 10.9: Kjerag 257

Appendix: Useful Resources 261
About the Authors 269
Acknowledgements 269

Introduction
How to use this book

Since you have picked up this guidebook in English, the chances are that you are either a visitor to the region or have moved here for reasons of study, work or family and don't (yet) feel comfortable enough in your Norwegian language skills to navigate the hiking landscape by yourself. Or maybe you have hiked the 'famous' hikes and are now looking for less busy places that offer a true taste of what this accessible wilderness has to offer.

The book is intended as a 'how to' and 'where to' guide. The first five chapters are dedicated to the 'how to' of enjoying hiking in this particular part of the world. Whether you are new to hiking or have many years of experience of hiking elsewhere, there is important information here. Local weather considerations, information on how to find the way and obtain adequate maps as well as equipment matters are covered. Additionally, we provide ideas for eating well on the trail and ways to entice children, teenagers, and others to join in.

The second part of the book is devoted to presenting 50 hikes in detail. They have been chosen from among the many because each offers something special. For every hike, there are directions to the start or parking area, a summary of important information, a sketch map, a detailed description of the hike including navigation tips, and any other highlights not to be missed. The hikes have been grouped according to length, height climbed and general difficulty. Chapter 6 showcases the urban walks on the doorstep, many with Sunday afternoon "waffle cafes". Shorter walks are the subject of Chapter 7: here nature can be enjoyed without hiking very far. Chapter 8 introduces local hills: some much loved by visitors and some lesser known, but all with stunning views and exhilarating trails. Chapter 9 suggests ideas for longer hikes and overnight adventures. These are experiences for when you have broken in your boots and are ready to explore! Chapter 10 is dedicated to hikes around the wonderful Lysefjord: here you will find some of everything. There are shorter walks, tops that provide vantage points to view Lysefjord and its surroundings, and longer adventures around the fjord.

Finally, for those who, after these experiences, wish for more, the Appendix provides resources for taking your hiking passion further. In the famous quote of John Muir, "[...] find out going to the mountains is going home; that wildness is a necessity".

Chapter 1: Making the Most of the Weather in Rogaland

The weather in Rogaland is rarely still. It shifts through the seasons and from day to day: sometimes sun, sometimes rain and often something in the middle. Cooler northerly winds swing around to warmer southerly winds; morning mist can disappear by noon. Learn a little about the local climate, and this will help you to choose a walk that lets you appreciate the beauty of the region, whatever the weather brings.

The Climate in Rogaland
Rogaland straddles two climatic zones. The dominant climate, around Stavanger and the areas near the sea, is oceanic and mild. Influenced by the warm Atlantic Gulf Stream, winters aren't as cold as might be expected this far north. Summer temperatures remain cool and pleasant, often with sea breezes.

Further inland, towards the mountains, the climate shifts a little, towards a humid, mid, continental climate. We see this difference most in the winter.

During the months of January, February, March and partly through April, the mountains become a playground for snow sports. Hiking is not possible due to the snow, but both cross-country skiing and snowshoeing are options instead. The coastal areas do expect a little snow each winter, but it tends to last only a few days. So, even when the higher mountains are inaccessible for hikers, the lower areas are not: with the exception of only a handful of days each year, Stavanger is a year-round hiking destination. The weather conditions and the clothes you will need to stay comfortable do change through the year though!

Temperature and Rainfall
The average temperature in Stavanger varies between a low of -1 and a high of 3°C in January and February, the coldest months, and between 12-18°C in July and August, the warmest months. Expect temperatures

to be a few degrees colder than this up in the mountains.
Although Rogaland doesn't enjoy the legendary rainfall of Bergen to the north, hikers can expect to experience some rain in any month of the year. With an average annual precipitation of 1180mm and an average of 214 days of the year with some rain, Stavanger is more than occasionally wet! The driest months are April and May, whilst the wettest tend to be in the autumn, when storms roll in from the west. Sunshine mirrors the length of day in the area: the highest average sun per day coincides with the longest days in June, with the reverse happening in December. When it's neither raining nor bright sunshine, there are still many possibilities that will have you reaching for your camera: mist, hazy sun, and rainbows are barely a few of them. Each of the four distinct seasons offers its own opportunities for hiking and enjoying the outdoors.

The seasons in Rogaland

The year begins in January. Near the coast, frost alternates with milder weather and there may be some snow. This snow is usually "wet" snow, which sticks together well and makes excellent snowballs and snowmen.

The snow rarely stays for more than a few days: milder weather generally comes in, giving overnight freeze/thaw cycles that result in icy patches on footpaths during the day. In the hills, the snow usually stays and the skiing season begins. This is a great time to explore the hikes around Stavanger and in the Jaeren region. Shorter days mean low level sun and beautiful light that isn't seen at other times of the year.

As the days lengthen into March and April, the frost disappears from the hills closest to Stavanger. From these hills are views to the east of the higher mountains still clad in snow. In the more sheltered forests and valleys, the spring flowers bloom. Watch out for wood anemone, snowdrops and violets alongside the buds on the trees. An Easter tradition is to collect a sprig of catkins to bring inside in celebration of spring.

The snow begins to melt from the higher hills later in the spring. By late June, many of the trails in the mountains are usually clear of snow, and become accessible to hikers. With the long days, July and August are the perfect time for longer expeditions. Follow in the footsteps of ancient farmers over the high mountain passes or visit one of the many cabins in the area.

Shorter hikes can be enjoyed in the evenings or early mornings, and on clear days the views from the tops are always spectacular. Summertime is also the berry-picking season. Look for blueberries (blåbaer) everywhere in the forest, raspberries (bringebaer), and many others, some native only to Scandinavia.

In September, the days become noticeably shorter, and October usually brings the first frost of the year. With the higher tops still clear of snow, a nice autumn day can be an opportunity for a spectacular hike through autumn colours to a hilltop viewpoint. Abundant birch and rowan trees give beautiful oranges and yellows in the forests and along the town trails. Even on a stormy day, it can be fun to kick through fallen leaves and hunt for mushrooms. Towards Christmas, you may meet people in the woods collecting pine cones and fallen branches. These are for Christmas decorations and a fun way to enjoy a hike even when it's a little cold.

In-between the seasons in the higher hills

Both the beginning and the end of the summer season have special considerations to watch out for. High in the mountains, the snow may take several weeks to melt in the spring. Locals consider April still to be a part of the ski season, and during May and early June, the snow is slowly melting from the mountain tops. At this time of year, hiking the high routes is hampered by both the remaining snow and ice, and the fact that some roads are not yet open. In a heavy snow year, the last of the snow may not finally disappear until mid-July.

At the end of the summer, the new snow may not yet have arrived, but overnight frosts can lead to patches of ice in shady places on the trail. By the end of September and into October, the days are much shorter than in the summer, so it's important to carry a head torch on longer hikes, just in case progress is slower than expected and you find yourself returning to the end of the hike in the dusk!

Which hike for which weather?

Every season offers a variety of weather: you will never be bored here! Hiking on a stormy day can be exhilarating, if you choose the right hike. As a rule, on wetter and windier days, stay on the lower level hikes and be sure to dress appropriately.

If it's really wet, the shelter of a forest beckons, whilst drizzle and mist can be lovely in valleys. One exception to this rule: the Jaeren coast faces out to the North Sea. When the wind is westerly, the hiking trails can be very exposed to the wind and, in some places, waves may even splash on to the trail. If you aren't inclined to seek this excitement, choose the east-facing shores or inland walks on these days, and enjoy the hikes on Kongevegen on a calm day or when the wind is coming from another direction.

When it's cloudy, hiking can be nice just about anywhere. Free of sunscreen worries, you can hike all day as it's unlikely to get uncomfortably hot either. If the cloud is low, be careful of entering the cloud unless you are confident with a map and compass as finding the way can be tricky in low visibility. If you are new to navigation, it's best to stay below the cloud until you've had a little practice.

The clear, sunny days are the days to watch and wait for. They can happen at any time of year, but are most frequent in May and June. On a good day, the Jaeren beaches can rival any in southern Europe and the hills can rival any in the world. Sometimes, an area of high pressure can sit over Scandinavia, giving several days of clear, sunny weather in a row. This gives time to plan and organise an extraordinary expedition. At other times, the nice weather comes at short notice and doesn't stay for more than a day. These are the days to drop everything and go! The reward comes in happy hikes and great memories.

Don't be scared to take an opportunity to hike whenever the weather gives you one. If you are able to store your hiking gear "ready to go", you can be off very quickly!

Where to find the weather forecast

The weather in this part of the world is notoriously unpredictable. There are several sources of forecasts: our favourites are www.yr.no and windy.com. Both offer remarkably accurate forecasts given the complexity of the weather patterns in the area. Windy.com gives all sorts of data as

well as the weather forecast, including things like sea temperature, wind patterns, and sea swell. The abundance of data makes for complicated screens, but is worth learning to navigate, and fascinating.

In general, the "long-term" forecasts will change as the day approaches. This is because weather fronts can arrive faster or more slowly than initially predicted, or sometimes even not at all if another pressure system "blocks" them from arriving in Scandinavia. Luckily, both of these weather forecasting services are very accessible via the internet and/or the app, allowing for frequent checking very easily!

Severe weather warnings

For generations, Norwegians have thrived in a country that is often inhospitable. They are experts at coping with difficult weather conditions, so when they say that severe weather is coming, take heed! The "severe weather warning" is called an "advarsel", and appears at the top of the screen in the weather forecast, denoted by a triangle caution sign. Expect to see a warning if:

- icy/slippery conditions on roads are expected
- winter storms are expected, which will make driving conditions potentially dangerous
- severe winds are expected (such that you should check boats on their moorings and items in your garden)
- there is significant flood risk
- any other adverse weather is expected

The adverse weather warnings will always give details of the area(s) affected, and for how long the adverse conditions are expected to last. Ignore them at your peril! Often the adverse weather will be in the mountains and, closer to the Stavanger conurbation, some hiking will be possible. Occasionally only coastal areas are affected, particularly if storms are coming in from the North Sea.

A little local temperature variation

If you've ever moved from a sunny place to a shady one and found yourself shivering, you'll know that the temperature outside changes according to where you are: shade, direct sun, local drafts and whether you are next to water all play a part.

It's essential to check the weather forecast before you set out on a hike, and, when you do, you'll see the forecast temperature. The weather forecast channels offer forecasts for many places in Rogaland: you'll be able to find forecasts for places such as Tau, Jørpeland, Lysebotn and others near to where you plan to hike. A word of caution: many of these places are at sea level, whereas many of the hikes will take you high into the mountains.

*Temperature decreases as you climb in **all** conditions!*

At sea level, where it is warmest, our hiker wears a T-shirt and shorts Higher on the hill, it is a little cooler, and our hiker puts on a fleece and long trousers. At the top of the mountain, our hiker wears a jacket, hat and mittens to stay warm.

> **If all else is equal, then as a general rule:**
>
> *If there is no rain or snow and you aren't in a cloud, assume that the temperature will decrease by about 5 degrees centigrade for every 500 metres you climb.*
> *If there is rain, snow or you are in cloud, assume that the temperature will decrease by approx. 3 degrees centigrade for every 500 metres you climb.*

The key to staying comfortable while the temperature varies is to dress in layers that can be removed and put back on: Chapter 3 shows you how to do this!

Inversions: the one exception to this rule. Cold air is more dense than warm air, and sometimes when it is very still, a mass of cold air will sink into a valley. The temperature in the valley then becomes colder than that higher up. Often there will also be mist in the valley, which looks beautiful when seen from above as you are hiking. In Rogaland inversions can happen at any time of year, but particularly during calm spells in autumn and winter.

A word about Wind

Epic tales of Arctic exploration and winter adventures often mention the "wind chill" factor. As wind blows across skin, it draws heat away from the body and cools you down. In other words, your skin feels colder than it should for the air temperature. There are formulas for calculating the temperature that you effectively experience by taking into account the air temperature and the wind speed. This is how weather forecasters try to give an idea of how the outside will feel taking the "wind chill" factor into account.

These formulas assume that there is no sun (i.e. it's dark), and you are walking directly into the wind at a speed of around 3 miles per hour. In Rogaland that's not very realistic, but it's still crucial to recognise the difference wind will make.

A "moderate breeze" of 5-6 metres per second will feel much colder as you hike, even if you are only exposed to it for a short stretch. As you go higher up, the wind often increases. A "fresh breeze" at sea level often turns into a gale in the mountains. Beware of gusts, which can reach high speeds on the hilltops and leave you feeling cold and uncomfortable if you are wearing the wrong clothes. Some weather forecasts will include the phrase "with gusts of up to.......metres per second". Take this seriously, and choose a lower level hike if you aren't sure!

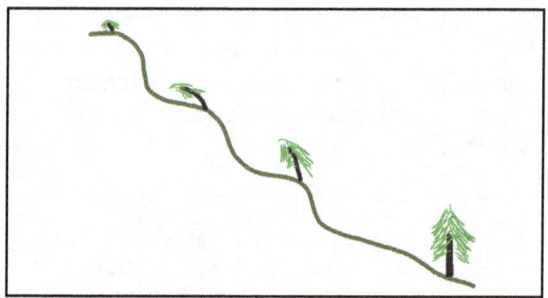

The mountains will still be there another day!
Sometimes a hike doesn't go to plan: you forget the food or the raincoat, you didn't realise how rough the trail would be, or the weather deteriorates rapidly despite a decent forecast. Determination to finish a hike is usually a good thing, but not if it comes at the expense of safety. If you ever feel that you aren't prepared for the conditions you are in, or a member of your party is severely uncomfortable, injured or becoming sick, take a "safety moment" and turn back. The hike will be there next time, when the conditions are better or you are better prepared. Don't let a fun hike become a survival epic just because you weren't inclined to change your plans!

Chapter 2: Finding the Way
(GPS Not Necessary)

This chapter is about navigating without 21st century aids. GPS systems and internet maps don't always help in the hills, and there will always be a day when the batteries are dead and/or the phone is out of range. Since the start of the hike is the first thing that must be found, the chapter begins with towns, counties, and the road, rail and ferry network in this region. Then some basic route-finding techniques are discussed. Finding the way on a hike in Norway is easier than in many other parts of the world, thanks to the local tradition of marking the trails.

The layout of the region

Norway is divided into regions, called Fylkes (Counties), which are subdivided into Kommunes. Each Kommune has its own local authority, but of course cooperation is common. Rogaland Fylke is located in the southwest of Norway. The area includes several fjords, some of which reach far inland. The longest, and most loved, is Lysefjord, which is 42km long, but there are several others nearly as long and no less scenic. The largest towns in Rogaland are located on the coast, with Haugesund at the far north and Egersund near the south of the area. Between these towns, the area around Stavanger and Sandnes forms the largest conurbation in Rogaland and the third largest in Norway. Stavanger is located on a peninsula, which is separated from the mountainous area to the east by Gandsfjord and Høgsfjord.

Rogaland county is located in the southwest of Norway.
The county is divided into 26 kommunes, from Sauda in the north to Sokndal in the south. The hikes in this guide are in Hjelmeland, Randaberg, Stavanger, Strand, Sandnes, Sola, Klepp, Hå, Bjerkreim, and Gjesdal.

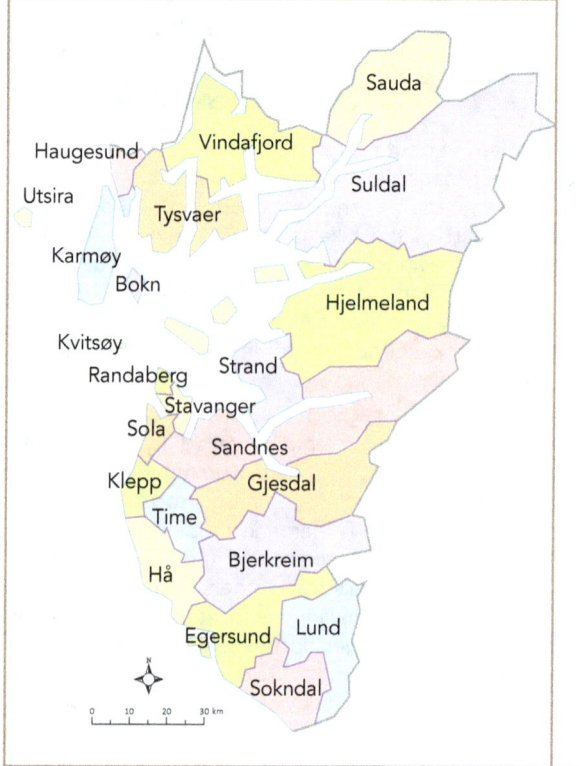

© Kartverket

To the north and east of Stavanger is an area of sea, within which there are many islands. The largest of these are connected to the mainland via bridges, tunnels or ferries, and several of the hikes in this guide explore them.

The area is well served by roads, with the E39 running north and south from Stavanger, and the RV13 heading from the island of Hundvåg through tunnels to Tau, and from there to the mountains in the east. Further to the south, at Ålgård, the Fv450 leaves the E39 and goes eastwards towards the mountain valley of Sirdal. The easiest way to

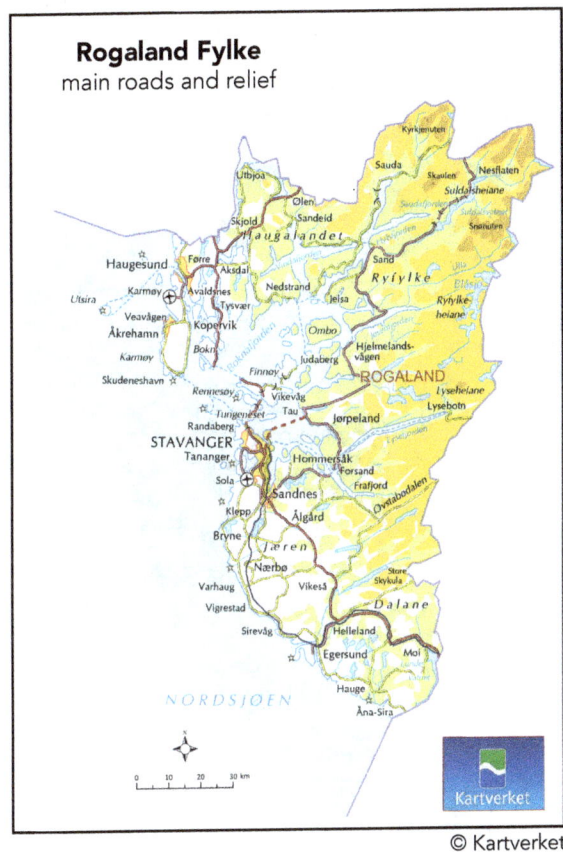

© Kartverket

meet the RV13 from Stavanger is to take the Hundvåg and Ryfylke tunnels to Solbakk and Tau.

The bompenger system

Norway has a system of road tolls, which are collected at bompenger stations. "bompenger" translates literally as "gate money". Many of the bompenger stations are currently located at boundaries between Kommunes (municipalities), but there are plans to add more in other locations. If you are driving a rental car, ask about the arrangements for bompenger. If you are driving a car that is not registered, no cross is displayed as you drive through a toll station, and a picture of your car registration is taken. If you do nothing, a bill will automatically be sent to the registered owner of the vehicle, even if they are a foreigner. Alternatively, you can register a credit card at www.autopass.no and follow the instructions on the site; this is worth doing in advance in order to pay the correct rate, since the default rate (if your car is not pre-registered) is always the most expensive.

The bus system

The local buses are run by Kolumbus. Timetables and fare information are available on their website, www.kolumbus.no, and through the Kolumbus apps (search for "Kolumbus Sanntid" and "Kolumbus Billett"). At the time of writing, the buses do accept payment in cash if you don't have the app or a bus pass, and a heavy supplement is applied (approx. 20 NOK per fare). Even if you are only planning to use the buses for a week, it's worth dropping by the bus station in the centre of Stavanger or Sandnes to purchase a bus pass, or downloading and using the mobile phone app for payment. It is possible to register a foreign bank card on the app for payment.

There are also coaches to the start of one or two very popular hikes, particularly Preikestolen. These run during the summer tourist season, and in winter are replaced by buses to the ski areas in Sirdal and Røldal. Hikes that are accessible via buses are denoted with a bus symbol in the guide.

The local ferries and tunnels

There are three kinds of ferry in the area: car ferries, where you drive your car on the ferry, but pedestrians and cyclists are very welcome, passenger-only ferries, and tourist cruise boats.

The car ferries were a local institution, but are being replaced slowly by bridges and tunnels, such as the Hundvåg and Ryfylke tunnels across the fjords to the eastern parts of Rogaland and Ryfylke. There are also fast passenger-only ferries that are operated as part of the bus system. They mainly link Stavanger to the surrounding islands. Timetables are available at www.kolumbus.no, and also in the ferry terminal building in the centre of Stavanger. Bus passes may be used on these ferries. Walk number 7.2 (Around Vassøy) is the only walk in this book that can only be accessed via ferry. The local tourist boats can sometimes be used as a ferry service as well, such as to access the Flørli steps (hike 10.8).

The local trains

There is one train line in the region, which begins in the centre of Stavanger, heads south to the town of Egersund, and from there to Kristiansand and, finally, Oslo. The trains are a mixture of local commuter trains that run between Stavanger, Sandnes, and further to Egersund, and the express trains going further south. Hikes in this book that can be accessed from the train line are noted with a train symbol.

Hikes accessible by tours

Some companies offer dedicated transport to and from particular hikes, with or without tour guides. Most of these are in the Preikestolen and Lysefjord areas. For details, check with the companies listed in the "Useful Resources" section of this book. Of particular interest may be the Preikestolen BaseCamp area, which is accessible via a fjord cruise and bus tour. The Tourist Office offers information on these, and an internet search will also yield information.

The hike grading system in Norway

In Norway, hikes are graded according to a colour system. This system will be followed in the guide. The levels are:

Green hikes

These are easy hikes with no special skills required. They are mostly short, at less than 5 km, and have not more than 300m of height gain (climb). They are on tarmac, gravel or other paths that are easy to walk along and receive maintenance. The paths are firm and free from obstructions, with no streams to cross, other than by bridge. Although there may be some ascent (climbing), the climbs are not steep or difficult.

Blue hikes

These are hikes of medium difficulty. They are suitable for beginners, people with average fitness and require only basic skills. They are mostly between 5 and 10 km in length, with a height gain of not more than 600m. The types of path are mostly similar to green hikes, although there may be some more challenging sections, e.g. some stretches of the path might be rocky, but there is no demanding scree. Most of the ascents are moderate, but there might be one or two steep sections, possibly with certain sections that some might consider precipitous.

Red hikes

These are challenging hikes. They are suitable for experienced hikers with good stamina. Good hiking boots and other equipment is necessary. They are up to 20km in length, with a height gain of up to 1000m. They can traverse paths, marsh, rocky sections and may cross up to two streams. They could include several steep ascents and/or challenging sections that may require some scrambling. There may be precipitous and/or exposed sections.

Black hikes
These are expert hikes. They are suitable for experienced hikers with good stamina and knowledge of how to use a map and compass. Good hiking and other equipment are required. In Norway, this designation is used mostly for serious ascents on steep routes with uneven paths. There are no limits to length or height gain. There may be a number of streams to be crossed, as well as steep, exposed sections of the trail such as scree or narrow ridges where scrambling is required. No black hikes are included in this book.

Trails in Norway
Given the vast number of hiking trails in Norway, it is reasonable to expect a great deal of variation in the conditions underfoot. Urban trails tend to be well-maintained gravel paths, and the most popular of these will be floodlit during the dark winter months. Away from the towns, in the mountains and forests, the word "trail" takes on a slightly different meaning. Hugely popular trails, such as the trail up Preikestolen (Hike 10.1), have had extensive work carried out on them to minimise erosion. Walkways have been placed across fragile bogs, and stone steps have been built into the steeper sections by Sherpas hired in from Nepal. This is the exception rather than the rule! Most of the mountain trails receive little or no maintenance, as they are relatively infrequently used. Bridges are *usually* safe and well cared for, but in many places, "trail" means a marked route through a bog or across an area of exposed rock. Expect some uneven ground, and enjoy the hopping and occasional scrambling!

The trail marking system in Norway

The local network of trails is generally very well marked via the volunteer efforts of willing hikers, and local Kommunes. Almost all of the regularly used trails are marked. Sometimes you may have to search for a marker, but they have been laid by hikers for hikers and will usually show the way. In addition, trail junctions in the popular areas are marked with signposts giving the direction of each trail. A word of caution to those who are red/green colour blind though: it may be difficult to see red markers against the gray rock!

Cairns are a very useful in seeing where the trail goes, especially higher in the mountains where the path is not easy to trace along rock and/or in poor visibility. Know though, that local children build sand castles on the beach, and rock cairns in the mountains. It is possible to spot popular lunch spots by the large number of small cairns in the vicinity! If you see a cairn, especially a little one, that does not also have a trail marker, such as a red T, on it, then it may or may not be a trail marker.

Maps for hiking in Norway

Even though the trails are well marked, it's still necessary to take a good map on every trip. **The sketch maps in this book are included as a general guide only, and are NOT intended to be used for navigation.** It's very easy to stray away from a trail, or find yourself on the wrong one. Many a hiker has followed a marked trail for several kilometres, only to discover that it was not the trail they thought they were on! The map is needed to check that the trail is the correct one, or to relocate and find the way back if lost.

There are traditional maps of hiking areas in circulation, at 1:50,000 scale. They are easily recognised by their red covers and the title "Norge 1:50,000" on the cover. The map on the front cover also shows, via a dark square, which area of Norway the map covers. In autumn 2015, the Norwegian Kartverket stopped producing these printed maps. It is now possible to obtain maps printed on demand at licensed retailers. A list of them, both within Norway and international, may be found on their website: www.kartverket.no.

If you are prepared to find a friendly translator or know a little Norwegian, the site www.norgeskart.no provides free downloads of maps from any part of Norway for printing at home at a scale of 1:25,000, which is ideal for hiking. The website is designed with the needs of outdoor enthusiasts in mind, and you can select maps with hiking, cycling and other leisure features included. The maps use the Norwegian Kartverket (government) database, which is continually updated, and at the time of writing, the maps are of excellent quality when printed on a decent home printer.

Some of the shorter, urban hikes in this guide are also part of the "Stavanger 52 Tur" program. They are in the built-up areas where a more detailed map is very useful. There are excellent maps available for download and home printing on the Stavanger Kommune website: http://www.stavanger.kommune.no/52. There are "52 Tur" maps available for hikes 6.7 (Store Stokkavatn), 7.1 (The Lundesnes Tour) and 7.2 (Around Vassøy).

It's important to have your map out of your pocket or rucksack, so that you can glance at it often as you walk. A ziplock bag or waterproof map carrier with a transparent window to read the map through is very useful.

Navigation basics

When hiking in the hills, always know where you are!

Yes, you can just follow the trail markers, especially on the hikes where there are not many other trails nearby. But, if you have an idea how far you've come, how far you have to go and whether there are any shortcuts back to transport home, you'll be far more in control of your trip. You'll be able to time the breaks and snacks, answer the "are we nearly there yet" question and of course return the quickest way if you need to.

Always take a map and compass

A map gives you an overview of the terrain, or the hills, valleys, rivers, and trails that you'll be traversing. With a map and compass, it is much easier to relocate when lost, or find the way in bad weather or fog. Before you begin your hike, check that you can see the route you plan to hike on the map. Make a mental note of where the hills are in relation to where you will be walking, and where any steep slopes, river crossings, or similar features are.

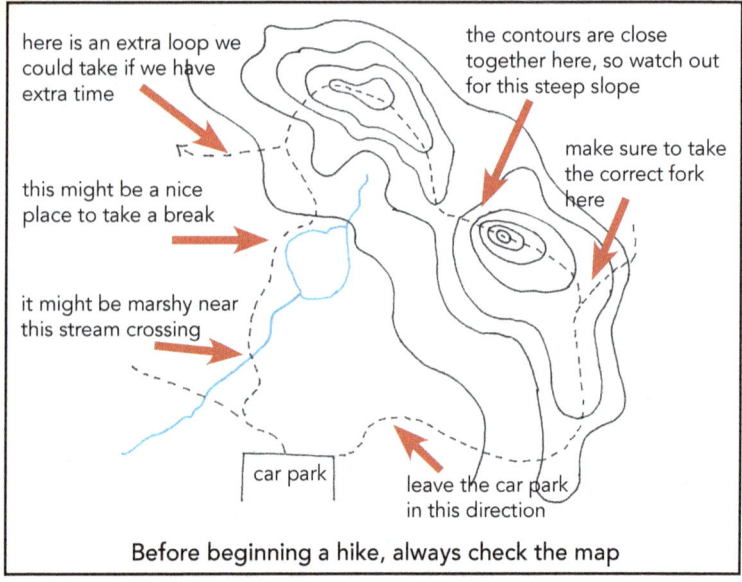

Before beginning a hike, always check the map

As you hike, check in regularly with the map. Features such as bridges, major path junctions, and lakes will be quite easy to see on the map, and will allow you to check your progress. Other features, such as knolls or crags, may not be as easy to find on the map, but it's still worth doing this and checking that they are where you think they should be.

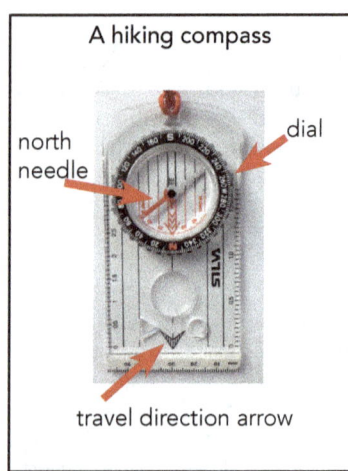

A hiking compass

Using a compass

A compass uses a magnetised needle to align with the Earth's magnetic field. The "north" end of the needle aligns with the Earth's north magnetic pole. The Earth's magnetic pole moves very slowly with time, and is not in quite the same place as the geographical North Pole itself. On hiking maps you'll see the slight variations between magnetic north, grid north and true north (the direction of the North Pole) shown on the legend at the bottom of the Norwegian 1:50,000 maps. In Norway, and for the kind of navigation required here, "magnetic north" is close enough to true north that a correction is not needed.

To use a compass with a map, hold the map flat with the compass on top of it. Wait until the needle of the compass has settled, and then turn the map so that the grid lines pointing north align with the needle on the compass. It is a common mistake to align north with south instead of north with north, giving a "180 degree" error: avoid this! You can now check the map against the features that you are seeing (because you now know which direction they are in!), and figure out where you want to go next.

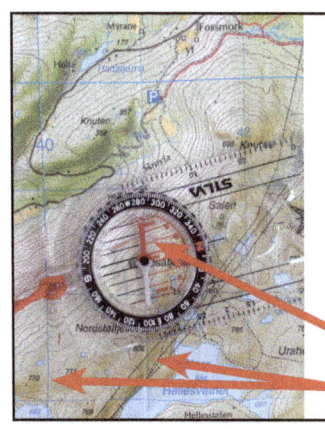

Here, the north arrow of the compass is aligned with the north grid arrows on the map. You now know which direction to look in to check which features are which on the ground. Note that the other lines and arrow on the compass are for finding bearings, and aren't necessary for this.

north arrow on the compass

north grid lines (in blue)

Finding a compass bearing

Sometimes you'll want to use the compass to tell you which direction you should be heading in. This can happen if a mist descends, if you're in a forest and can't see far, or if you suspect you may be on the wrong trail, or on the right trail but going in the wrong direction. To do this, begin with the map. Lay it flat, and then lay the compass on top of it with the lines on the *base* of the compass (not the north arrow) facing in the direction you want to go. Now, allow the needle of the compass to settle, and then turn the dial so that the lines on the dial align with the north arrow. With the lines on the dial of the compass aligned with the north arrow, the large arrow at the front of the compass is pointing you in the direction that you want to go in. Look in that direction, choose an object (e.g. a lone tree) near the horizon that is aligned with the arrow, and walk towards it. When you reach the object, take another compass bearing and repeat.

Finding a compass bearing

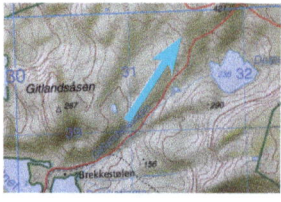

1. Identify the direction you want to go in on the map (indicated by the blue arrow here)

2. Align the arrow on the base of the compass in this direction

3. Turn the dial of the compass until the north line on the dial is aligned with the north arrow of the compass (lay the compass flat!)

4. Keeping the grid lines on the compass dial aligned with the north arrow, use the arrow on the base of the compass as a pointer to identify something near the horizon in the direction you are going.

Bending the map
Often in life we see what we expect to see, and maps are no different. People who have taken a wrong turn and are a long way away from where they think they are can still convince themselves that they are on track by doing what is called "bending the map": taking the features in front of you and convincing yourself that they are what is on the map, even though they aren't. With experience, it gets easier to spot this self-delusion, figure out from the map where you actually are, and navigate back to the correct trail.

Relocation: how to figure out where you are when you're lost
When you realise that you aren't where you thought you were, the first thing to do is begin to think about what might have gone wrong. Did you climb the wrong hill? Did you turn left along a path instead of right? Could you have missed a path junction? If it becomes clear what happened, just return to the trail you wanted to follow and carry on, or plan a new route from where you are now to where you want to be.

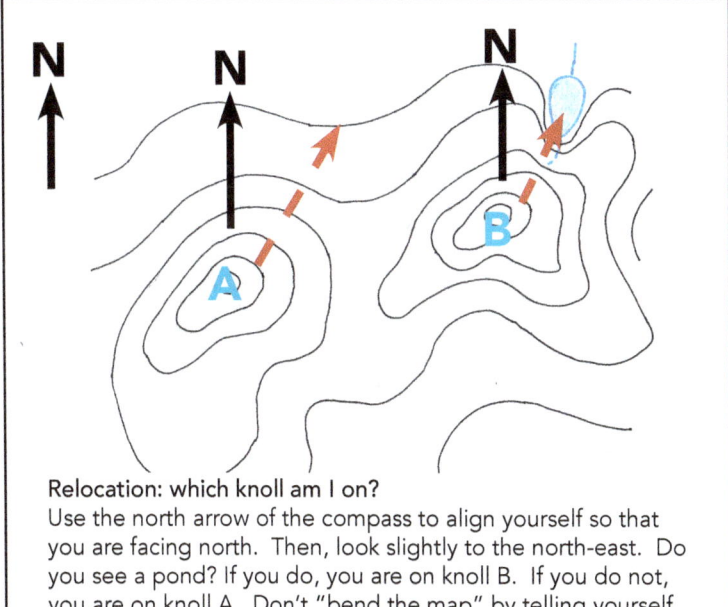

Relocation: which knoll am I on?
Use the north arrow of the compass to align yourself so that you are facing north. Then, look slightly to the north-east. Do you see a pond? If you do, you are on knoll B. If you do not, you are on knoll A. Don't "bend the map" by telling yourself that the lake is just "hiding" in the valley and you're still at B.

Finding the Way (GPS Not Necessary)

If it doesn't become clear what went wrong, look around for a large feature nearby, such as a lake, bridge or hilltop. Then, look to see what else is near this feature. Look at the map, and try to see where the nearby features might be on the map. For instance, if you see a bridge over a stream next to a lake, try to find this bridge on the map. When you think you have found the feature on the map, compare the location of the feature according to the map with where you are standing. Is this the same lake, bridge or hilltop?

Once you are sure you have found where you are on the map, you can use the map to choose a route that will take you from where you are to where you need to be. This might not be the original route that you had planned to take. If necessary, take a compass bearing to make sure that you set off in the right direction.

"Safety" Navigation in poor visibility

Sometimes a route goes close to a hazard, such as a cliff or deep river. If you are near the hazard in poor visibility, be careful to choose a route that won't put you in danger if you stray slightly off course. It's much better to walk an extra kilometre or two than risk getting too close to a cliff!

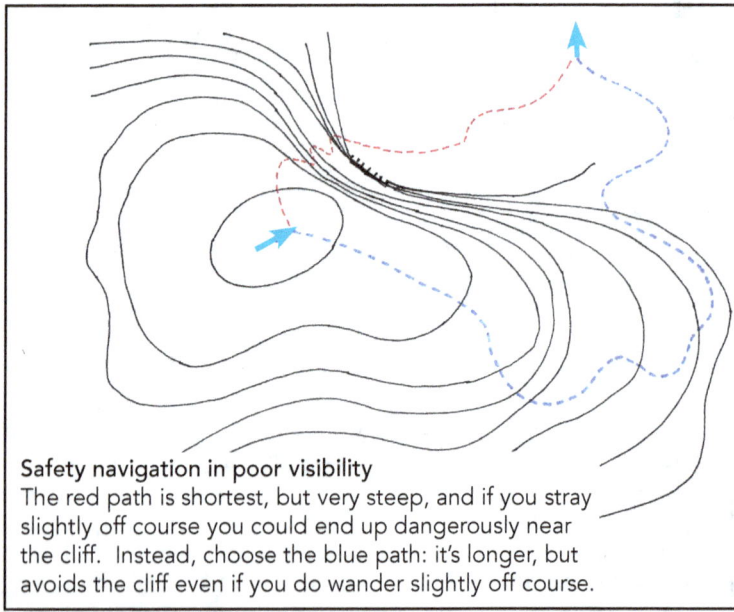

Safety navigation in poor visibility
The red path is shortest, but very steep, and if you stray slightly off course you could end up dangerously near the cliff. Instead, choose the blue path: it's longer, but avoids the cliff even if you do wander slightly off course.

The maps in this guide and legends used in this book

The maps in this guide are intended as sketch maps, to help you link the descriptions in the book to places of interest on the hikes. It is essential that you also take a map with you. In this book, you'll find the following symbols used in the hike descriptions:

 Green level (easy) hike

 Blue level (medium) hike

 Red level (challenging) hike

 This hike may be accessed via bus

 This hike is accessed via a ferry

 This hike may be accessed by train

 This hike may be accessed by car

 Point of interest or navigational landmark on a hike. The number in the circle corresponds to the number in the hike description.

 Car park

How long will the hike take?

Everyone walks at a different speed, and some people go more slowly over rough and/or steep terrain than others. It's impossible to predict how long any individual person will take to complete a hike, so in this book times have been calculated for an average hiker. A walking speed of 4 km per hour on easy, flat terrain is assumed, plus an additional 10 mins per 100m of climbing. This corresponds to a moderately fit person carrying a rucksack weighing 10kg. It *doesn't* include rest and refreshment stops. To get an idea of how long to allow for any particular hike, think of the following:

Finding the Way (GPS Not Necessary)

Rest and refreshment stops: hike times don't include these breaks, so extra time must be allowed. As a guide, for every 5 hours hiking time, allow at least one hour rest time. In good weather, allow for longer stops; conversely in cold or wet weather stops are likely to be shorter.

Fitness level and experience: if you are new to hiking, or not accustomed to exercise, allow extra time, especially on rougher trails and steep slopes.

How heavy is your rucksack? The more weight you are carrying, the slower you will go, especially up hills. If you have people of mixed fitness levels in your party, consider asking the fitter members to carry more of the weight, so that everyone travels at a similar speed.

How large is your party? Larger groups travel more slowly, because break stops tend to be more frequent, and the group as a whole must travel at the pace of the slowest member.

Are you hiking with children? In general, if you are hiking with children aged between 0 and 10, allow double the time in this guide. If you are hiking with children between the age of 10 and 14, allow 50% extra time.

Does someone in your party have special considerations? For example, older relatives may have balance issues on rough terrain and need extra time just on these stretches of the trail.

If you are new to hiking and you begin with the shorter hikes in this book, you'll be able to see how your own hiking time compares to the hike times given here. Then, as you progress to the longer hikes, you'll have more of an idea how much time to allow.

A final word: don't be confused by local signs!
If you are learning Norwegian, or have picked up a few words as you travel or research your visit to Norway, don't be confused if you can't read some of the local signs. Norway has three official languages and many more dialects. The spellings can vary considerably, and Norwegian

placenames are often repeated around the country, adding to the potential confusion for foreigners. If in doubt, double check to be sure you are looking where you should be. Also, many local information signs are written in Nynorsk, whereas most Norwegian language learners begin with another official language, Bokmål. Nynorsk is phonetic though, so looking carefully and sounding out the words will usually help.

Chapter 3:
Equipment Matters
Local secrets for staying warm, dry and comfortable

Equipment can make the difference between an unhappy and a happy hiker!

The equipment needed for hiking will to some extent depend on the length of the hike, its location and the weather/season. Nevertheless it is important to note some overarching principles. For the trails presented in Chapter 6, city clothes and comfortable, sturdy shoes will mostly do the job, provided it is not too wet outside.

But for the hikes in Chapters 7-10, you would need to consider your outfit a bit more carefully. 'There is no bad weather, just bad clothing' goes a Norwegian saying. While hiking in other climates might be more forgiving to suboptimal gear, hiking in Norway can become uncomfortable, or possibly unwise, if one is not prepared for weather changes and differing conditions along the trail. Due to its high geographical latitude, Norway is considered alpine area over 600m above sea level. Hikes above this height do require good outdoor clothing. Wearing the right clothing will almost certainly make hiking much more fun.

Chapter 1 describes the variability of weather patterns in Rogaland. Due to this changeability, the most important clothing principle for hiking in Norway is layering. We describe the details of the layering system below after a general overview of fabrics used in (outdoor) clothing. We also offer some specific advice on equipment and provide a checklist at the end of the chapter.

Fabric Materials

Cotton clothing is not suitable for hiking. Although it is soft, comfortable, and the most used natural fibre in clothes today, cotton readily absorbs and retains water . It leaves the hiker feeling damp, which is uncomfortable in both cold and hot weather. Wearing cotton socks can quickly lead to blisters even in the best-fitting hiking shoes.

Wool has traditionally had a reputation for being itchy. New breeds of sheep and new methods of manufacturing have changed this in the past 20 years. The wool used in outdoor clothing today is much softer on the skin. It is the base layer fabric of choice in Norway due to its many benefits. Wool can absorb up to 40% of its own weight in water before feeling wet. It transports moisture away from the skin, making it an ideal fabric for socks and base layers. Even when wet, wool does retain body heat. All these attributes make wool particularly suitable for the cooler Norwegian weather. When worn next to the skin it dries quickly. One can find summer and winter wool base layers even at box retailers that are inexpensive, durable and easy care. An added benefit of wool is that it does not retain odours as much as synthetics do.

Today, synthetic fabrics are used in the majority of sports clothing. Synthetics encompass a wide array of different materials. These materials are good at pulling moisture away from the skin and transporting it outwards, to where it can evaporate in the air. As base layer material, synthetics can feel cold on the skin when wet. In terms of price to performance ratio, a good wool base layer will still be more economical, when compared to a high-performance synthetic base layer.

Synthetic materials really come into their own for the outer layers. A good rain jacket will keep you comfortable while protecting you from wind and rain. This is a key part of the hiking equipment here in Norway so advice on rain jackets will be covered in more detail later in the chapter.

Fleece is a very lightweight fabric when compared to wool. It can be tightly woven to provide greater wind protection or knitted loftier for additional warmth. It is very easy care. It is water repellent, but also a less breathable material, meaning it does not naturally transport moisture from the inside out. Fleece garments come in an ever-increasing variety of thicknesses, colours, and shapes and are a great way to make a fashion statement without breaking the bank (see "Enticing reluctant teenagers", in Chapter 5).

Down comes in many different specifications and is experiencing a revival due to new technology that prevents down from losing its qualities when faced with some moisture. It provides a lot of warmth and wind protection. It is a very light material, and easy to pack and compress. It is generally expensive, but a potential addition to consider once you have your basic set of hiking clothing, and want to increase comfort levels and reduce weight. If animal welfare is a concern, new alternatives to down made from recycled polyester are now available. They do not compromise on warmth, comfort, or weight, and are priced similarly to down jackets.

The Layering System: Practicality and Functionality

The layering system involves

Base layer
Depending on the time of year this could be a long or short sleeved top and bottom. Wool or synthetic base layers come in many thicknesses and price points. Wool is seen as the best material for a base layer in this temperate climate.

Mid-layer
Typically a fleece of varying thickness depending on season/hike/temperature. Some hikers do like to wear a down jacket as a mid-layer, due to its weight to warmth ratio. This is generally the more expensive option and more of a "nice to have".

Outer layer
A rain jacket and rain trousers that have good wind stopper characteristics as well as water resistance and breathability.

Additional layer
of either wool, fleece or down in the backpack to put on in case of cooler weather or for comfort during resting times and breaks.

The layering system works to keep you warm because air is trapped between the layers. If fabrics are breathable, the layers transport the body moisture away from the skin towards the outer layers where it can evaporate.

Norwegians will often advise fellow hikers to begin their hike slightly cool, as the body will warm up through the activity. If one does prefer to be comfortable at the start, a 'clothes stop' after 15 minutes to shed one layer is a good idea. Don't hesitate to do this. Be assured that most hikers in your party will feel the same and it is advisable to stay as dry as possible.

When taking breaks, make them either short enough that you will not feel chilled, or put on an extra layer when you stop that you then remove after increasing activity levels again. This 'off and on again' approach depends on weather and to some extent also on personal feelings of hot and cold. Additionally, some fellow hikers we have met take an extra base layer along, to change into at the end of the ascent. Although changing into the new layer is a little cumbersome, it does ensure comfort while resting, enjoying views, and on the way down.

Specific Advice on Equipment

Rain jacket and trousers

Outerwear designed for active sports has varying degrees of water resistance, but will eventually leak given enough water, time, and pressure. A rubber raincoat is completely waterproof, and may be the ideal garment for standing in a downpour waiting for the bus, but if you tried to hike in it, you'd be wet in no time from your own perspiration. The trick is to balance protection from rain and snow on the outside with the ability to let water vapour (from perspiration) escape from the inside. The best breathability of your outer shell will come from side zips or vents. This means they can be opened under the armpits towards the elbow and hip, or, in trousers, along the thighs. This mechanical ventilation works far more efficiently than any technical fabric. This means that a jacket with vents as opposed to one that claims high breathability is advisable.

For the rain jacket in spring/autumn and winter, we recommend a waterproof rating of 20000^+mm, with at least partially sealed seams, venting zips and waterproof zips. It is also important to take rain gear along in summer whenever hiking in the mountains. Over 600m above sea level Norway is considered to be an alpine environment, and the weather can change quickly. The wind might be stronger than expected and the rain jacket will provide good protection against wind even if it doesn't rain. Having a good rain jacket is money well spent.

> **Waterproofing and breathability numbers**
> Manufacturers typically describe the waterproof breathability of fabrics using two numbers. The first is in millimetres and is a measure of how waterproof a fabric is. In the case of a 10k or 10,000 mm fabric, if you put a square tube with inner dimensions of 1" x 1" over a piece of said fabric, you could fill it with water to a height of 10,000 mm before water would begin to leak through. The higher the number, the more waterproof the fabric.
>
> The second number is a measure of how breathable the fabric is, and is normally expressed in terms of how many grams of water vapor can pass through a square metre of the fabric from the inside to the outside in a 24 hour period. In the case of a 20k (20,000 g) fabric, this would be 20,000 grams. The larger the number, the more breathable the fabric.

Rain trousers should be easy to put on and take off on the trail, especially as you might already be wearing muddy boots. The best ones would have full length waterproof zippers on either side for ease of handling: naturally these will tend to be the most expensive. Alternatively, test whether you can put them on wearing your boots: look for big enough openings to take your boots through, waterproof zippers, and sealed seams.

Given enough rain, no rain gear will keep you dry. This is because moisture also starts to build inside and cannot be transported out due to higher humidity outside the garment. In this case you have some mitigation options. Keep moving to stay warm, take short breaks, keep hydrated and eat snacks to keep your core temperature up. Put on more medium or base layers if you have any and seek shelter if necessary.

Hiking trousers

Hiking trousers are not necessary when out on urban walks, coastal walks or shorter hikes in good weather conditions. Once temperature drops, and when it gets wet or muddy underground, they will greatly increase comfort. Consider levels of water resistance and fast drying fabrics. The fit of hiking pants should not be restrictive and allow full range of motion.

Boots

Boots are the key piece of equipment for hiking of course, but also one that can be talked about the most. Preferences vary a lot and there is not a "one-fits-all" answer. We have met fellow Norwegian hikers that own five pairs of boots for different kinds of hiking, just as a Dutch national will likely own different kinds of bicycles, and the Swiss different kinds of skis.

One thing that can be said is that it is never a good idea to go on a long hike with new boots, as even the most comfortable boots might need to be worn in. Always attempt to keep your feet dry to avoid blisters. Consider taking a spare pair of socks along to change into.

Gaiters

Gaiters are a very useful piece of gear to keep shoes and feet dry in muddy or rainy conditions. Even when it is not raining, walking through damp grass/heather can leave the hiker with the lower part of the trousers damp or wet.

When choosing gaiters, ease of use and sturdiness are the things to look for. Gaiters have attachments that go under the sole of the hiking boot, so any poor stitching will make these straps break away easily and reduce the life of the gaiters significantly. Test them before you need them, as they will be useless on the trail if you can't figure how to put them on.

Walking or trekking pole

The use of a walking or trekking pole comes down to personal preference. We have hiked with and without, and some key differences are worth mentioning. As a hiker, you develop a greater sense of balance and possibly strength when not using a pole. Without a pole you have both hands free to help you with ascents and descents if needed. When crossing small streams or marshy areas, the pole will have the advantage of prodding the way for depth and stability in front of you, and using the pole will provide additional stability in those situations. Some people find a pole helpful on ascents/descents to alleviate strain on joints. This is probably a matter of training of the surrounding muscles and with more strength and practice the pole might be needed less.

Walking poles are becoming increasingly common as a pair, but we would not recommend this on Norwegian mountain trails. These tracks tend to be narrower and having to manage two walking poles means you don't have any free hands any more. Taking one along might be a compromise. They come in different materials and can be adjusted in length, which makes them easier to store away when not needed, especially if your daypack has a pole holder. More importantly, an extendable pole can be adjusted to match the terrain, and the steepness of the ascent/descent.

Water carriers, bottles, cup and vacuum flask

Taking water along when hiking is very important to prevent dehydration. People have different preferences but good quality plastic water bottles are the most inexpensive option. Some people prefer water carriers so to avoid having to stop and get the water bottle out while on the trail. Be aware that these systems do require more care to keep hygienic.

Norway might be one of the few countries where drinking water out of streams is generally still a safe option and the water tastes fantastic. Do this only when in the mountains and when you don't see animals grazing in the vicinity. Be careful only to take water out of fast running streams, or where one can see that it has been filtered in a natural way.

A thermos with a hot drink (see Chapter 4 for options) is almost always a good idea. When choosing a thermos flask make sure it does not leak when upside down, and has a good insulation. Double-walled vacuum-insulated stainless steel flasks will do this best. Check the opening mechanism to ensure you find it practical and not prone to leaking.

Daypack

A good daypack will make any hike more enjoyable, because it will distribute the weight of water, food, drinks and any extra equipment onto the hiker's back in the most ergonomic way.

For day hikes, a 20-40 litre backpack with a hip belt, and straps that are not too narrow on the shoulders works well. A sternum strap helps reduce the weight on the shoulders and makes the carrying easier. Make sure that the daypack fits the length of your back. Preferably, there should be some space between the pack and the back of the hiker (a ventilation panel) so that air can circulate and sweat buildup is reduced. Daypacks are not made of waterproof material, so a waterproof cover is recommended if the pack does not come with one. Daypacks designed for hiking might have additional features such as attachments for a walking pole or ice axe, a hydration system compartment, or extra outside pockets and/or loops to put things where they are more easily accessible while hiking.

Other Gear
Beanie, hat, buffs and gloves
Taking along a beanie and gloves is always recommended. It is advisable to use beanies (or a padded hat) and gloves that are water and windproof for hiking in cooler months and on rainy summer days. Buffs are incredibly versatile and light to carry. They are made of light wool, soft fleece or cotton. Consider having a spare in your daypack for extra warmth. They can be manipulated to serve a multitude of purposes and most of them will come with illustrations of at least ten ways to use them.

Sun protection
Even in this northern climate, sun protection is a necessity, not a luxury. In summer, or when the sun is shining on snow, take sunglasses and sunscreen. Depending on the season, a brimmed hat would also be useful on bright sunny days.

Whistle, telephone
Generally a whistle to attract attention is only needed when going off into more remote areas. Mobile coverage is increasing all the time but can not be guaranteed in the mountains.

Map, compass, GPS
For information on these items see Chapter 2 on Navigation. There are waterproof sleeves available for maps, so that they can be taken out and consulted in rainy conditions. A map is of no use if it stays in the daypack!

Sitting mats
Sitting mats can be really small and lightweight. They will provide comfort on the trail on breaks if the underground is damp and they are an effective barrier against cold. When hiking with smaller children a bigger camping mat might come in very useful for building a camp where the kids can come back to and sit warmly, maybe around a fire roasting some bread on a stick or a marshmallow.

Camera
Many phones these days have excellent cameras, but the photography aficionado will of course always want a better shot. The landscapes, skies, and colours you encounter will probably make you take many more photos than you initially intended. Don't say you were not warned!

Small first aid kit
At the very least, a small first aid kit should have some blister relief patches, (adhesive) bandages, a few gauzes of disinfectant or a disinfectant spray, some painkillers and antihistamines, an insect bite relief cream, and a pair of tweezers. A tick remover is also needed as ticks that spread Lyme disease are increasingly also found in Norway.
There are many small kits available for purchase or one can assemble one's own. Keeping basic first aid skills fresh is always a good idea.

Headlamp
At the very height of summer, it doesn't really get properly dark at night in Rogaland. At all other times of year, a headlamp comes in useful for those days when it takes longer than expected to get back.

Ice spikes
From October onwards it can freeze on higher elevation and boots may not have enough grip. Make sure the spikes ("broders" in Norwegian) fit your boots and can withstand the pressure of use. Buying cheap will likely not pay off here, as the cheaper models are liable to slip off boots. A good pair will give you grip on those slippery slopes.

A word on maintenance
The soil in Norway is often acidic and on lower elevations you will likely encounter sheep, cows and sometimes goats. Their droppings are also acidic and will over time be detrimental to the performance fabric or leather of your boots. Therefore cleaning off your boots after hiking is recommended. Read the instructions and if you buy in a store with knowledgeable staff they will most likely be happy to give you advice.
After some time all performance fabrics will lose some of their water repellent quality. There are some excellent spray-on water repellent products available that work with most synthetic fabrics and can extend the life of your rain jacket, trousers, and boots. Your outdoor clothing will come with specific instructions on washing and maintenance and a little care goes a long way in keeping your gear in good shape.

Summary checklist of equipment

This is intended as a handy reference list. Not all of this equipment is needed for every hike, especially not for the shorter, urban walks.

- Base layer of wool or synthetic (long johns not always needed, weather/season dependent)
- Middle layer of fleece, wool or down
- Hiking pants
- Outer layer windproof, rainproof rain jacket, rain trousers (also in summer)
- Hiking socks and boots
- Beanies or hat (summer/winter), buff, gloves
- Daypack and rain cover (if not built-in)
- Gaiters
- Water bottles
- Vacuum flask
- Food and drink (see Chapter 4)
- Sitting mats
- First aid kit, whistle, telephone
- Headlamp
- Ice spikes (in cooler months)
- Camera
- Walking pole (if preferred)
- Map, compass, (GPS if using)
- Mobile phone
- In summer or on bright winter days in the snow, sun protection, sunglasses
- Some spare clothing such as socks, buffs or gloves and an additional mid-layer

Chapter 4:
Easy Ways to Eat Well on the Trail

Hiking in Norway is about more than the trails and the views: it's about the fun of eating al fresco in the midst of unspoiled nature, and relaxing with friends and family as the treats are shared around. The mountains in Rogaland haven't been extensively built up, so the delicious food that you eat on the trail will be whatever you carry with you. There are no restaurants at the top of any peaks, nor are there kiosks at viewpoints offering coffee or beer to hikers passing by. This chapter begins with the rare exceptions to the "there is no restaurant" rule, and then shares local secrets for good hiking food. Don't be daunted: you can be your own caterer even if you don't have time to prepare in advance or shop around for delicacies.

The exceptions: Preikestolen Fjellstue, Øygardstøl (Kjerag), Flørli, and the Sunday waffle cafes

In the area we cover in this book, there is one "mountain restaurant". This is Preikestolen Fjellstue, located at the main car park and "base area" for hikes 10.1 (Preikestolen), 10.4 (Gryteknuten) and 10.3 (Moslifjellet), and at the end of hike 10.2 (Fantapytten). Here, there is both cabin-style accommodation and hotel rooms, a cafe/restaurant and a kiosk selling drinks, ice cream and local souvenirs. The restaurant has a view over the lake and is a lovely way to relax after a hike in the area! It serves a variety of coffee, snacks and meals prepared from local ingredients by the resident chef.

There is also a cafe at Øygardstøl, the car park and "base area" for hike 10.9, Kjerag. This cafe is perched above Lysefjord, and has such a wonderful view that it has a special viewing platform in addition to window tables.

The view is rather different at the start and end of hike 10.8, the Flørli steps. Here there is a small cafe located in the old power station building right next to Lysefjord. It is possible to eat dinner in the museum here.

These eateries are open during the week, and cater to tourists as well as locals. Rather fewer tourists encounter the "Sunday waffle cafes".

Sunday afternoon is a great time for hiking in Rogaland. Most shops and businesses are closed, and with fewer people at work, locals of all ages can enjoy the vast outdoors on the doorstep. A local tradition is the "Sunday waffle cafe". These small cafes pop op only on Sunday afternoons. They serve drinks, Norwegian waffles, usually with jam and sour cream ("rømme" in Norwegian), and sometimes other snacks. The cafes appear in areas with hiking trails or other attractions, so that the break for waffles becomes part of the outing. On warmer days, there is always somewhere to relax outside and enjoy the views and the sun. When it's cooler or wet, they provide an opportunity to remove the outer layers and chat around the table with hot drinks and snacks. The staff are often volunteers, with the money raised going to local charities. Opening hours are from around 12 noon until 3pm, and the cafes open on most Sundays of the year except for the month of July and holiday periods. The walks in this book that pass alongside or near to a waffle cafe are:

- 6.1 Lille Stokkavatn and Byhaug
- 6.4 Sørmarka and Ullandhaug Tarn
- 6.7 Store Stokkavatn
- 6.9 The Arboretum
- 6.10 Ørre Friluftshuset and beach
- 6.11 Hå Gamle Prestegård to Obrestad Havn
- 7.3 The Tungenes Peninsula
- 8.1 Dalsnuten
- 8.5 Bjørndalsfjellet

These convenient cafes with their delicious snacks are the exception though, and, for the most part, you will be carrying your own refreshments with you when you hike.

The first thing to bring: plenty of water

On the shortest hikes in this book, you may not need to take a snack, especially if you are hiking without kids. The one thing you do want to have is water! Even in this cool climate, you need more water when hiking than when at rest, especially if it is warm, when you are climbing hills, or when moving fast enough to get out of breath. We recommend a sturdy water bottle, of at least 1 litre capacity, for every adult. Very young children will only need a smaller bottle, and might even want to carry it themselves. On cold or very wet days, you might want to substitute the water with a hot drink such as hot chocolate, tea or hot juice (see below), or take the hot drink as an extra. If the hike is a long one, don't forget to take note of where you might refill your bottle if necessary.

Getting enough energy

Hiking requires energy, i.e. it burns calories, especially when carrying weight and/or climbing hills. Exactly how many calories depends on a person's weight, how much they carry, how fast they go, how high they climb, and how fit they are in the first place. A full day's climb up a decently high hill burns a lot of calories! It's essential to eat enough energy food on the trail on longer hikes. Carry plenty of snacks in a place where they can easily be reached: in the top of a rucksack or a coat pocket. Grumpiness, in children or adults, is often a sign of low blood sugar.

Happy hikers take regular snack breaks

A dose of a favourite snack may solve a grumpiness problem! Snack breaks also give everyone a rest and a chance to stop and appreciate the view, waterfall, berries or whatever else is near. With kids, snack breaks are also a chance to play games and alleviate the feeling of constant marching. If you are moving fast (enough to be slightly out of breath), your blood will be diverted away from your digestive system and to your muscles. For most people, this is the uphill part of the hike! Here, limit snacks to easily digested, high-energy foods (bananas, chocolate etc), and catch up on other nutrients later. During longer meal stops or when traveling at a more leisurely pace, any food can be enjoyed.

Snacks to try

Fruit is one of the best snack foods: it's easily digestible and high in energy. Local supermarkets usually have apples, bananas and some kind of citrus (orange, mandarin, clementine) available all year. For the dedicated banana-lover, it's even possible to buy "banana protectors": banana-shaped plastic boxes that prevent your banana from being squished in your rucksack! Dried fruit is also easy to buy in local supermarkets. If you are new to hiking, you may not yet have heard of GORP. GORP is "Good Old Raisins and Peanuts". This mixture of peanuts and raisins is the original trail mix. It's easy to carry, nutritious, and perfect for grabbing quick handfuls at rest points. Nowadays trail mix can include any number of nuts, dried fruit, chocolate pieces, and sweets. It can be purchased ready-mixed in many varieties, or you can mix your own. Sometimes salted nuts are added: the combination of salt and sweet really hits the spot when you are outdoors and active! Chocolate bars make good snacks, in moderation, as do biscuits, cake, crisps and cookies. A plastic container will stop baked goods from being squashed in transit. If you are baking at home, cookies, cupcakes and tray bakes all make excellent snacks on the trail.

Make Your Own Trail Mix
Put out packets of a variety of trail mix ingredients such as nuts, dried fruit, and some chocolate and/or sweets. Give everyone their own poly bag or other container, and let them make up their own mix to carry on the hike. Everyone's will be slightly different!

Liquid snacks and hot drinks

Fruit juices, smoothies, and milk drinks are great "liquid snacks" in the hills. They are easily available pre-packaged in supermarkets and petrol stations, or you can make your own favourite. A thermos flask takes a few minutes to prepare, but hot drinks bring a big feel-good factor in the hills and are usually very welcome when served. Traditionally, Norwegians will bring along a flask of hot cocoa or "saft". In local supermarkets, you'll see containers for reformulated cocoa drinks for sale: all you need to add is hot milk or water (or a mixture of the two). Hot "saft" is a Scandinavian drink, popular with both adults and children. Look for bottles of dark saft concentrate in the drinks section of supermarkets. It is most often made from blackcurrant juice. The concentrate is diluted with hot (or cold) water to give a delicious fruit drink.

Coffee and tea are good alternatives, but if you take either with milk, take the milk in a separate container rather than premixing the drink: sometimes the milk can curdle in the thermos and the result is not tasty! Thermos flasks are also good for bringing hot soup: either your own homemade creation, or mixed from a powder packet base. Tomato soup and chicken broth both travel well.

Foraging for snacks

The mountains and forests in Rogaland are famous for their berries. If you are lucky enough to be hiking in late summer, you can expect to find raspberries (bringebær), blueberries (blåbær), lingonberries (tyttebær) and possibly even blackberries (bjørnebær). Cloudberries (møltebær) are quite rare here, but, if you do find any, please remember that picking unripe cloudberries damages the plants. You need to wait until they are ripe, to make sure that they will come back next year!

Berry picking is especially popular with kids, and they will usually enjoy making something with the berries afterwards at home. The local blueberries are famous and delicious; you may meet people picking them with special "berry combs" that you can purchase in local shops.

Berry picking expeditions can in themselves make great hikes. You can stop at a good patch for a pick-it-yourself snack, grab a couple of berries as you pass by, or take along a container to fill with berries to enjoy later or freeze.

Asking a local where to find good berries usually results in an answer along the lines of "anywhere" or "everywhere"! This is partly because most locals are reluctant to give away the location of their favourite berry spot for fear that all the berries will disappear, but really the truth is that each year is different, and you may chance upon a good patch of blueberries on any hike at the right time of year.

Meals in the mountains

The meal eaten most often in the mountains is lunch. "Lunch" can mean anything from a sumptuous picnic in glorious surroundings on a warm day, to an extra-large snack with a good serving of a hot drink (usually in rain or cold weather). If there isn't much time to prepare, sandwiches work well, and all of the local bakeries sell delicious "brødskiver": single or double sandwiches on their own, locally made bread. If there is more preparation time, there are no limits to creativity! Here are a few ideas for things that are easy to carry:

Quiches and pies were made for picnics! Cut them into portions in advance, and carry in rigid plastic containers. If they can't be eaten with fingers, carry forks, preferably reusable plastic ones to reduce weight without resorting to throwaway single use items.

Vegetable sticks and dips (e.g. hummus) work well: prepare the sticks in advance and take them in plastic sandwich bags.

Wraps and pitta pockets make a good alternative to traditional sandwiches, especially as they fall apart less as they are eaten!

Wide necked thermos flasks can be used to take along hot food, e.g. macaroni, chunky soups or stews: very welcome on colder days!

Choosing a lunch spot
On warmer days, when you plan to stop for a while, look for spots with views, by the side of rivers, or with good opportunities for games if you are with kids. South facing slopes are ideal for soaking up the sun while you picnic. Often you'll find a lovely, secluded place if you move a few metres away from the trail.

On cooler days, the most important part of stopping for lunch is staying warm. Look for sheltered places that are out of the wind before you stop and get comfortable. The windiest spot is usually the top of the hill, so retreat a few metres down in the lee of any wind to look for a good spot that is sheltered by rocks or a well-positioned crag.

If you plan to build a fire
First, the law in Norway: When lighting a fire, you are legally responsible for it. You need to be able to control it at all times, and extinguish it completely before you leave. Additionally, open fires are not permitted in, or near, the forest between 15 April and 15 September, and at times of general fire bans. Ask the locals if you are unsure of the current regulations. If you plan to build a fire when and where it is legal, here are a few ideas for food:

"Firepit chicken": prepare marinaded strips of chicken breast using your favourite homemade marinade or one purchased from a local supermarket. Take along pointed wooden skewers or barbecue forks if you have them. When you are ready to cook, dampen the skewers (so that they won't burn!) and poke a chicken strip onto each skewer. Hold them near the fire to roast until the meat is well cooked through. Remove from the skewers and put in pitta pockets to serve.

Fish tacos: take along prepared taco filling (lettuce, cheese, salsa etc) and tacos. Cut unsmoked fish (salmon, trout or white fish) into strips, season and cook on dampened wooden skewers or barbecue forks as above. When the fish is cooked, load it into a taco together with the desired fillings, and eat.

Roasted banana and chocolate: peel a banana, cut it in half, and put it in tin foil with a few pieces of chocolate between the two halves. Put the foil package at the edge of the fire. Turn around a few times during cooking so that both sides cook evenly. After about 10-15 minutes, open the foil package: the banana will be roasted and the chocolate melted. Eat it from the foil package with a spoon.

Toasted marshmallows: a campfire wouldn't be a campfire without these! Remember either to use a "green" stick to toast them on, or dampen a wooden skewer (don't forget that metal forks or skewers conduct heat and may burn you hand!). Toast the marshmallows slowly, near the flames rather than in them, and turn the stick often to get a marshmallow that is beautifully toasted on the outside and gooey inside.

Barbecue pits and portable barbecues

Many recreational areas have barbecue pits for public use. You'll need to bring along your own charcoal, firelighters and of course barbecue food. You can also buy "one time use" barbecues in supermarkets locally. All you need to light it is a match, but, before you do, place the tray carefully on rocks so that it can't scorch and kill the plants underneath it. Some areas have experienced so much damage from single use barbecues that they have banned them: please respect this and only use yours in areas where they are allowed. Beaches are good portable barbecue spots as you won't damage the sand, but please don't use them on the fragile grass in the dunes. Allow time for the coals to cool down after the meal. Also, this is rubbish that needs to be carried back with you and not left behind.

Advice for stormy weather

When the weather is wild and wonderful, abandon any plans for stopping anywhere for very long. Enjoy the views on the move as you appreciate the exhilaration of being out in the elements. In lousy weather, it's better to forget about a "lunch stop" as such, and take a substantial snack in any place where it's sheltered enough to stop for a few minutes. A thermos with a hot drink (cocoa, coffee, tea or soup) is well worth bringing along on stormy days! Later, when you are back in the warmth of a building, there will be plenty of time to eat more slowly and laugh about the day's experiences.

Something in the car for when you return

A snack waiting in the car can be the perfect way to finish the day. Since this snack doesn't have to be carried, it can be kept warm in extra thermos flasks or cool in a cool box. Ideas to try include soup, hot dogs, baked goods, hot drinks or even a camping stove and fuel to make a fresh brew of hot tea or coffee.

Food packaging doesn't belong in the hills!

Please don't forget that the nature you are enjoying is pristine because the hikers who came before you took **everything** home with them. Orange peel can take up to **two years** to decompose on a mountain top! Please be kind to the environment and take all your food packaging and waste home with you. As a bonus, in Stavanger, all food waste is collected and composted. Your picnic scraps will be put to good use when you put them in the correct bin back home.

Chapter 5:
Enticing Reluctant Kids, Teenagers (and possibly dogs)

"Are we nearly there yet?" and its cousin "How much further do I have to go?" are two questions that may be a standing joke, but aren't funny if they're repeatedly uttered by an unhappy hiker. Even companions who usually love hiking aren't always in the mood, and children in particular are apt to enjoy the outdoors, and hiking, in different ways than their parents. Here we describe some tried and tested techniques for helping the youngest and more reluctant hikers to enjoy their experience. Even though all children, and their families, are different, these tips have been successful in many situations, and hopefully will help you too!

In order to entice others, less enthusiastic than yourself, to come out hiking, you could focus on something that your toddler/child/teenager or reluctant adult likes doing already. Start by incorporating this activity or let it even be centre stage of the hike to begin with.

Bring the baby doll or toy that your toddler adores. If they love to dig, bring a shovel and go somewhere

where they can dig. If your children like scavenger or treasure hunts, organise one in nature. If they love to draw, bring drawing supplies along, stop and draw. If they love challenges, give them a challenge! If they have favourite foods, bring those along and have an extensive picnic. If they love games, play games as you move along.

It might take you longer before you are able to complete that five-hour hike with your group, but it will increase your chances that everyone is on board and can complete it once you decide to give it a go. As long as you can make it a shared and regular activity it is likely that the common enjoyment, together with the probable increase in range, interest and skills, becomes a positive feedback loop in itself.

'Hiking' with toddlers

Norwegian toddlers are out in all kinds of weather, often seen wearing waterproof 'onesies' that even include the rubber boots. No one that has seen them roaming in the forest or digging on the beach can doubt their enjoyment in being outside, playing and exploring. Starting small, not being in any hurry, taking plenty of snacks, (hot) drinks and wrapping oneself up are key at this stage.

Toddlers can be very active, but will not cover distance in the traditional sense of a hike. There is almost no point in setting a goal as to wanting to complete a hike. By walking on and off trails you will build your toddlers' strength and motor skills. Let them walk on their own two feet whenever they are willing to and take your time to explore the natural surroundings. Everything will be of interest to your toddler, from stones to trees, leaves, bugs etc. Engaging with your toddler in this exploration of the natural world is likely to bring you pleasure in sharing the sense of discovery and wonder with this age group. Local guidebooks on flora, fauna and geology can be a good source of information.

Many Norwegian families with children in this age group make up a sort of 'base camp' together. This can include setting up a tent, making a fire, and bringing some toys along. Then a few adults will mind the children, exploring the closer surroundings together, while others go out and complete a hike, taking turns next time. A good number of hikes readily offer this opportunity, e.g. 7.6 (Røssdalen, on the meadow), 9.2 (Storaberget longer route, at the lake), 6.10 (Orre Friluftshuset, at the beach), 9.1 (Reinaknuten, at the lakes near the start), 8.8 (Øykjafjellet, at the Alsvik Naturcenter), and 8.10 (Rennesøyhodet, at the Daledammen Lake). These and other possibilities are mentioned in the individual hike descriptions.

If you do want to gain some mileage, getting a back carrier and carrying your toddler will help. As your toddler grows you will also gain strength for those expeditions later on, when they can walk the longer distances but you might have to carry everything else. For walks in town and on some of the beach trails bring a tricycle or miniscooter along if you have one. Your toddler will be able to cover a longer distance by themselves. Hikes in this book that are good for tricycles are: 6.6 (Mariero to Jåttå), 6.7 (Store Stokkavatn, or part of this walk) and 6.9 (The Arboretum, apart from the very last section of the hike), and 7.8 (Frøylandsvatnet).

Hiking with older children

Given enough time, and some experience, older children (age 5 and up) should be able to complete most of the hikes described in this book. In Chapter 2, we give some guidance on how to adjust expected timings to walking with children. This age group is potentially the easiest one to hike with. They naturally seem to thrive on 'challenges', 'adventures' and 'expeditions' and it is possible to build on that when hiking in Norway. Hiking trails are left natural as much as possible. Crossing the occasional stream, walking on rocks, and climbing over boulders are all obstacles that usually appeal to this age group. There are also activities like geocaching that build skills in navigation and yet feel like a treasure hunt.

Activities such as crossing obstacles and signing "summit" books are often fun and challenging for children.

Children in this age group often enjoy sharing a responsibility and it makes them feel an important part of the successful hike – which they are! Therefore, give every child their own small backpack, even if it contains very little. It could contain a small water bottle, a snack and a spare warm piece of clothing. Bring lots of food and water; children will eat even before you have started on the hike, quite possibly feeling hungry the moment you step out of the car or bus. If feasible, regularly involve them in food preparation and baking. Children usually love to eat what they have made. Consider having a few special treats, baked goods or other that you only make or take for hiking. Having these special occasion foods will motivate and create strong memories, not just in children. How often do we associate smells, tastes or noises with childhood memories? This is the time to create them.

Keeping your hiking gear organised and stored in a way that makes it easy for you to get it out will increase the chances of spontaneous shorter walks and prevent children from becoming impatient as adults potter around seemingly forever before getting out of the door.

Let children be the lead of activities, adjust to their needs, pace and interest. It is a good idea to keep tuned in to what the child is currently reading or the (online) games they are currently playing. Keep some specific questions you can ask when the time comes that they are tired and you still have some time to go. When prompted like that on a favourite topic they might just surprise you with a detailed explanation of the plot-line, the character in the game or the intricacies of getting to the next level. Before you (and they) know it, the boredom/fatigue has passed. Games, songs, making up stories are all activities that can be done in these situations. Have a few up your sleeve, just in case, or take the lead from what the children are proposing.

Adults are more boring to most children than other children are, so bringing friends along on a hike will certainly increase their enjoyment. Hiking with a larger group will add to the preparation time as you need to co-ordinate and plan more, but it will feel more of an expedition or adventure to children in this age group.

Post-hike activities are a good way to reflect on the experience and embed the memories. This can include journaling, creating albums, drawing, sorting through any new items that are being collected, sharing stories and photographs with friends and family. In years to come they become the tangible part of your adventures together.

Enticing teenagers to join in with hiking

For teenagers, the challenge moves from the physical to the emotional/mental arena. Getting teenagers to do something together with adults is not going to be straightforward. Yet the potential rewards are worth persevering for. Often, the literal change of scenery and physical activity will clear the mind and significantly improve moods, and you might find yourself with an opportunity to interact with your teenager in a relaxed way.

According to teenagers that we asked the biggest barrier you face

"Vertigo" hikes and photo opportunities can be fun for teenagers.

is actually to get them on the hike. Once they are at it, they do tend to enjoy themselves. The common hurdles are the dislike of doing something away from the social media environment, having to cope with potential discomfort (being sweaty, wet or cold) and having no interest in the outdoors.

Here the 'vertigo' hikes in the region: 10.1 (Preikestolen), 10.9 (Kjerag), 10.8 (the Flørli Steps) and Trolltunga (not covered in this guide) could help in getting your teenager interested in joining in the other hikes. While Preikestolen or the Flørli Steps can be completed by most teenagers without any preparation in terms of fitness, this is not necessarily true for Kjerag and certainly not for Trolltunga (not covered in this book). You could propose the hikes in this book as 'training' hikes. 8.5 Bjørndalsfjellet and 9.1 Reinaknuten can be training for Preikestolen; 9.5 Vådlandsknuten, 9.3 Bynuten, 9.4 Selvigstakken, and 9.8 Vinjakula can be training for Kjerag (5-6 hr return), and nothing other than regular hiking prepares you for the challenge of Trolltunga (8-10 hr return)!

While children will just need good solid equipment, teenagers (like adults) need clothing that they feel comfortable in. See Chapter 3 for more information on equipment and the layering system. Most importantly, their clothing also has to 'fit' both with their current look and their self-perception. While we don't advocate spending a fortune on designer hiking wear, you might be able to get one or two outer layer pieces that make your teenager feel ok being seen in. This may also prevent them from hiding whenever a camera appears, and perhaps indeed encourage selfies for sharing on social media.

And yes, teenagers will still probably get wet at times, and be uncomfortable, but this will most probably be forgotten at the end of the day, or become 'experience' stories in due time. Be prepared to listen to a grumpy teenager at times and you are likely to be rewarded with a young adult who is delighted you took them on these explorations of Norwegian landscapes. They truly are exceptional and have to be experienced to believe it.

Many of the ideas that work for older children still apply to teenagers, such as bringing a friend or even going with two or more families. There is safety in numbers, especially if your teenager regards the activity as potentially uncool in their peer group. Imposing activities such as navigation etc., will probably not work, but keep the option open for your teenager to try.

Good food, and plenty of it, is an absolute must when hiking with teenagers.

Reluctant adults

If you like hiking but your partner doesn't yet, some compromise will be needed. Generally speaking, trying out something new together such as geocaching, setting targets for length, metres climbed etc., which involves gadgets and technology could appeal to some. Others might value a barter, where they get some time 'off' to do something they love on their own, or being able to 'call the shots' next weekend. Some of the hikes presented here give stunning views for minimal exertion, and might be a great introduction to hiking and whet the appetite. These include 8.1 Dalsnuten, 8.2 Vårlivarden, 8.4 Lifjell, 7.2 Around Vassøy, and 8.6 Storaberget. If lack of knowledge of the area, confidence or hiking skills are the issue than hopefully this book can be of help.

Hiking with dogs

Your four-legged friend could well be your most enthusiastic hiking companion! Be aware that Norwegian Law stipulates that dogs are to be kept on a leash between 1 April and 20 August, so as to not disturb any wildlife or animals such as sheep, goats and cows that are left to roam in the countryside. In addition, dog walkers have to be in control of their dogs at any time so as to avoid unwanted contact of their dog with another person. This means that your fellow hikers will not react kindly if your dog runs up to them and tries to make friends by jumping up or sniffing them. If you do take your dog off the leash when the law and any local regulations allow it, you need to be sure it will return to you when called.

For the details of the law refer to: https://lovdata.no/dokument/NL/lov/2003-07-04-74.

Chapter 6:
Urban Fresh Air and Sunday Waffles

The hikes in this chapter explore the nature on Stavanger's doorstep. Despite being close to the city, they are varied in their terrain and all have fresh air and open spaces to offer. They are easy to reach, making them an ideal outing for any time of year and all kinds of weather. Many of them pass close to Sunday "Waffle Cafes" (See Chapter 5); these hikes are particularly enticing on Sunday afternoons. Whether you are new to hiking, or looking for a short excursion, they are a good place to begin.

Hike 6.1: Lille Stokkavatn and Byhaug Cafe

Lakeside, woods, and views: all within 5 minutes of Stavanger city centre!

Despite being in the Stavanger conurbation, this jewel of a little lake combines well with the viewpoint and Sunday afternoon cafe at Byhaug. For most of the time, you won't know you're in a city.

Access 🚗 or 🚌	Grading 🚶
Terrain: gravel path, road, forest path	Length: 4.5km
Facilities: Sunday cafe at Byhaug	Time: 1 hour 20 min

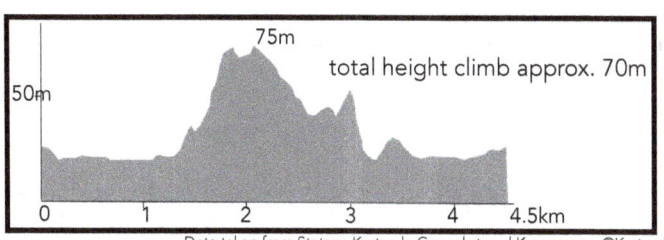

Data taken from Statens Kartverk, Geovekst and Kommunes, ©Kartverket

Urban Fresh Air and Sunday Waffles

Hike 6.1 | Lille Stokkavatn and Byhaug Cafe

To reach the start of the hike:

By car: Exit Stavanger city centre travelling west along Madlaveien (Rv 441). Drive past Mossvatnet to the left, and at the next roundabout (this is a large roundabout with bridges for bicycles overhead), take the first exit north into Rv 440, Ytre Ringvei Vest. Turn left at the next roundabout along Adjunkt Hauglands Gate, and continue along this road as it turns sharp right. The road ends at a T-junction: turn left, into Gustav Vigelands Vei, and the car park is signposted 300m along on the right hand side of the road.

By bus: local bus services run close to the start of this hike. The nearest bus stop is Gustav Vigelands Vei. Check www.kolumbus.no for current routes, prices, and schedules.

Hike directions:

Parts of this hike are marked with Stavanger "52 Tur" signs.

From the car park, face towards the field and turn right. The path starts between two houses (the one on your left is modern looking), and makes a right hand turn after just a few metres. You will pass an open field between the houses and will soon reach a marsh. The path goes along the side of this marsh, which is one of the biggest in the area. You'll see grasses, lilies and various birds, depending on the time of year.

At the corner of the marsh (the bus stop at Gustav Vigelands Vei is here), take the path left (1) along the side of the lake, where you'll pass a recreational area with picnic tables. From here you'll see the hill of Byhaug to the right and Lille Stokkavatn lake to the left. When you reach a bench by the side of the path, look right for a path leading away from the lake and into the woods. This path is marked with a T and walk no 43, "Tastaturen". You should find yourself going uphill along a path that is muddy in most conditions. There will be an open field to your right, and woods to your left. Follow the path with the Tur 43 signs uphill and over the Byhaug tunnel, passing a small picnic table with lovely open views into town. After a short while you reach a tarmac road: turn left to reach the parking and recreational area around the Byhaug Cafe.

When you are ready, continue past the cafe building and straight ahead along the road (3). Follow the Tur 43 signs towards a playing field. Cross

Lille Stokkavatn and Byhaug Cafe | Hike 6.1

© Kartverket

the field, cross the road diagonally in the same direction that you are walking, and look for a T-sign pointing into the woods opposite (4). Follow this path until it ends in a T-junction. Take the left hand turn, and continue until you reach a road.

Turn right along the road and look for a T-sign pointing right after approximately 100m (5). Take this path to the right: it goes past a marsh on the right hand side. As soon as you have passed this marsh, look for a path to the left.

Take this path, which leads to a quiet area with trees and a sheltered fireplace. There are various benches and props for games here. On Mondays and Thursdays, the area is used by a local nursery. At other times, everyone is welcome to use the space, but please don't forget to clean up after yourself and leave everything as you found it.

The trail leads from the far end of the hollow, to the right hand side of the rope swings (6). Look left up the hill to see a large boulder,

Urban Fresh Air and Sunday Waffles

Hike 6.1 | Lille Stokkavatn and Byhaug Cafe

and follow the path (marked with a T) up the hill and past it. You will reach another good viewpoint at the top of the hill. The path continues straight over the crest of the hill and veers right down a steep slope on the other side. Be careful in wet or damp weather: the rocks on this path are slippery when wet!

At the bottom of the hill, you will see Store Stokkavatn on your right. Turn sharp left up a gravel trail. Continue straight until this trail ends in a T-junction (7).

Here, turn right and follow the gravel trail with the lake (Lille Stokkavatn) on your left. The trail turns around the outline of the lake, and then leads up a short slope and down again to reach a picnic area on the left hand side. There are benches here, a stream leaving the lake, and opportunities for refreshment and games (8). When you leave this area, turn left and follow the tarmac road approximately 500m back to the car park.

The Byhaug Cafe is open from 12-3pm on Sundays, apart from the month of July and on holiday weekends. The area has picnic tables and a decking so that everyone can enjoy the fine views from this high spot. If the weather is clear, you should be able to see the high mountains of Hjelmeland, Rennesøy and the communications tower on Ullandhaug. Even if it isn't very clear, on most days a panorama of Lille Stokkavatn with Store Stokkavatn behind is usually visible from the decking area.

Hike 6.2: The Kvernevik Coast

An easy path with open views across the North Sea and Hafrsfjord

This is an open, airy stretch of coastline dotted with small beaches and harbours. Easy bus access allows for a one-way hike, with the option of continuing along hike 6.3 if a longer outing is wanted.

Access 🚗 or 🚌	Grading 🚶
Terrain: gravel path	Length: 6.5km
Facilities: none	Time: 1hr 40mins

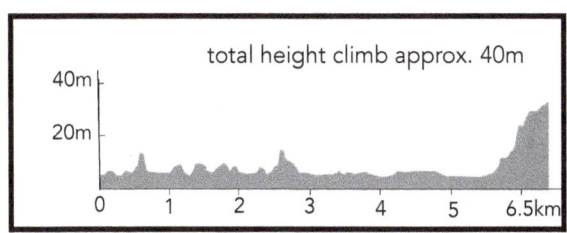

Data taken from Statens Kartverk, Geovekst and Kommunes, ©Kartverket

Urban Fresh Air and Sunday Waffles

Hike 6.2 | The Kvernevik Coast

To reach the start of the hike:

By bus: This hike is best reached by bus, as this allows for hiking in one direction. At the time of writing, the end of the bus line (no 3) was at Viste Hageby, approximately 500m along the road, and opposite the car park described below. Travelling from Stavanger, you can alight the bus at Endrestø Nord, right in front of Hålandsvatnet. Take the pedestrian bridge over Kvernevikveien and you will see "T" signs for the walk "Tur 26, Kvernevikturen". They will take you south into Kvernbekkveien, Kvernbergveien, and finally Kvernevikveien, to the Endrestø bus stop. The hike description starts here. If you do miss the bus stop at Endrestø Nord, simply alight at Viste Hageby and cross the road. For current schedules, routes and prices, see: www.kolumbus.no.

By car: If you prefer to drive, there is a car park close to the start of the hike at the side of Hålandsvatnet. From Stavanger centre, take the E39 towards Randaberg. After about 5.5 km, turn left into Rv 509 towards Tananger, into Kvernevikveien. Follow this for about 2 km until you reach the Hålandsvatnet car park on your left. To reach the start of the hike, follow the directions above from Endrestø Nord bus stop. Note that if you are hiking from a car, you will need to double back and retrace your steps to return as the hike is described in one direction only.

Hike directions

Parts of this hike are marked with Stavanger "52 Tur" signs

From the Endrestø bus stop **(1)**, turn south with the sea on your right hand side. The path is marked with a T just to the seaward side of a rose hedge. Take it along the side of the inlet. The path follows the shore line past houses and up a short hill. From here, you can see a little harbour. Continue down the hill, past the harbour, and follow the winding trail, keeping the sea to your right. On the top of the next hill, you'll see a sculpture of a giant chain link. This is called the "Broken Link" **(2)**.

From the top of this bluff are views north towards the Viste coast, and also south to Tananger and the channel into Hafrsfjord. Continue along the path as it wiggles and winds further south, until approximately 1km from the Broken Chain it meets the Kvernevik Ring Road **(3)**. Turn right onto the road, and stay on the pavement until you are nearly at the large bridge. Look for a T-sign that points to a trail leading under the bridge

The Kvernevik Coast | Hike 6.2

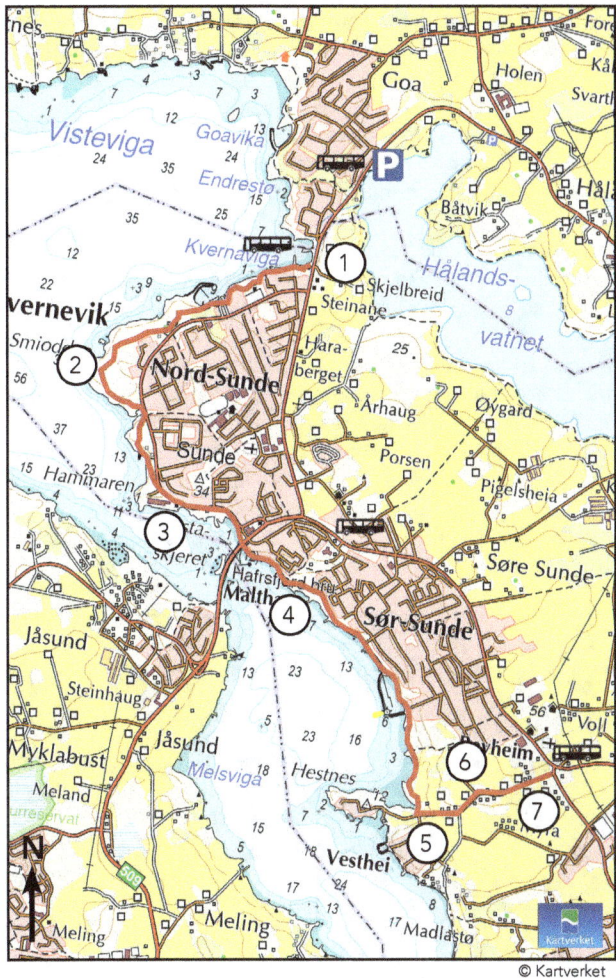
© Kartverket

on the right hand side. The Hafrsfjord bridge connects Stavanger with Tananger. By the side of the new, modern bridge, you'll see the remains of an older one.

Take the trail under the bridge, and continue along the coastal path. Soon you reach a small beach, with a picnic and recreation area (4). It is a good place to stop and appreciate the views along the fjord towards Madlasandnes. If you are finished hiking at this point and would like to

Urban Fresh Air and Sunday Waffles

Hike 6.2 | The Kvernevik Coast

cut your walk short, turn back towards the bridge and look for a T-sign pointing up the hill. This path leads back to the main road where you can catch the bus home.

The remainder of the hike follows the coastal trail along the shore of Hafrsfjord. The trail goes past several small harbours and beaches, which provide more opportunities for picnics, swimming and other fun.

When you reach a junction with a tarmac road (5), you have a choice. Either turn right, to join hike 6.3 at point (2) of the hike, or turn left into Hestnesveien to finish your walk.

If you choose to finish here, the road passes a house on the left hand side, which has an information board in the garden by the side of the road (6). If you have a few minutes to spare, take the time to stop and view the rock carvings here. Afterwards, rejoin the road and follow it straight uphill until it reaches Revheimsveien, the main, busy road (7). This road is on the bus routes to and from Kvernevik and Tananger, and you should be able to catch a bus. The nearest bus stop is slightly uphill at Revheim church.

The "Broken Link"
On 27 March 1980, the Alexander Kielland platform collapsed in the North Sea. For a short time, it was held to the seabed by one of the 6 anchor chains (the other 5 having snapped), but eventually the one remaining chain was unable to hold the structure and it also snapped. In all 123 people lost their lives. The broken chain sculpture, situated here on a bluff facing the North Sea, is a memorial to the people who died in the disaster.

Madlasandnes | Hike 6.3

Hike 6.3: Madlasandnes

An easy trail with views over Hafrsfjord, finishing at the "Three Swords" beach

This is a stretch of coastline dotted with little harbours, beaches, and an amazing "bridge" around a corner. Easy bus access allows for a one way hike, with the option of beginning with hike 6.2 for a longer outing.

Access 🚗 or 🚌	Grading 🚶
Terrain: gravel path	Length: 5.6km
Facilities: toilet, ice cream stand in summer, and picnic tables at Møllebukta	Time: 1hr 40mins

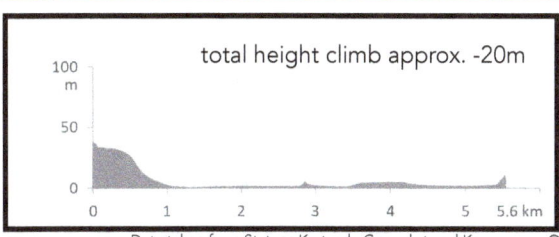

Data taken from Statens Kartverk, Geovekst and Kommunes, ©Kartverket

Urban Fresh Air and Sunday Waffles

Hike 6.3 | Madlasandnes

To reach the start of the hike:

By bus: This hike is best reached by bus, as this allows for hiking in one direction. The hike begins from the bus stop at Revheim Kirke, on Revheimsveien. On the way back, there are buses from Madlaleieren, Madlaforen, or Amfi Madla bus stops. For current schedules, routes and prices, see: www.kolumbus.no.

By car: If you prefer to drive, the simplest way is to park at the end of the hike, at Møllebukta, and walk "there and back" to Hestnes, at point (2). Although the walk is described only in the direction from Hestnes to Møllebukta, the route is straightforward to follow in the other direction. From Stavanger centre, drive west along Rv 441 towards Tananger. Take the second exit at the roundabout where Rv 441 intersects with the Rv440, continuing towards Tananger. About 1.5km beyond this junction, turn left along Madlaveien. After a few hundred metres, just before reaching Møllebukta, turn right into Regimentveien. The car park is signposted on the left.

Hike directions

Parts of this hike are marked with Stavanger "52 Tur" signs

From the bus stop (1), with your back to the Revheim church, either cross the road or immediately walk towards the pedestrian underpass on your left and towards the fjord and into Hestnesveien, where you walk downhill towards Hafrsfjord. Near the bottom of the hill, you will see an information board describing the ancient carvings in a rock outcrop just above the road. These are the Fluberget rock carvings. If you have a few minutes, it is worth stopping to see them. When you are ready, continue along the road. After a few metres more, a gravel track meets the road from the right (2). If you are joining this hike from hike 6.2, this is where you join.

Continue along the road until you see a signpost marking a track to the left, which goes along the shore of Hafrsfjord. Continue along the shore with the fjord on your right hand side. The path goes past some houses, and then meets another track coming in from the left. Continue to the right, along the shore. At Madlasandnes, the path goes between private harbours and private gardens (3). This might be slightly unusual to you, but the trail is well marked and you should be able to follow it

Madlasandnes | Hike 6.3

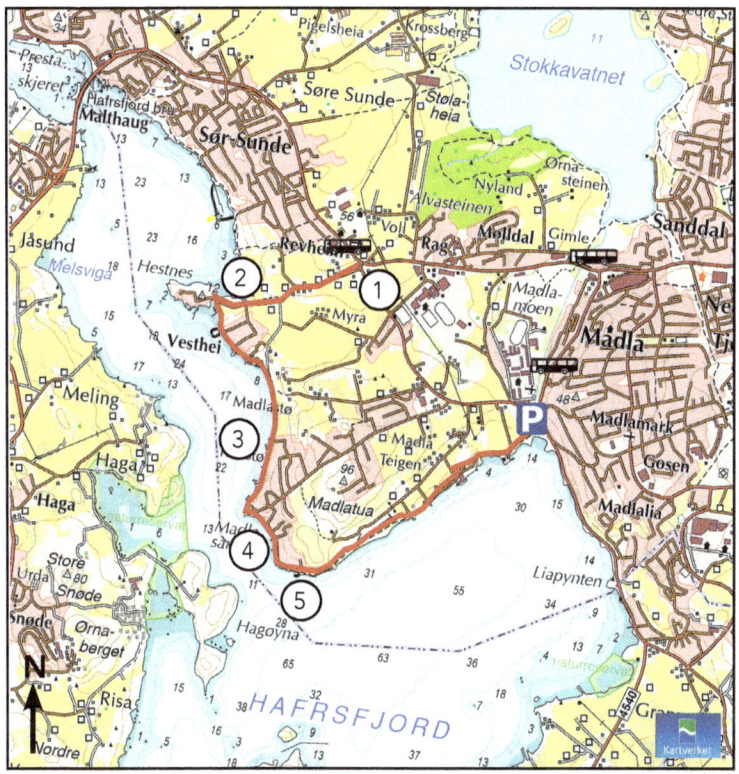

© Kartverket

around the headland until it joins a narrow road (4).

Continue along the road until you come to a most unusual "bridge" (5). There is a steep rocky headland here, which was impassable, but everyone wanted to be able to walk along the shore. The solution, in 2016, was to build an overhanging "bridge" around the rocks, followed by a steep cutting. This gives an easy path that allows for wheels as well as foot traffic. Enjoy both the bridge and the cutting, and afterwards continue along the shore. From here the trail is easy to follow as it passes houses, a small harbour, and finishes at the beach at Møllebukta.

Møllebukta offers toilets, an ice cream stand (in summer), picnic tables, and the famous "Three Swords" sculpture. Linger for a while and enjoy, before catching a bus back into town.

Hike 6.3 | Madlasandnes

To go back to town by bus, follow the stream from the beach up towards Regimentveien, cross and pass by the military training camp. Cross the road and you will find the Madlaleieren bus stop ahead. Alternatively, turn left into the walking path and follow the stream past the houses until you reach a small underpass. Madlaforen bus stop will be on your left, and there are also stops at Amfi Madla shopping centre.

The Fluberget Rock Carvings
This is a set of rock carvings from the Bronze Age (around 1800-500 BC). The carvings have been painted in red to make them easier to see. There are several motifs here that are also found in other places around Norway: boats, hands, circles and tally marks. More information is available both from the information board adjacent to the carvings, and in the Archaeological Museum in Stavanger.

The Three Swords
On a rocky outcrop just south of the beach at Møllebukta, three enormous bronze swords a plunged into the rock. This sculpture commemorates the battle of Hafrsfjord in 872. After this battle, Harald Hårfargre (Harold the Fair Headed) united Norway into one kingdom. The swords were designed by Jaeren artist Fritz Røed (1928-2002), and the monument was unveiled by King Olav of Norway in 1983.

Sørmarka and Ullandhaug Tarn | Hike 6.4

Hike 6.4: Sørmarka and Ullandhaug Tarn

A much-loved local wood that makes a fine outing in any season

Sørmarka has been preserved and cherished as the city of Stavanger grew around it. It offers gentle hills, easy walking, fine views and a Sunday afternoon cafe.

Access 🚗 or 🚌	Grading 🚶
Terrain: gravel path	Length: 5.1km
Facilities: Toilet at point (6) on map	Time: 1hr 20mins

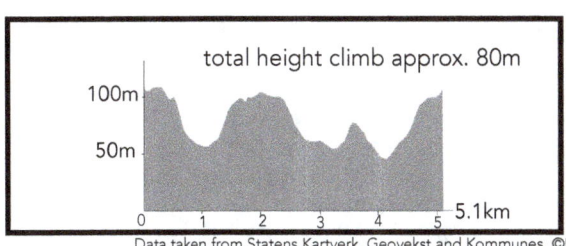

Data taken from Statens Kartverk, Geovekst and Kommunes, ©Kartverket

Urban Fresh Air and Sunday Waffles

Hike 6.4 | Sørmarka and Ullandhaug Tarn

To reach the start of the hike:

By car: From Stavanger, take the E39 south towards Kristiansand. Leave at the first exit signposted Ullandhaug, and turn right at the roundabout at the end of the slip road onto Rv 440. Turn left at the next roundabout, and proceed up the hill along Ullandhaugveien. Go straight over the set of traffic lights, then turn right at the next mini-roundabout into Folkeviseveien. Turn immediately right again (signposted "Ullandhaugtårnet" and "Botanisk Hage". You will be on a narrow road that turns sharp right to go underneath Ullandhaugveien. The car park is on the right hand side of the road shortly beyond the underpass.

By bus: local buses run along Ullandhaugveien, Madlamarkveien, and Tjodveien. Bus stops Jernaldergården, Tjodveien, and Gosen are near the start of the walk (at the time of writing, bus routes 4, 6, 7, and X60, among others). If you are unsure about where to get off the bus, ask the bus driver for "Sørmarka". For current schedules, routes and prices, see: www.kolumbus.no

Hike directions

Parts of this hike are marked with Stavanger "52 Tur" signs.

From the car park, turn so that you are facing towards the telecoms tower at the top of the hill. Look to your left, and you should see a road called "Ullandhaugleitet". Follow this road along fields and down a steep hill, which can be very icy in winter. The road ends in a T-junction (1). Turn right. You will come to a metal barrier that prevents cars from going further, and a "no motor vehicles allowed" sign. Just past these, turn left along a gravel track.

In about 20m, past some trees, you will see another track leading slightly to the left. It is marked with a T-sign, and Tur 37 (2). Follow this track to the left and around the side of the hill. (Beware! You may be tempted to follow a second track that goes to the right and UP the hill. Avoid this!).

The track leads to the top of the tunnel where the E39, the main road from Kristiansand to Bergen, goes under the hill. Above the tunnel entrance, the track turns sharp right and up the hill. Near the top of the hill is a path junction. Turn right and then immediately left here: you should end up on a track marked with a T-sign and Tur 37. This track winds through the woods and past the knoll of Hinnaberget to the left.

Sørmarka and Ullandhaug Tarn | Hike 6.4

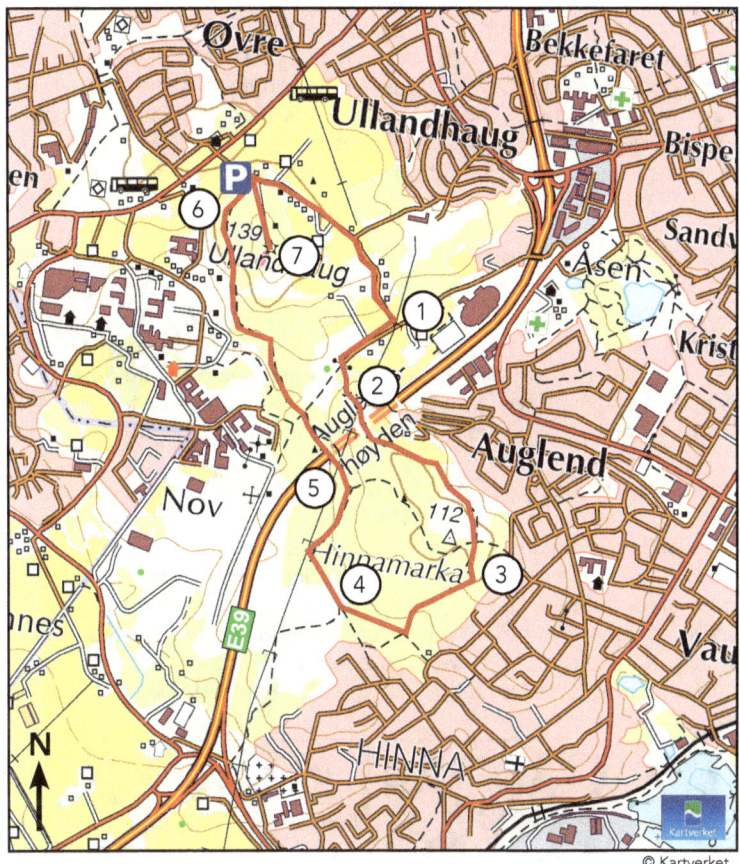

© Kartverket

Shortly after Hinnaberget there is a lovely area for picnics and games. Carry on when you are ready, down a little hill and past a small pond on your left. Just after the pond is a path crossroads. Continue straight across, and then turn sharp right down the first track after the crossroad: it's only about 20m further along (3). You should still be on the track marked with T-signs and Tur 37, but you are now very close to a bridle path that runs parallel to the track for a short while.

Continue through the woods until you reach another path junction, with a bridle path. Go straight here, following signs for Turs 37 and 28. At the bottom, there will be several paths, both walking and bridle. Take the

Urban Fresh Air and Sunday Waffles

Hike 6.4 | Sørmarka and Ullandhaug Tarn

first path to your right, and follow it until you see a little cabin just after another path junction. Bear right past the cabin, on a trail marked with a T-sign and Tur 28 (4). This track continues straight for a stretch, then turns right up a hill. Continue uphill until you reach a fork in the track. Take the left hand fork, and straight after this the right hand fork (marked with a T-sign and Tur 46). Continue walking straight, underneath some electricity lines and across a bridle path to pass over the south end of the E39 tunnel (5).

Carry on straight over the next crossing, past a small cabin (with basic WC facilities) on the right. Stay on the main gravel track, going straight over the next junction and following signs for Turs 37 and 5. As Tur 37 veers to the left, continue uphill along Tur 5. When you reach a bicycle rack, look to the left. Here is the Stavanger Botanical Garden (6). It is open 24 hours a day, free to visit, and well worth a detour or snack break. There are also public toilets within the garden area.

When you are ready, return to the main track the way you came in, and turn left to continue the hike. The track returns to the car park, but if the weather is decent or it's a Sunday afternoon, the fun isn't over yet. Follow the road up the hill to the communications tower that is visible from all over Stavanger (7). Enjoy the views of the city and perhaps some refreshments before you return to the car park. At the time of writing, the cafe in the tower was open on Sundays from February to June and August to December between 12noon and 3pm.

Stavanger Botanic Garden
Stavanger Botanic Garden is located on a south-facing slope adjacent to Sørmarka area. It is well tended, and there is usually plenty to see here. The trees and plants in the beds are labelled, and there is a toilet and picnic area. Entrance is free, and everyone is welcome to visit at any time of day.

The Viste Coastline | Hike 6.5

Hike 6.5: The Viste Coastline

Easy walking along a south-facing coast that has been inhabited since Stone Age times

This easy coastal walk offers views, an occasional beach and remnants of previous centuries, all within 15 minutes of the centre of Stavanger. It is a lovely walk at any time of day, but especially at sunset or when the wind is moderate and clouds are flying by. A wooded area and an STF day cabin at the far end of the hike give shelter from any inclement weather, and space for games. The first half kilometre of the hike is along a gravel path, and is ideal for wheelchairs and prams. However, beyond this the path does get quite rough underfoot.

Access 🚗 or 🚌	Grading 🚶
Terrain: gravel path, field and forest trail	Length: 4.8km
Facilities: Toilets at car park and Vistnes	Time: 1hr 10mins

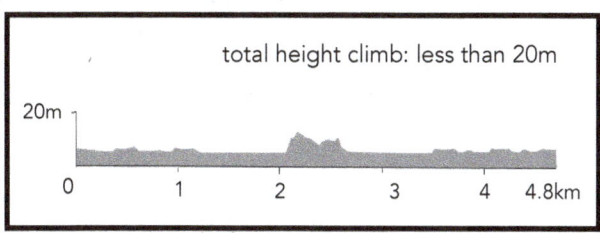

Data taken from Statens Kartverk, Geovekst and Kommunes, ©Kartverket

Urban Fresh Air and Sunday Waffles

Hike 6.5 | The Viste Coastline

To reach the start of the hike:

By car: from Stavanger centre, take the E39 towards Randaberg and Bergen. Continue along the E39 for just over 3km, and at Dusavik roundabout, take the third exit, signposted "Randaberg", into Randabergveien. The road turns sharp right just beyond the roundabout. Continue past some shops on the left hand side of the road, and immediately beyond these, turn left along "Goaveien" (signposted "Goa"). Continue straight over the first roundabout, then fork right at the next roundabout. Continue down a small hill, and turn left at the T-junction. The car park is straight ahead.

By bus: At the time of writing, bus number 15 from Stavanger stops at Viste Strandhotell, and bus number 3 stops at Viste Hageby, which is a 10 minute walk away from the start of the hike. For current schedules, routes, and prices, see www.kolumbus.no

Hike directions

Parts of this hike are marked with arrows on wooden boards.

Viste beach is located in front of the car park. It is a popular place for picnics, games and watersports. To the right hand side as you face the water are the buildings of the Viste Strandhotel. At the time of writing, the hotel cafe was open on occasion. To begin the hike, stand facing the sea just beside the car park. You will see the beach in front of you, extending away to the left. Look for the gravel track, which heads westwards along the coast, between the hotel on the right and the beach on the left.

Follow the track up a short hill **(1)**, and then down again to a little beach and harbour **(2)**. Shortly after the harbour, there is a yellow building. Continue straight, around the building, ignoring the gravel track that leads up the hill to your right, unless you want to take a short detour to Vistehola **(3)**. As you continue along the coast, look for lines of rocks leading into the sea. These are old boat pull-ins, and some still lead to boathouses on the shore. Carry on along the shoreline, up a short flight of stone steps and along the edge of a field. The path continues to hug the shoreline. Just after more stone boat pull-ins, there is a notice board at the side of the path with a map showing the trails around the farm of Vistnes **(4)**.

The Viste Coastline | Hike 6.5

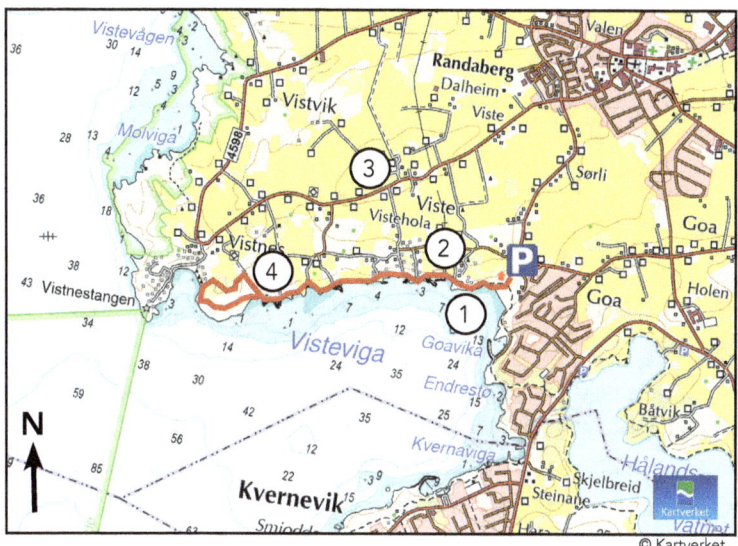

© Kartverket

Here the path forks: take the right hand fork, signposted "Vistnestunet". This track leads to the farming museum at Vistnestunet, which is well worth visiting if open (see box). Otherwise, walk down the track and then take the first path on the left, leading up a little hill and to a WC. Just past the WC on the right is a shelter built in amongst some trees. This is a good place for a break when the weather is windy or wet. When you are ready, turn right past the shelter, heading away from the sea and into the woods. Follow the path along the wall that forms the boundary between the wood and the farming land beyond. When you reach a stile on your right, turn left back through the woods.

From here, there are many small paths, and it doesn't really matter which you take up the hill and back towards the sea. If you see them, there are some small wooden signs with yellow arrows marked "ut". If you follow these, you will stay on the trail. However you get there, when you come out of the woods and on to the rocks, you should see the sea in front of you. This is a great place for a break in all weathers, since the beautiful wooden STF day cabin on the promontory provides shade or shelter as needed. The trail continues to the left, with the sea on your right hand side, across the rocks and back to the signpost at (4).

Urban Fresh Air and Sunday Waffles 73

Hike 6.5 | The Viste Coastline

Return to the car park along the same track: everything will look different from this direction. At the end of the hike, the beach at Viste is a lovely place to picnic, play or swim.

Vistehola
Vistehola is a 9 metre deep cave located approximately 200m inland from this hike. The site itself may look a little underwhelming, but the cave was inhabited during the Stone Age. Archaeological digs have discovered many artefacts and revealed much about how ancient people lived in this area. The skeleton of a young person who lived around 8,200 years ago was found in the cave. The remains are among the best preserved in Norway, and are housed today in the Archaeological Museum in Stavanger. There you will find more information about this remarkable site.

Vistnestunet
This area has been farmed for millennia: a local saying says that "Spring comes first to Randaberg, and there it comes first to the (south facing) Viste coastline". Vistnestunet is a farm museum that shows daily farming life at the end of the 1800s. On several weekends a year, it opens for theme days. Details are posted on www.jaermuseet.no (in Norwegian), and on their Facebook page, "Vistnestunet museumgård". The open days include activities for children, and are well worth a visit. At other times, Vistnestunet is a working farm. Please respect this, and restrict your visits to the open days.

Hike 6.6: Mariero to Jåttå

Sheltered coast with beach facilities at Vaulen and views to Lifjell and Dalsnuten

One of the most sheltered stretches of coast in the area, this hike offers something in every season. In summer, there is a beach with shallow swimming and water fun. When days are short, enjoy twilight skies and the moon rising over the hills on the opposite side of Gandsfjord.

Access 🚆 or 🚗	Grading 🚶
Terrain: gravel path	Length: 4.3km
Facilities: toilets, seasonal kiosk and water park at Vaulen, shops at Jåttå	Time: 1hr 15mins

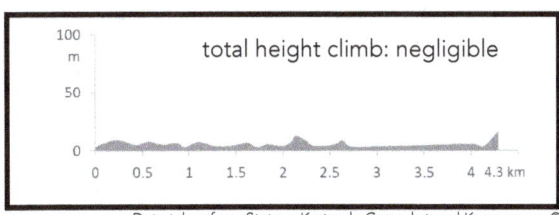

Data taken from Statens Kartverk, Geovekst and Kommunes, ©Kartverket

Urban Fresh Air and Sunday Waffles

Hike 6.6 | Mariero to Jåttå

To reach the start of the hike:

By train: This hike is best reached by train, as this allows for hiking in one direction. The hike begins from the train station at Mariero, on the train line between Stavanger and Sandnes. Note though, that not all trains between Stavanger and Sandnes will stop at Mariero: some of the express trains will be direct between the two centres. For current schedules, routes, and prices, see: www.kolumbus.no (although Kolumbus is the local bus company, they also include the local trains on their website).

By car: If you prefer to drive, there is a car park at Vaulen, near point (2) on the hike. Although this does put you in the middle of the walk, it may be an excellent option for those with very young children or others in the group who might prefer to enjoy the beach rather than hike. To get there from Stavanger: leave the town centre travelling south on Rv 44 towards Hinna. After about 5km, turn left along Stasjonsveien, signposted to Vaulen badeplass. Take care as this road is narrow and has speed humps. The road goes over a railway bridge, swings left, and ends at the car park about 800m from the junction with the Rv 44.

Hike directions

Parts of this hike are marked with Stavanger "52 Tur" signs

From Mariero train station, turn south along the cycle route that runs between the railway track and the shore of the fjord. Depending on which platform you alighted from, you may need to cross under the railway line via the underpass just to the north of the station. You should end up walking along the track with Gandsfjord on your left hand side. If visibility is good, you'll see a hill with a radio mast on top on the opposite side of Gandsfjord. This is Lifjell (hike 8.4). Soon the track will veer to the left, away from the railway line into a wood (1). Continue to follow it straight through the woods. Just before the woods open on to a beach, there is a trail to the left. This is a dead end along a little peninsula, but by all means explore it before returning to the main track. The track continues along a beach (2). Here there are water slides and diving platforms for everyone to enjoy, and if the day is warm there are likely to be swimmers of all ages here.

At the end of the beach, follow the shoreline around the car park, and look for the trail that follows the shore to the left. The path continues

Mariero to Jåttå | Hike 6.6

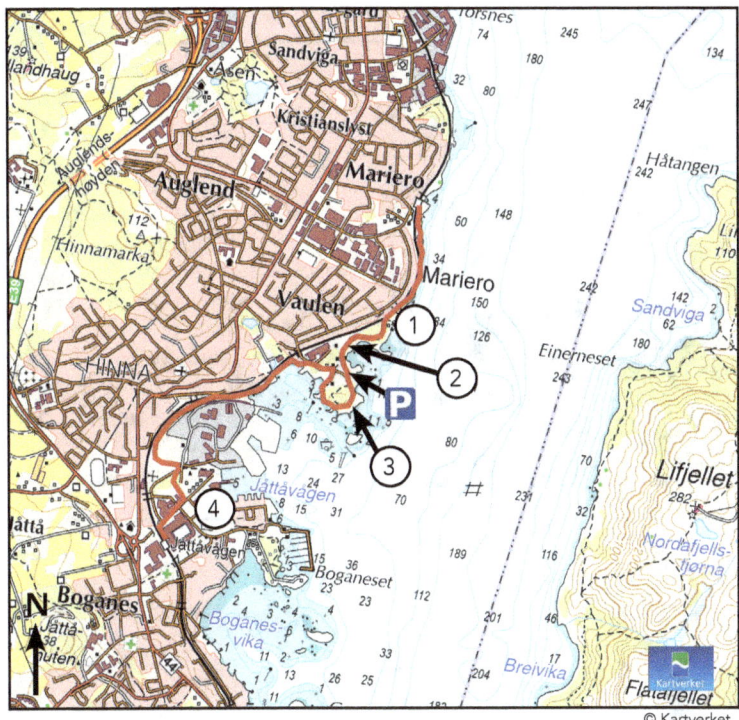
© Kartverket

around a small peninsula (3). The peninsula has woods, tiny coves, and is liberally dotted with picnic benches as well as a small playground on the far side. The path goes all the way around the headland, then loops back towards the car park. Turn left here, and follow the road away from the shore until you see a track on the left. Take this track past a tiny harbour and around a small bay to another tiny harbour. Here, the track turns inland but remains leafy as it goes between some buildings and the railway line. Stay on the track as it turns sharp left. You will emerge at a small car park and road junction.

Cross straight over the road and take the path on the right hand side that goes through the parkland towards the shops and offices at Jåttå. When you reach the main thoroughfare at Jåttå (4), turn right. Here there are restaurants and a shopping centre. When you are ready to take the train home, Jåttå train station is at the end of this road on the left hand side.

Urban Fresh Air and Sunday Waffles

Hike 6.6 | Mariero to Jåttå

Vaulen Beach

Vaulen beach is a much-loved local resource. Its location on the eastern side of the Stavanger peninsula shelters it from the worst of the Atlantic gales, and the shallow water becomes (relatively) warm on sunny days. There is permanent water play equipment, a seasonal kiosk, volleyball nets, toilets, and more: an easy place to spend a summer evening or a day outdoors, without travelling miles away from the city.

Store Stokkavatn | Hike 6.7

Hike 6.7: Store Stokkavatn

A beautiful lake, accessible to all

Store Stokkavatn is a large freshwater lake in the suburbs of Stavanger. It is much loved, and used by locals at all times of the day. During the dark winter months, the main trail around the lake is lit; this trail is rarely (if ever) empty of people. The trail is easy, and accessible to pushchairs.

Access 🚗 or 🚌	Grading 🏃, but longer than usual for this level of hike
Terrain: gravel path	Length: 8.2km
Facilities: Toilet at the Scout Camp **(5)**	Time: 2hr 10mins

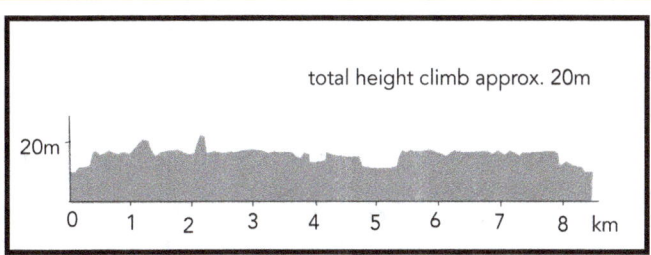

Data taken from Statens Kartverk, Geovekst and Kommunes, ©Kartverket

Urban Fresh Air and Sunday Waffles

Hike 6.7 | Store Stokkavatn

To reach the start of the hike:
By car: From Stavanger centre, take Madlaveien (Rv 441) westwards. Continue past a large roundabout with a flyover for cyclists and pedestrians. Go straight across and continue straight over the next two roundabouts. Turn right into Ragbakken at the next roundabout, and right again to enter the car park. The car park is notable for the adjacent electricity substation, which is decorated with modernist graffiti.

By bus: Several bus routes, such as 2 and 3, run very close to the start of this hike. Good places to alight from the bus are the large shopping centre at Madla Amfi or Møldalsveien. From there, follow the cycle lane under the main road and turn right to reach the start of the hike. For current bus routes, prices, and schedules, see www.kolumbus.no

Hike Description

This hike is marked with Stavanger 52 Tur signs

From the car park, take the trail past the electricity substation and through woods. Turn right at the T-junction to begin an anti-clockwise circuit of the lake. The first thing you will come across is a bridge over an inlet, where the local duck population is often being fed by enthusiastic toddlers. A little further along, on the right hand side of the trail, is an adult "playground". This training area has been built so that people can incorporate strength and flexibility training into their outdoor workouts (1).

Continue along the trail, keeping the lake to your left hand side. Soon you will reach an outdoor deck, from which you can access the lake for a swim, which is very popular on warm summer days. As you ascend a small hill, look for the specimen trees in the little arboretum here (2). There is a sign (in Norwegian) explaining a little about the society that maintains the area, and some of the trees are labelled. From here, the path descends a hill and enters a short stretch of thick woods. It emerges into a wetland area: continue straight at the next two path junctions, then follow the trail to the right and up another small hill (3).

At the top of the hill the trail ends at a tarmac road. Continue straight, and follow the road downhill. In winter, this hill is sometimes icy, so care may be needed. At the bottom of the hill, turn right, keeping the lake to your left. For most of the rest of the hike, the trail hugs the shoreline.

Store Stokkavatn | Hike 6.7

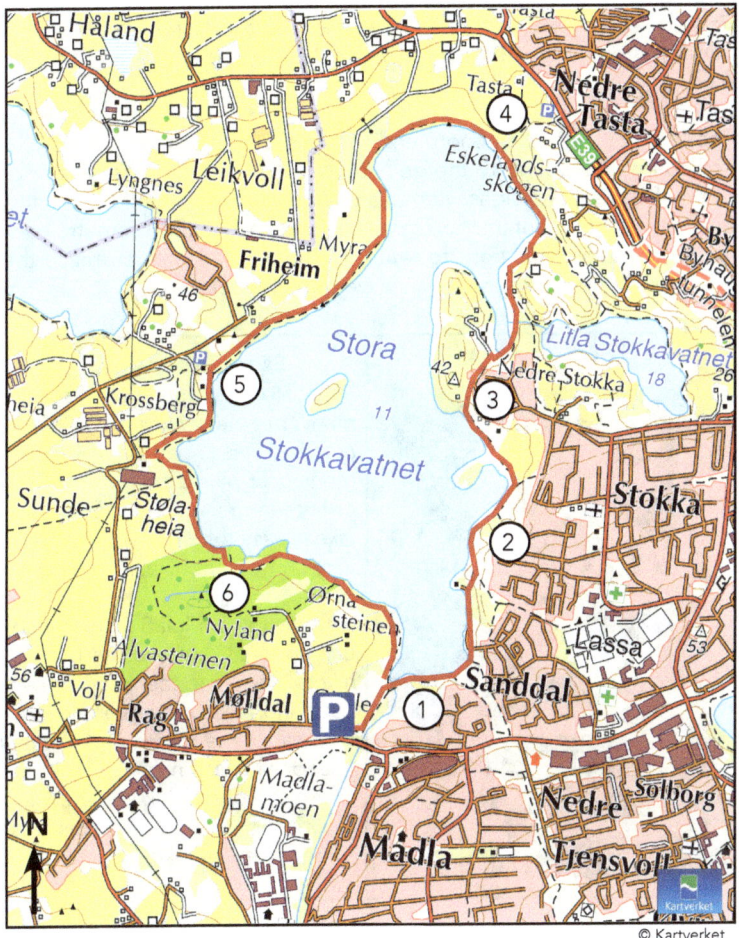

© Kartverket

The next 3km of trail follow the north shore of the lake. Enjoy the picnic areas (4) and any wildlife you spot: there are deer living in this area. As you near the areas of Friheim and Krossberg, there are a couple of small hills. When you emerge form the woods into a field, you have reached the Scout area, Speidermarka (5). You may see canoes stacked by the side of the field, and also the toilet block at the far side. The area is frequently used by school, youth and community groups.

Urban Fresh Air and Sunday Waffles

Hike 6.7 | Store Stokkavatn

Another 50m or so along the path lies Stavanger Roklubb (Stavanger Rowing Club). The clubhouse is set back from the shore slightly. On Sunday afternoons, the club serves waffles from here as a way to raise funds.

The trail continues through undulating woods, past a junction to Krossberg and around to the golf course (6). The trail crosses parts of the golf course, and signs warn trail users to beware of golf balls in this area. From the end of the golf course, it is just over half a kilometre back to the trail that turns right to return to the car park. If you reach the bridge with the ducks again, you have gone too far.

Store Stokkavatn

This area is many things to many people: an outdoor gym, picnic and barbecue area, running or hiking trail, cycle trail, orienteering area and more. The lake is easy to reach, and makes a very convenient hike.

However, it is a full 8.2km around the edge of the lake, and some hikers find that the easy gravel path and mostly level terrain lack interest for the length of the hike. Younger hikers, in particular, may find it tedious to hike all the way around without games or activities to break up the hiking.

Hike 6.8 Hålandsvatnet

Hålandsvatnet is a beautiful, tranquil lake with a gravel track around the perimeter

This lake, just to the north west of the better-known Store Stokkavatn, provides an undulating gravel track all the way around its perimeter. Whilst at Store Stokkavatn the walking is more through forest than open land, here there are fewer trees and more open views. The terrain is generally gentle, with just the odd short slope, giving a very popular hike at all times of the year.

Access 🚗 or 🚌	Grading 🚶
Terrain: gravel path	Length: 7.0km
Facilities: none	Time: 1hr 45mins

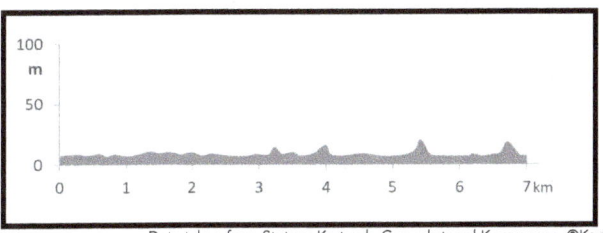

Data taken from Statens Kartverk, Geovekst and Kommunes, ©Kartverket

Urban Fresh Air and Sunday Waffles

Hike 6.8 | Hålandsvatnet

To reach the start of the hike:

By car: The car park is at the start of the hike at the side of Hålandsvatnet. From Stavanger centre, drive west along Madlaveien Rv 441. Take the exit into Kvernevikveien at the roundabout where Rv 509 intersects with the RV 441, just before the Hafrsfjord bridge. The car park is signposted on the right hand side of the road after approximately 2km.

By bus: From Stavanger, take the bus (at the time of writing, this was number 3) to Viste Hageby, and alight at Endrestø Nord. The start of the hike is just ahead of you, by the car park information board. For current schedules, routes, and prices, see www.kolumbus.no

Hike directions

Parts of this hike are marked with arrows on wooden boards.

There is an information board at the car park. Stand in front of this, facing the lake, and look for the start of the track around the lake on your right hand side. Take this track (you should have the lake on your left hand side). You will enter a wood and, just after crossing a stream, a path leaves the track to the right (1). Continue straight here, keeping the lake on your left hand side.

At the next path junction, bear left (staying close to the shore), and follow the trail over a little bluff and along the shore to another path junction (2). Again, keep straight, staying close to the shore. The path will come to a junction with a narrow road (3). Here, you are very close to Store Stokkavatn. Take the track to the left, which winds up through a small wood and along beside the houses at Friheim. Just after the houses, the trail meets another road. Again, take the trail to the left, keeping close to the shore. The trail becomes a little more undulating, as it winds along the north shore of the lake.

As you begin to get near the car park again, a path junction shows another track leading north up a (quite steep) hill (4). This track leads to an alternative car park. Rather than take this track, fork left to follow the shore of the lake again. The trail goes up a short, steep hill before descending back down to the car park.

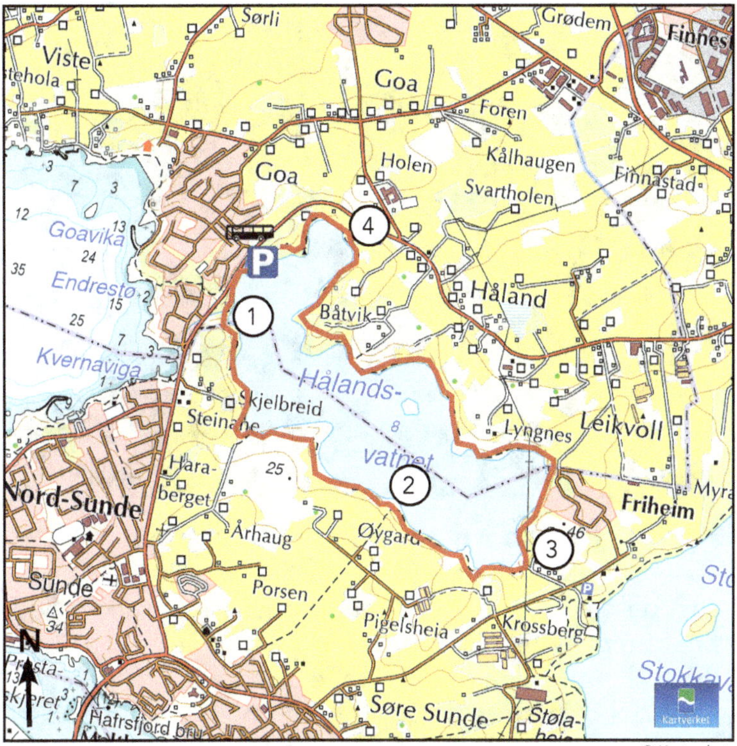

Hålandsvatnet | Hike 6.8

Urban Fresh Air and Sunday Waffles

Hike 6.8 | Hålandsvatnet

Krossberg and the modern cross

Just before point (3) on the hike, there is a place called Krossberg. The word "kross" in the name implies that this is the site of an ancient stone cross, and oral tradition had told of a cross on top of the knoll. In the 1920s, there was a search for the remains of a cross. Nothing was found on the knoll. When a wider area was scoured, broken fragments of the top of a cross were discovered at the side of Hålandsvatnet. These fragments are on display at the Archaeological Museum in Stavanger, and a modern stone cross has been erected on the original knoll (pictured here).

The Arboretum and Steinfjellet | Hike 6.9

Hike 6.9: The Arboretum and Steinfjellet

A calming labyrinth of trails, trees, ponds and flowers, with a little hill and viewpoint

Nestled in the hills to the south of Sandnes lies the Arboretum ("Arboret" in Norwegian). On Sundays, there is a waffle cafe. The area is perfect for a leisurely stroll. Almost all of the trails within the Arboretum are suitable for push chairs or wheelchairs, as is all but the final 200m of the hike described here. This hike goes through one of the nicest areas of the Arboretum and then climbs Steinfjellet to enjoy the views of the surrounding low hills and fields.

Access 🚗	Grading 🚶
Terrain: gravel path	Length: 4.0km
Facilities: Sunday cafe and toilets (1)	Time: 1hr 15mins

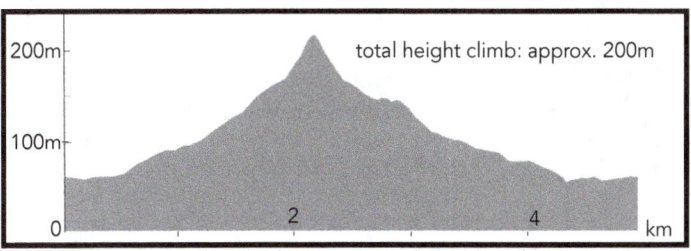

Data taken from Statens Kartverk, Geovekst and Kommunes, ©Kartverket

Urban Fresh Air and Sunday Waffles

Hike 6.9 | The Arboretum and Steinfjellet

To reach the start of the hike:

By car: From Stavanger, drive south on the E39 towards Kristiansand. Just under 4km south of exit number 27 (Lauvvik/Hommersåk), turn left on to Rv 333 ("Espelandveien"); there is a signpost saying "Arboret". Follow Rv 333 for 1.2 km, and then turn left into the signposted parking lot for the Arboretum.

This car park is large and convenient, but it is not free! Please use a ticket machine to pay, and display your ticket in the windscreen of your car. All proceeds from car parking fees go towards the expenses of maintaining this wonderful Arboretum.

Hike Description

This hike is marked with wooden signposts, many of which were faded at the time of writing. The Arboretum is a relatively small area containing many, many paths: route finding can be tricky because it might not be obvious which path you are on! It may help to remember that uphill is away from the car park, and downhill is towards it.

From the section of the car park nearest to the road, face the ticket machine and turn right along the track to the main Arboretum entrance. Continue straight through the metal gates on the track and two green "welcome" signs. On the left, there is a little wooden sign saying "Solstien". Follow the arrow straight ahead.

The path bends to the right. Follow it, again following the "Solstien" arrow. You will see a lake on your right. Continue past the lake, and past a track that goes off to the right. (If you want to make a detour to the waffle cafe (1), take the track to the right here).

The Arboretum and Steinfjellet | Hike 6.9

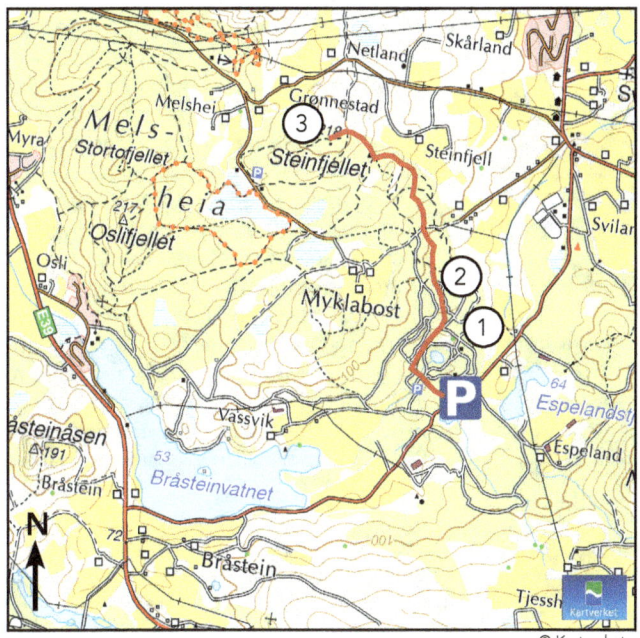

© Kartverket

At the next path crossroads, turn left uphill (a right turn at this crossroads will also take you to the waffle cafe), and then immediately branch right, along a trail signposted "Poppelstien". Continue straight, past a pond on the right hand side. Further up the hill is a second pond, also on the right. This area is planted with rhododendrons and is spectacular in spring. The second pond is lovely for picnics and games.

After the second pond, there is a path junction. Cross straight over and over the little bridge, signposted "Kjaerlighetstien"(2). Carry straight on at the next path junction, along a track with a large boulder on the right hand side. After approximately 200m, the trail forks: take the left hand fork up the hill. Continue straight over the next junction in about 25m, signposted

Urban Fresh Air and Sunday Waffles

Hike 6.9 | The Arboretum and Steinfjellet

"Rundgangen".

Continue straight again at the next path junction. The path bends to the left uphill. Turn right at the next junction, signposted "Fjellveien". Follow the "Fjellveien" straight across the next junction, and then fork left twice, to keep on the main trail. Keep straight as you leave the Arboretum, and then turn right when you reach a junction, signposted "Steinfjellet". At the time of writing, the sign was almost hidden by a large bush. If you miss the turn, you will find yourself descending gently through the forest towards a car park at Melshei. If this happens, retrace your steps to the path junction and take the turn marked "Steinfjellet". The path continues uphill: the final 200m of trail is over stones, marked with red dots.

From the top of Steinfjellet (3), enjoy looking down over the Arboretum and across to the surrounding hills. There are several sheltered spots for picnics and snacks.

Return the way you came, following signs marked "Arboret". Once you are back in the Arboretum area, either continue the way you came, or explore some of the other trails in the Arboret.

The waffle cafe (located on the east side of the lake nearest the car park) is usually open on Sundays.

Orre Friluftshuset and Beach | Hike 6.10

Hike 6.10: Orre Friluftshuset and Beach

Pristine beaches and dunes with views across Jaeren to the mountains beyond

An easy stroll along beach, dune and coastline. The views are spectacular here: out to sea you'll watch supply boats, cruise ships, fishing boats and others as they traverse the Jaeren coast. Inland, the views cross the local farmland to the hills and mountains beyond. This is a fine hike for everyone to enjoy at any time of year, and particularly on Sundays when the Sunday cafe at the Friluftshuset offers a range of drinks and snacks.

Access 🚗	Grading 🚶, but long for this level
Terrain: sand dunes, path	Length: 9.2km, (easy to shorten)
Facilities: Cafe, toilet at the car park	Time: 2hrs 20mins

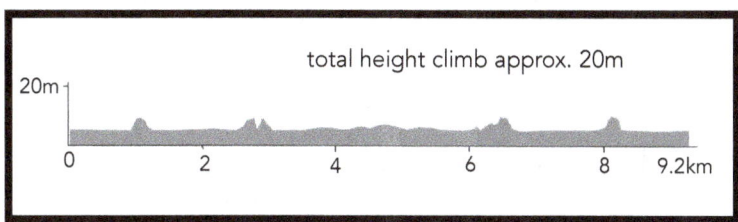

Data taken from Statens Kartverk, Geovekst and Kommunes, ©Kartverket

Urban Fresh Air and Sunday Waffles

Hike 6.10 | Orre Friluftshuset and Beach

To reach the start of the hike:

By car: From the centre of Stavanger, take the E39 south in the direction of Kristiansand. After about 6.5km, exit on Rv 509 (signposted Sola and Sola airport) Continue through a tunnel, and just after leaving it (about 3.5km after leaving the E39), exit and take Rv 510 south towards Rege. Continue along until you reach a junction with Rv 507 (just over 14km). Here you will see Orre Friluftshuset signposted to the right. Turn right along the Rv 507 and follow this road. You will see the large freshwater lake of Orrevatnet on your left hand side. Beyond the lake, after you pass the gokart track (signposted Gokart bane), look for another sign for Orre Friluftshuset on the right hand side. The signposted track leads to the car park 300m along on the right.

Hike Description

This hike is not marked, but the trail is straightforward to find

From the car park, follow the track towards the sand dunes and over a ditch. As soon as you have crossed the ditch, fork left along a trail that heads across the sand dunes. There are many small paths that cross one another: it doesn't matter which you take, or even if you cross over the dunes and walk along the beach, provided you keep the sea on your left hand side and the fields on your right hand side! Continue northwards up the coast for approx. 1km. Here Orre beach ends at a spit facing out towards the sea (1). On the other side of the spit is another beach: this one has more pebbles than Orre beach, but is no less lovely.

Following either the beach or the dunes, walk along to the next spit. This one has a concrete bunker on the far side of it (2), and a metal tower about 200m further inland. Follow any path past the metal tower. Here, the beaches turn to pebbles and the path follows along the side of fields. In approximately one more kilometre, the path joins a gravel track. When the path turns sharp right towards a large house, leave it and look for a path along the coast. Follow this until it ends at a little harbour.

This harbour is Revehammen (3). It comes as a surprise that there is a place along this windswept coast calm enough to slip a small boat in and tie up. The harbour is very old: it was one of few places along the Jaeren coast to launch fishing boats from. The coastal path continues from here to Borestranden and then to Hellestø beach (see Hike 7.4). If you

Orre Friluftshuset and Beach | Hike 6.10

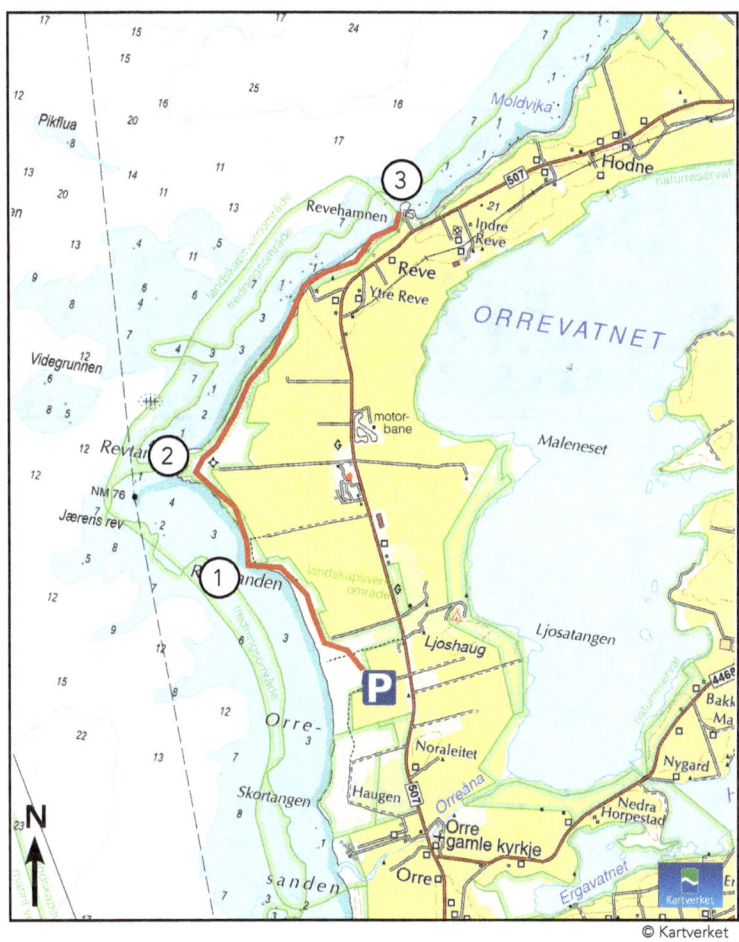

© Kartverket

have energy, or perhaps can arrange one-way transport, it's perfectly possible to continue. Otherwise, this is a good place to turn around and follow the coast back to Orre Friluftshuset and the car park. Although the return is along the same coast, walking back offers different views, especially if you choose another path along the dunes and beaches.

The track back across the dunes to the car park can sometimes be difficult to find. It is about halfway along the beach: look for the wooden boardwalk that has been built to protect the dunes. If you reach a river

Hike 6.10 | Orre Friluftshuset and Beach

crossing, you have found Orreåna, the river that drains the lake you passed on the way to the car park. Turn around and look again for the Friluftshuset about 1km back along the beach.

Orre Friluftshuset
is nestled in the sand dunes to the side of the car park. On Sundays, there is a snack bar here, with waffles, snacks, hot and cold drinks and a piano to play. On cold or windy Sundays it is an ideal place to warm up. For more information (in Norwegian) see: www.jaerenfri.no/friluftsenter

Hike 6.11: Hå Gamle Prestegard to Obrestad Havn

A classic stretch of Jaeren coastline

This stretch of coastline showcases the classic Jaeren shore. Although the hike is quite short, it offers beautiful pebble beaches, a harbour in use since antiquity and an old farm now put to use as an art centre and coffee shop. It's worth the drive from the Stavanger area at any time of year, especially on a summer evening or weekend in winter. The coffee shop is open during the week as well as at weekends.

Access	Grading
Terrain: fields, rocky shore	Length: 3.4km
Facilities: Cafe, toilet at the car park	Time: 50mins

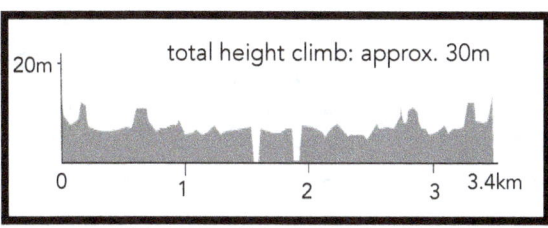

Data taken from Statens Kartverk, Geovekst and Kommunes, ©Kartverket

Urban Fresh Air and Sunday Waffles

Hike 6.11 | Hå Gamle Prestegard to Obrestad Havn

To reach the start of the hike:

By car: The hike starts and finishes at Hå Gamle Prestegard. From Stavanger, take the E39 south in the direction of Kristiansand. After 12km, leave the motorway on the Rv 44 towards Bryne. After 25km, turn right, signposted Hå Gamle Prestegard and Obrestadt Fyr. This road ends at Hå Gamle Prestegård after 3.4km. The car park is on the left.

Hike Description

This hike is marked with blue posts and blue dots on rocks.

From the car park, face the sea and look to your left for a blue trail marker. You will climb over a fence into a field. The blue markers show the way across the field and along the coast. Follow them around the bay called "Fuglavike". After about 1km, you will come around a headland and see a track uphill signposted "Obrestad Fyr" (1). This is an old lighthouse and is just a short detour up the hill. The main trail continues around the coastline, and is well marked with blue dots.

Just less than another kilometre brings you to the beautiful bay at Obrestad. You can choose to walk along the sandy beach, or keep your feet dry on the pebbles above the sand. At the far side of the bay is Obrestad Havn (2).

This may be far enough for a Sunday afternoon stroll. If you wish to walk further, the trail does continue beyond Obrestad Havn along the "Kongevegen", (see overleaf), although it is less well marked in places. From here, or beyond if you choose to go further, turn and return the way you came.

Obrestad Havn
This is a harbour that has been in use since antiquity. If you look carefully up the hillside, you can make out a mound, which is the ruin of an ancient boathouse. It is thought that this boathouse was in use during the Iron Age.

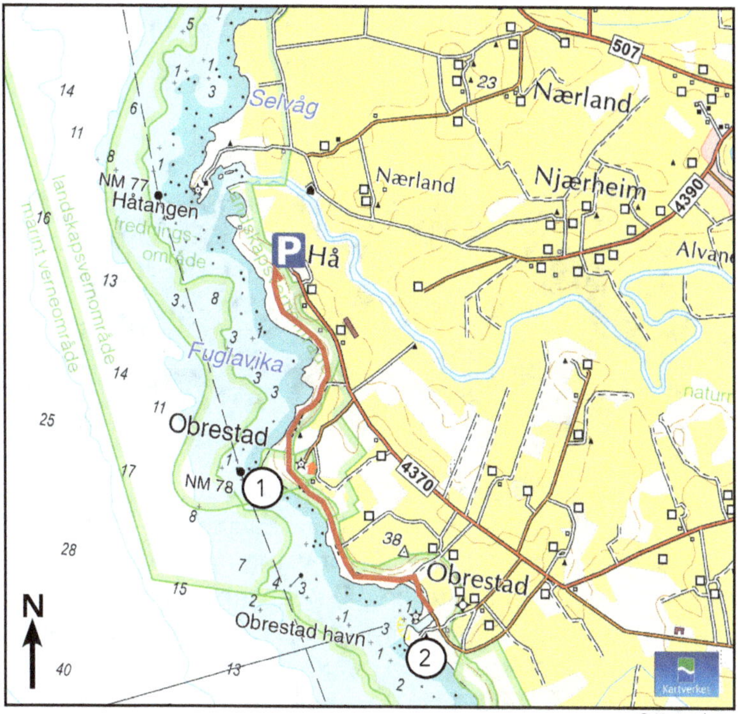

Hå Gamle Prestegard to Obrestad Havn | Hike 6.11

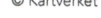

© Kartverket

Hå Gamle Prestegard

Hå Gamle Prestegard translates literally as ""Hå Old Priest's Farm". It is a farm dating back to ancient times. Today it is used as an art centre by Hå Kommune. There is always an exhibition to see, and there are often classes and workshops happening here too. A cafe serves home-made goodies in one of the farm buildings: see www.hågamleprestegard.no for more information.

Urban Fresh Air and Sunday Waffles

Hike 6.11 | Hå Gamle Prestegard to Obrestad Havn

South of Obrestad Havn: discovering the Kongevegen

The coastal trail continues for miles south of Obrestad Havn: to the farm museum at Grødaland, the beautiful chapel and ancient graveyard at Varhaug, and eventually meeting the main road (Rv44) near the tiny harbour of Madlandshamma. Parts of this stretch of the trail were once part of the main road between Ogna and Sandnes. The road is ancient, and the level terrain allows it to be wide enough for horses and wagon to traverse. Anywhere that a horse and wagon can go, a king in a carriage can also go, and the road was named "Kongevegen", because royalty travelled along it.

The walking along Kongevegen is gentle, and the path is good in most places, although it is not all compatible with buggies or wheels, and there are one or two muddy fields to cross. If you would like to explore it, there are car parks at Grødaland and Varhaug Gamle Kirkegard (Varhaug Old Graveyard) as well as at Hå Gamle Prestegard.

Chapter 7:
Shorter Hikes, Stunning Scenery

The hikes in this chapter seek to take you out of the urban areas and into the countryside. They are between 4 to 8.3km long, are all graded easy and have negligible climb. For the large part, they take you to the coast, from the North Sea to the fjords, visiting some of the Ryfylke islands on the way. That said, this chapter also finds the way to a delightful mountain valley (Røssdalen), the shore of an inland lake (Frøylandsvatnet), and a high walk in the Jaeren moors (Synesvarden).

The Lundesnes Tour | Hike 7.1

Hike 7.1: The Lundesnes Tour

Fine coastline and excellent views

The island of Hundvåg may be a dormitory suburb for Stavanger, but it still boasts wonderful coastal trails with inlets, rocks, views in three directions and beautiful sandy beaches. Of the several hiking trail loops on the island, this one showcases the best of the scenery and makes for an excellent hike with many places to stop, picnic and enjoy.

Access 🚗 OR 🚌	Grading 🚶
Terrain: gravel path, road, coast	Length: 8.3km
Facilities: none	Time: 2hr 10mins

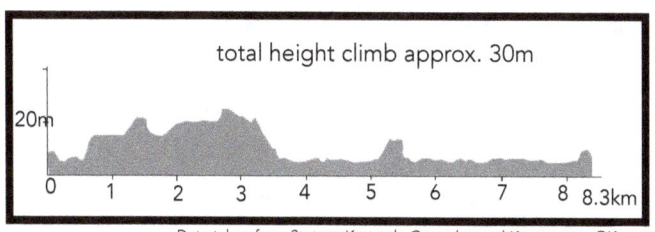

Data taken from Statens Kartverk, Geovekst and Kommunes, ©Kartverket

Shorter Hikes, Stunning Scenery

Hike 7.1 | The Lundesnes Tour

To reach the start of the hike:

By car: The hike starts and finishes at the public car park close to Lundsvågen Marina. From Stavanger, travel across the bridges (there are three in total) to the island of Hundvåg. At the roundabout after the third bridge, turn left and continue 1.2km to the next roundabout. Turn right here, and then continue around the Hundvåg ring for 2.2km until you reach a roundabout with a supermarket on the left hand side. Turn right here into Lundabakken, and right again at the T-junction after 430m. The car park is on the left after approximately 350m on Kisteneset road. If you come to a large marina (Lundsvågen), you have gone too far.

By bus: There is a regular bus service that goes around the "Hundvåg Ring", which passes close to this hike at points (1) (bus stop Lundshagen) and (4) (bus stop Husabøåkeren). For current schedules, routes, and prices, see www.kolumbus.no

Hike Description

This hike is marked with Stavanger "52-Tur" signs.

From the car park, return to the road (Lundeveien), turn right and look for the path between the road and the shore, marked with a T-sign, next to houses numbered 23, 25, and 25B on Lundeveien. Follow this gravel trail (marked with T-signs) along the coast, past houses and following it as it makes a right turn slightly uphill into Lundsvågen street, until the trail meets a road crossing. Cross the road via the pedestrian crossing, and turn immediately right past the front of a supermarket. Take an immediate left turn, and after 50m take the next left up "Pepperhaugen"(1) with your back to "Lunde Skole", which is the school building behind you.

After 70m, just before the road bends to the left, turn right along a track, towards a tyre swing set. There will be a ditch to the left beside the track. Carry on straight past the houses and on to an open area. About 100m past the houses, turn left at the track crossing (signposted Tur no. 2) towards a small hill (2). Follow the track up the incline, past a gazebo on the left and turn right along the road where the track ends in a T-junction with a road (signposted Tur no. 2).

Continue to the white church and turn right just past it (signposted Tur no. 2) (3). Follow the road straight over a crossroads, and take the next

The Lundesnes Tour | Hike 7.1

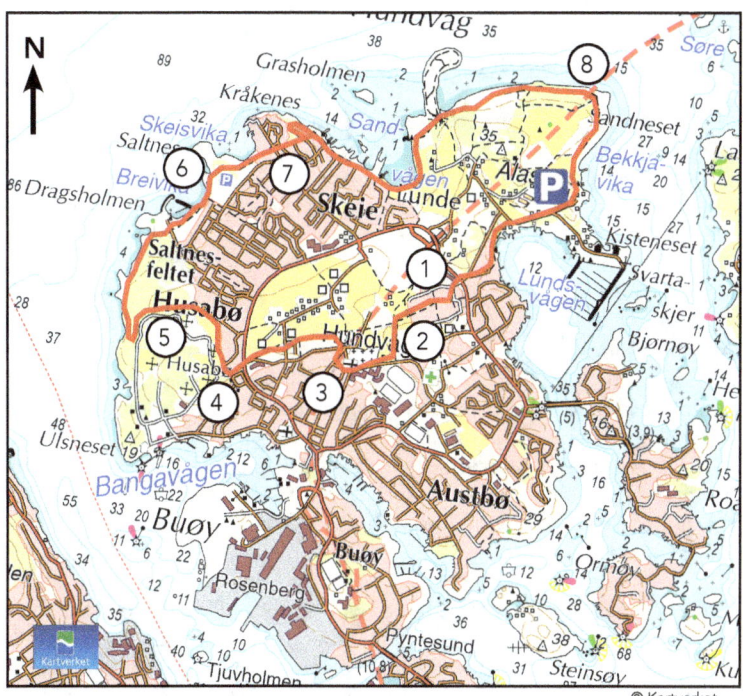

left down a cycle track (signposted Tur no. 2). At the next (busy) road crossing, fork right to go under the underpass. Once you have gone underneath, the track continues straight towards some tall trees. 80m beyond the underpass, turn right up a track that goes between houses (4). There is a sign marked Tur no. 2, but it is easy to miss. You should be heading towards a radio antenna.

Follow this track as it turns right alongside a perimeter fence. When the track ends at a road, turn left, still following the fence. This road ends in a car park. Cross the car parking area, and then fork left along a wood-chipped track (signposted Tur no. 2). The perimeter fence should still be to your left. This is "Trollskogen" (The Troll Wood), a local favourite for picnics and playing.

Where the wood-chip trails diverge, fork left (signposted Tur no. 2) (5). The path winds through the woods and to the shore, where it takes a U-turn and begins to follow the shoreline northwards. The trail emerges

Hike 7.1 | The Lundesnes Tour

from the trees; there are views across the Byfjord to Tasta and Dusavik. Continue along the path as it follows the rocky shoreline, perhaps making use of one of the barbecue pits or picnic tables.

In just over half a kilometre, there is a little inlet. Turn right and follow the T-sign along the track towards a building housing an electricity substation. The track ends in a tarmac road; turn left and then immediately right along a gravel track (6). You should be heading east, with a harbour on your left and houses on your right. Continue past the houses and along the track for the next kilometre. When the track ends at a road junction, turn right.

After 75m, look left for a narrow path between the houses. If you reach a pedestrian crossing, you have gone too far. Take this track (7), cross straight over a road, and continue straight past a playing field. Just after this, the path ends in a T-junction at a road. Turn left along the road in front of a line of garages. The next track is straight ahead, through a metal gate. Take this track, and follow it as it bends immediately to the right. The trail now follows the coast, past harbours and around a playing field.

Once you pass a set of picnic tables with a modern sculpture in the form of a ship, continue straight along the coast, enjoying the views towards Hjelmeland (8). Soon you pass an electric power station cladded in copper, and will reach the tip of the peninsula at Lundesneset, with its monument (see below). This part of the coast is used by the local Scouts, and has an amphitheatre that is perfect for games and picnics. Past this, the trail continues towards a playing field and along a gravel path back to the car park.

The Utøya monument

On the farthest reach of Lundesnes, in a place good for quiet reflection, stands a monument to the 77 people who were killed in the massacre at Utøya on 22 July 2011.

Around Vassøy | Hike 7.2

Hike 7.2: Around Vassøy

Discover one of the prettiest of the "city islands" (byøyene)

This walk takes you away from the city centre, and right into the fjords and islands known as byøyene, the "city islands" of Stavanger. The walk circumnavigates the island and takes you through both urban and natural parts of Vassøy. For this reason sturdy footwear is recommended.

Access	Grading
Terrain: paved road, moorland	Length: 5.7km
Facilities: picnic tables, barbecue pits	Time: 2hrs

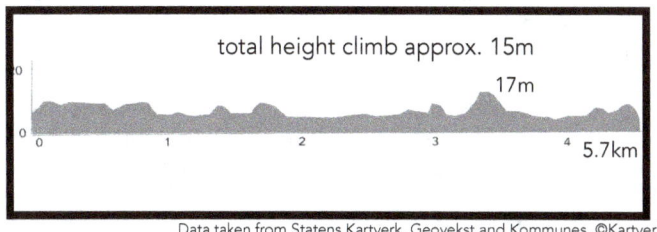

Data taken from Statens Kartverk, Geovekst and Kommunes, ©Kartverket

Shorter Hikes, Stunning Scenery

Hike 7.2 | Around Vassøy

To reach the start of the hike:

This hike may only be reached by ferry. Ferries leave from the boat/ferry terminal in Stavanger (Fiskepiren). Ferry route number 898 departs from Jorenholmen quay and Ferry route 800 leaves from the Bakerbrygga 1 quay. Travel times vary between 15min to 45min depending on the boat taken. You can plan your travel through the local public transport website www.kolumbus.no

Hike Description

This hike is marked with Stavanger "52-Tur" signs and red dots.

NB: *Generally, the signs for the '52 hverdagsturer' are well positioned and will help with navigation. Sometimes though they might be difficult to see due to having been overgrown by vegetation, might be damaged or fallen off. In addition to these 'T-signs', the path is also marked by red dots on rocks or trees beyond the areas that are built up. These are also a good navigation tool, but are starting to fade along the eastern shoreline.*

The hike starts from the ferry quay on Vassøy (1), where you will see a small kiosk/supermarket ahead as you leave the pier. There you will see the 'red T' and also the number of the walk as number '32' on the signpost at Nordstrandveien, pointing left towards the north of the island.
Turn left, and walk along Nordstrandveien (2) until the end of the road. The path then takes you in the direction of the northern tip of the island (3). The view opens towards the other "byøyene" (city-islands) to the west, and the fjords and mountains to the east.

As you move along the path on the eastern side of the island, you may observe all kinds of pleasure boats and yachts, which might be out on the fjords. The trail on this side of the island (4) can be surprisingly rough, muddy and wet at times. The path follows the coast weaving in and out of forested areas.

As you continue to walk in a southerly direction, you find yourself back in urban surroundings. Reaching Sørstrandveien (5), the path will lead towards Peisaren, a delightful small beach (6) with picnic tables, a beach volleyball court, pier and swimming opportunity. This is a perfect place to take a break if time and weather allow.

Around Vassøy | Hike 7.2

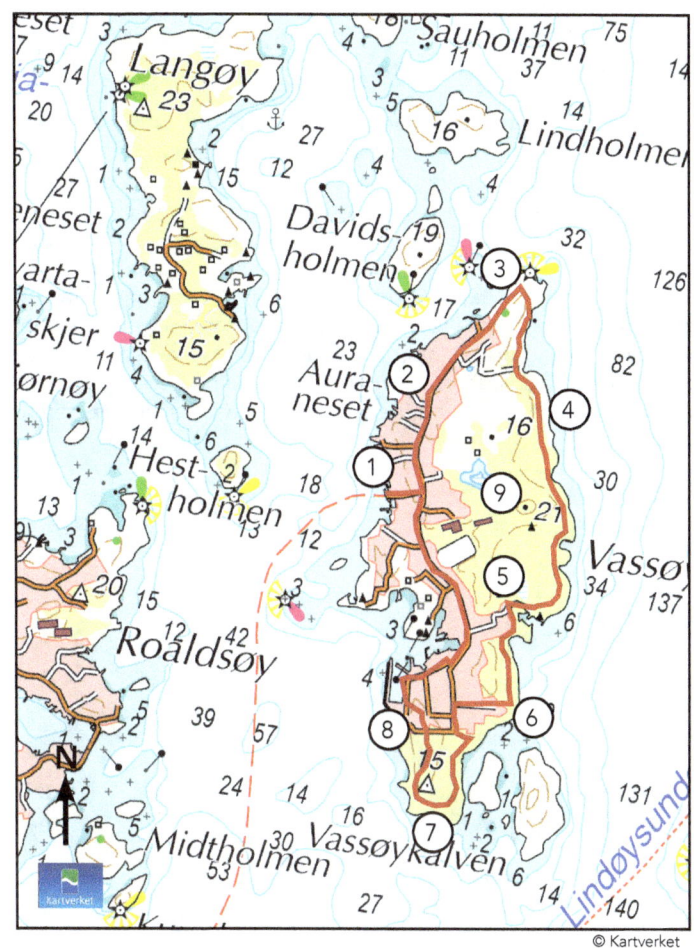

© Kartverket

From here, proceed to the southern tip of the island by crossing into a coastal wooded area, mainly following the red dot markings found on rocks. The vegetation here changes to coastal heather. The southern tip (7) of the island offers views to Stavanger, as well as the mountain tops of Sandnes such as Varlivården (Hikes 8.2 and 8.11), Dalsnuten (Hike 8.1), and Lifjell (Hike 8.4). As the trail turns, stay at height to get back out of the woods and return to urban surroundings once more, taking a left into Sørstrandveien (8). The path leads you towards and around the

Shorter Hikes, Stunning Scenery

Hike 7.2 | Around Vassøy

harbour of Makkavågen.
Proceed past Makkavågen along Sørstrandveien, towards the ferry pier and the end of the island circuit.

If you have time and don't mind possibly getting 'lost' for a while, the walk can be extended to include the bird nature reserve of Torvmyrå **(9)**. As you pass the fire department of the island, there is a path leading towards Vassøy School and Vassøy kindergarten. Paying close attention to the red dot markings, follow the trail towards the lake of Torvmyrå. It is possible to circumnavigate the lake, but the markings and the path are not obvious especially at the northern side of the lake. In spring, many birds nest here, and it is a very good spot to observe a variety of species (but please don't disturb them!). If you don't want to circumnavigate the lake, you could also just retrace your steps towards the fire department, and continue the walk in a northerly direction towards the ferry terminal.

The Tungenes Peninsula | Hike 7.3

Hike 7.3: The Tungenes Peninsula

Spectacular, rugged coast combined with views and beaches

The Tungenes peninsula feels remote and open, and yet is just a few minutes from the centre of Stavanger. On a fine day hikers are rewarded with views far to the north and west. The trail leads through a wonderful variety of terrain: you'll experience flat trails, beaches, ancient steps, rocky scrambles and marsh. Hiking meets history here: there's an old war lookout, a lighthouse, old fishing harbours and long-disused boat pull outs.

Access 🚗 (or 🚌 with extra walk)	Grading 🚶
Terrain: varies (see above)	Length: 7.4km
Facilities: toilet at Sandevigå, Sunday cafe and toilet at Tungenes Fyr	Time: 2hrs

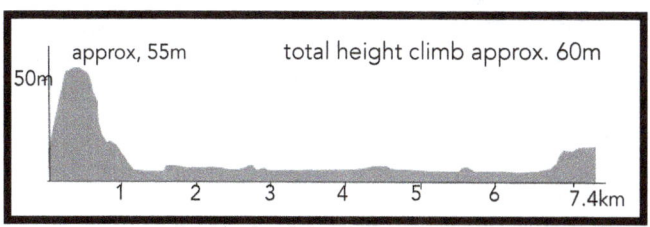

Data taken from Statens Kartverk, Geovekst and Kommunes, ©Kartverket

Shorter Hikes, Stunning Scenery

Hike 7.3 | The Tungenes Peninsula

To reach the start of the hike:

By car: from Stavanger, take the E39 north towards Bergen. The road goes through a short tunnel at Byhaug. 3.5km beyond the tunnel exit, turn left at the roundabout towards Randaberg. The road turns sharp right just after the roundabout. Proceed through the centre of Randaberg, turning left at the T-junction in the town and then immediately right towards Tungenes. The car park is on the left, signposted "Sandestranden", 2.7km after the road junction in Randaberg.

By bus: The nearest bus stop is "Sandeveien" (Randaberg), but this bus stop is serviced only a few times a day on school days. Otherwise, the nearest bus stop is "Randaberg Idrettshus" at the Randaberg stadium. It takes about half an hour to walk from here to Sandestranden beach and car park. For current schedules, routes, and prices, see www.kolumbus.no.

Hike Description

Parts of this hike are marked with signposts.

NB: The hike description begins from the car park at Sandevigå (Sandestranden) and goes anti-clockwise around the peninsula. There are also car parks at the foot of Randabergfjellet and at Tungevika. The hike could easily be done from either of these two car parks (marked P on the map), or in a clockwise direction if preferred. If arriving by bus and alighting at "Randaberg Idrettshus", walk north along Tungenesveien towards the beach. You will pass point (1) on the hike along the way, so you can turn up the hill here, thus avoiding backtracking from the car park at Sandestranden.

From the car park, turn away from the beach, return to the road, and turn right along the cycle path that runs by the side of the road towards Randaberg. The road curves to the left, with the hill "Randabergfjellet" to the left of it. After about 350m there is a car park on the left side of the road with bicycle racks **(1)**. Cross through this car park to find the trail, which goes steeply up the hill. The short climb goes past a small cave and forks, with both forks reaching a wide, tarmac area with space for parking **(2)**.

Follow the tarmac around the side of the hill. It soon becomes a gravel road, with gates and fences on either side, leaving only one direction to follow. Soon you reach a viewpoint overlooking Sandestranden. Follow the gravel path as it starts to descend towards a second lookout area.

The Tungenes Peninsula | Hike 7.3

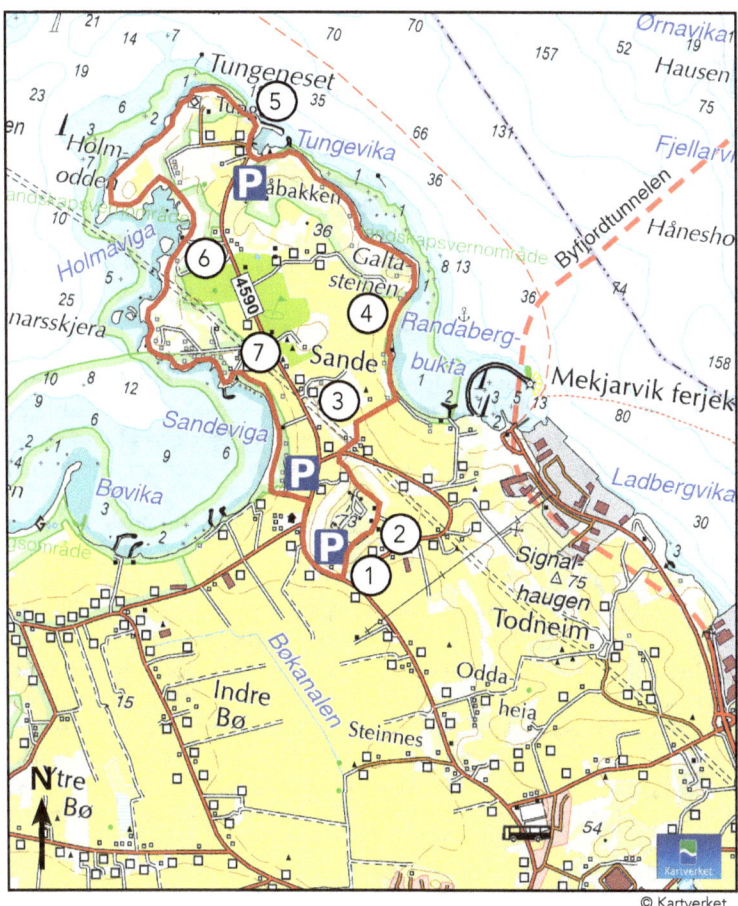

© Kartverket

From here, there are views across Byfjord to the islands of Åmøy, Sokn, Bru and Rennesøy. Nearer to the shore, there is a harbour with a curved stone wall enclosing it. In contrast with the peaceful scene, the main E39 road to Bergen goes under this harbour in a tunnel. An information board describes the history of the radio installation that is now fenced in on top of the hill.

The trail continues steeply downhill, at first on a grassy path, then down a series of old stone steps to the road crossing at the bottom of the hill. Go straight across the road, and take the tarmac road past two houses (3), following it to the beach. Turn left along the beach and continue to

Shorter Hikes, Stunning Scenery

Hike 7.3 | The Tungenes Peninsula

follow the path close to the shore past some cabins. After the cabins, the trail opens out on to the rocky shore (4).

For the next 1.2km, enjoy the easy scramble along the shoreline. This rock has quartz veins that stand out a little from the surface and improve your grip on the rock. The rocky section ends at the little harbour of Tungevika. Climb the stile and follow the trail around the edge of the harbour. Here there is a large car park with an area of benches overlooking the tie-ups for small boats. Turn right past the benches. A signpost says "Tungenes Fyr 0.4km". This path to Tungenes Fyr is suitable for wheelchairs and pushchairs, but you can carry on straight between the two buildings in front of you. The left hand one of these is a little seafaring museum, open during the afternoons in some school holidays.

Continue past the museum to the shore, and then turn left along the shoreline (5). On a fine day, the low islands of Kvitsøy will be visible on the horizon. You may also see the Kvitsøy ferry as it goes to and from the islands several times a day. To the left is the former lighthouse, Tungenes Fyr.

The hike continues around the coastal side of the lighthouse and from there along the coastline. Follow the coast around the little peninsula of Holmodden and into the bay at Holmaviga. The trail goes between the cabins and the shoreline, then along the marsh to the old boathouse at the south end of the bay (6). Don't be misled by a T sign pointing up the hill: this leads to the golf course! Continue along the indistinct trail that stays close to the shoreline, past the front of a few cabins and private boat piers (7). A few T-signs indicate the way towards the start of Sandestranden bay: cross the section of tall grasses to reach it (it may be tricky to keep one's feet dry at high tide!).

The beach has toilet facilities and is a popular picnicking, swimming and beach games spot on warm days. When you are ready, return to the car park at the far (south) end of the beach.

Tungenes Fyr
This historic lighthouse it always interesting to visit. It houses a Sunday afternoon cafe, concerts on Thursday evenings, and occasional exhibitions. Sometimes the exhibitions are in the grounds of the lighthouse, and so may be enjoyed even when the building is closed.

Hike 7.4: Hellestø

Superb beach and shoreline: one of Jaeren's "Pearls on a String"

Jæren County lies to the south of Stavanger, and has many beautiful, wide sandy beaches. Locals call them 'pearls on a string'. Walking on the beach is almost always possible, even when it is blowy and rainy. It offers different views and moods in any season or weather, and is generally easy to walk for hikers of different abilities. The walk described here goes from Hellestø beach to the small harbour of Tangarstø-Reve.

Access 🚗	Grading 🚶
Terrain: sand, pebbles	Length: 6.8km
Facilities: toilets at the car park, and at Tangarstø-Reve (point (3) on the hike)	Time: 1hr 45mins

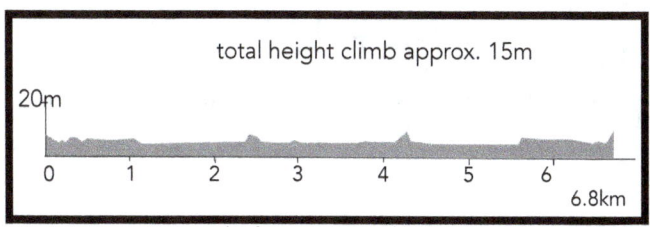

Shorter Hikes, Stunning Scenery

Hike 7.4 | Hellestø

To reach the start of the hike:

By car: from Stavanger, take the E39 south, in the direction of Kristiansand. Take the Rv444 exit towards Bryne, signposted towards Sola airport. At the roundabout take the first exit into Rv 509, towards Sola and the airport. After about 3.5km turn left into Kleppvegen/Rv 510. Follow for just under 3km and, at the roundabout in Stenebyen, turn right into Vigdelsvegen, signposted towards Vigden and Hålandsmarka, for another 2.5km until you come to the sign for Hellestø beach.

By bus: the nearest bus stop is Hellestøstranda in Vigdelsvegen at the entrance to the car park. Unfortunately it is only serviced, very infrequently, on school days. For current schedules, routes, and prices, see www.kolumbus.no.

Hike Description

This trail is not marked, but is straightforward to navigate

Starting from the car park, take the path that leads towards the beach. When you reach the beach, walk in a southerly direction along the sand **(1)**. The sea will be on your right.

Hellestø Beach
The beach at Hellestø is wide and long. The sea breezes make it a good place to fly kites, and on busy days there may be many. The beach is also open to the North Sea, and the waves can be high. Surfing isn't just for Hawaii: here at Hellestø the opportunities are also good. If you do decide to go into the water, check in first with the information board at the car park, which describes the currents in English as well as Norwegian.

At the end of the beach, either walk up into the dunes and continue along on top of the dunes, or stay on the pebble beaches that follow

Hellestø | Hike 7.4

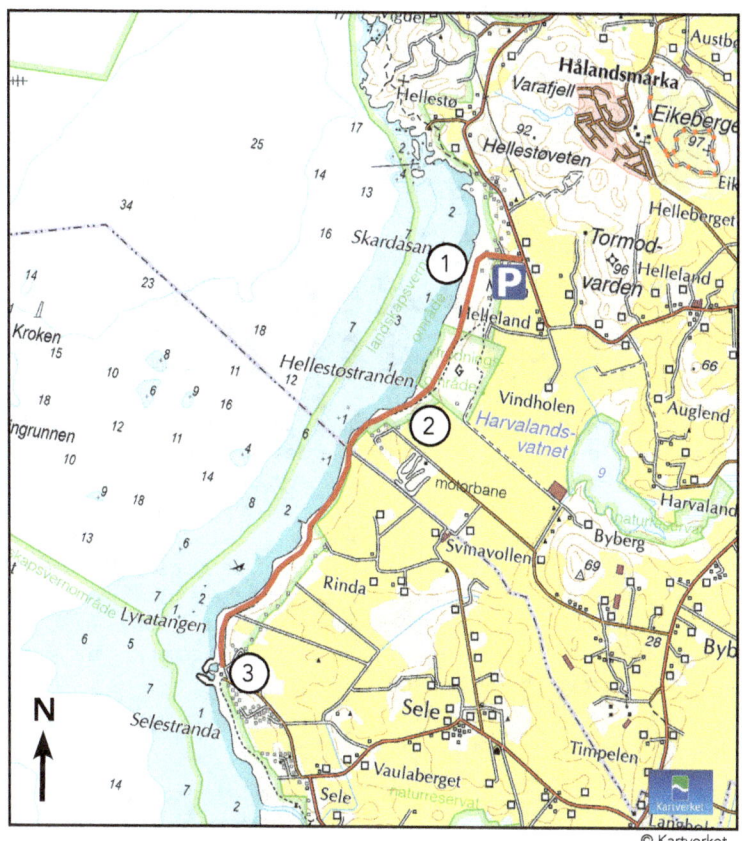

© Kartverket

(2). This choice can be made depending on weather conditions and the party that you are walking with.

You will reach the harbour of Tangarstø-Reve (3) about 3.4km from the car park. There are several picnic tables along the harbour, which are especially inviting in good weather. If you want to go further, you could continue along the coast to the beach at Sele. There is a spacious carpark here, where you could park a second car, if you want to walk the beaches in one direction only.

Going back towards Hellestø carpark, retrace your steps along the dunes and beaches, this time keeping the water on your left hand side.

Hike 7.4 | Hellestø

North of Hellestø beach

If you go to the north of Hellestø beach, you can have a very different walk indeed from the level coast and pebble beaches featured in this hike. The trail, marked with blue posts, starts at the north end of the beach and winds around, and up and down, the rocky shores, punctuated with charming little beaches at Vigdel (where there is a car park) and Ølberg (where there is a car park, campsite, restaurant, and kiosk). The coastal trail eventually meets Sola beach, just south of the airport runway. All the way there and back from Hellestø makes for a lengthly hike, but the car parks offer one-way opportunities, or a way to enjoy the whole length of coast via shorter expeditions.

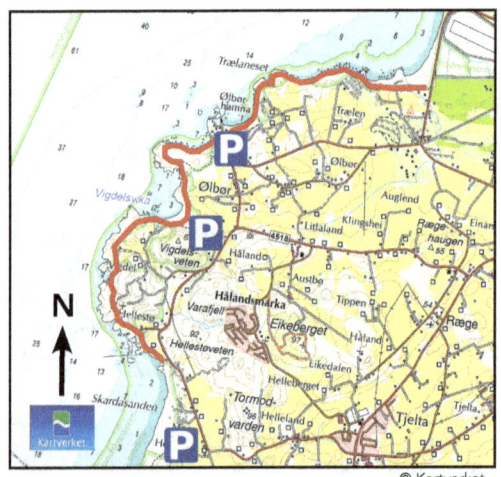

© Kartverket

Reianes | Hike 7.5

Hike 7.5: Reianes

A rugged moorland peninsula to the north of Stavanger

The Reianes peninsula lies at the far west of the island of Rennesøy. It is used as pastureland for sheep, and the absence of trees allows for sea views in all directions. Near the start of the hike, you may see the car ferries shuttling between Mortavika and Årsvågen. Later, as you reach the south of the peninsula, the views are across Mastrafjord towards Tungenes and Utstein Cloister.

Access 🚗	Grading 🚶
Terrain: moor, tarmac road	Length: 4.6km
Facilities: none	Time: 1hr 10mins

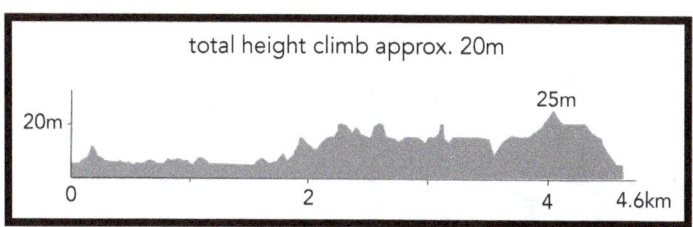

Data taken from Statens Kartverk, Geovekst and Kommunes, ©Kartverket

Hike 7.5 | Reianes

To reach the start of the hike:

By car: From Stavanger, follow the E39 north towards Bergen, through both the Byfjord tunnel and the Mastrafjord tunnel. After emerging from the Mastrafjord tunnel, continue along the E39 for about 5 km until you see a signpost for Sørbø and Reianes to the left. Take this turn, and continue towards Reianes. (If you reach the ferry terminal, you have overshot: double back and look for the turning on your right).

Follow this road for approximately 2.3km, past a sign for parking at Bø, and down a little hill. The parking area is at the bottom of the hill on the right hand side, and is signposted. If this car park is full, there is also a second parking area at the end of the road: this parking area is at point (4) on the hike.

Hike Description

This trail is marked with signposts, red dots and red T-markers.

From the car park, follow the road for about 50m until you see a trail leaving the road on the right hand side. The signpost marked "Reianes Rundt" indicating this trail was on the floor at the time of writing. If you reach some farm buildings, you have gone too far. Leave the road and take this trail, which is marked with red dots, as it follows the coastline to the north-west. There is a cabin on the left, and there might be spring flowers between the trees beyond this at the right time of year. The trail then climbs a short, rocky section, and views open up to the north (1).

Look for lines of cairns with T-markers painted on them, which show the way around this portion of the peninsula. However, be aware that there are several "extra" cairns near the trail that might lead you astray. If a cairn doesn't have a red T-marker on it, the cairn is not marking the trail! Near the tip of a headland, the trail swings to the south.

Spring primroses:
A treat if you pass this way in April or May!

Reianes | Hike 7.5

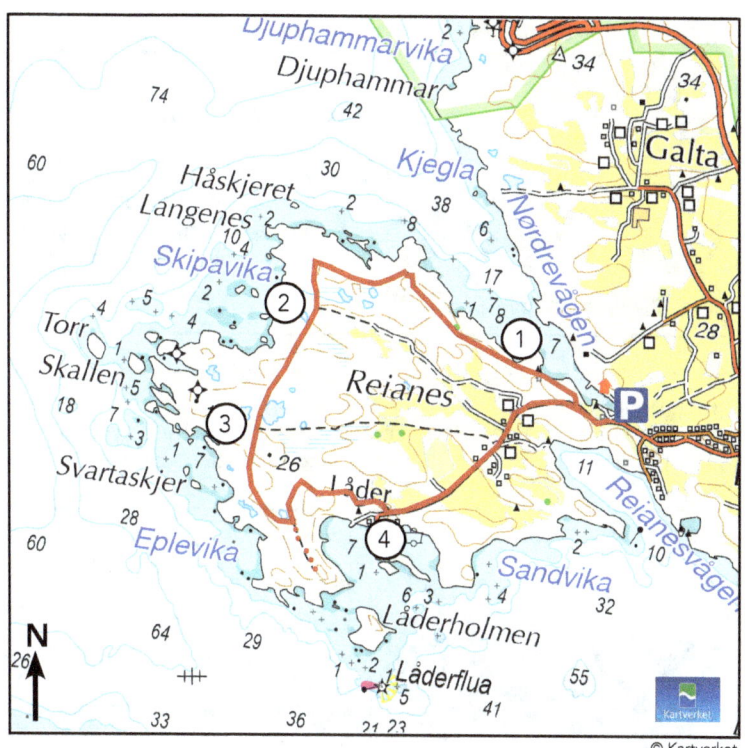

© Kartverket

Just after this turn, there is a stile over a wall (2), with a track junction on the other side. If you are ready to return by the quickest route, the track to the left will take you across the farmland and back to the road. However, we recommend continuing straight ahead to enjoy fine hiking and cliff views towards Utstein Cloister in the south and the islands of Kvitsøy to the south-west.

There is a second path junction as you begin to reach the south of the peninsula (3). Again, the shortest way back to the car park is to turn left, but we recommend continuing straight ahead.

Just as the path swings again to face east, there is another path junction. To the right is a knoll signposted "Selsnes". Take a short detour to the top of this knoll (marked with a dotted line on the sketch map) to appreciate the view along Mastrafjord and the remains of the iron age

Hike 7.5 | Reianes

fort here, before doubling back to the main path.

The beach at Låde
Near Låde there is a lovely pebble beach. The beach is protected from the sea breeze by the headland, and so makes a fine swimming spot in summer.

The path continues across the moor until it meets a farm track just above the harbour hamlet of Låde. Turn right along the track until it reaches the second parking area at the tarmac road (4). From here, turn left and follow the tarmac road across farmland and back to the car park.

Drystone walls
If you look carefully at the walls dividing the fields here, you will see that they are built without any mortar: the stones are carefully positioned so that they stay in place without any. Building these walls is an ancient art. A notice, in Norwegian and English, explains that stone walls have been in use in this part of the country for many centuries, and mark borders between farms.

Røssdalen | Hike 7.6

Hike 7.6: Røssdalen

A short valley walk to an idyllic meadow picnic spot

Røssdalen is a "classic" Norwegian U-shaped valley. This short, easy hike takes you alongside a lake and then through woods to a meadow. A river runs through this delightful spot, and there are picnic tables and barbecue pits. It is a wonderful summer outing for the youngest hikers and anyone who wants to enjoy the mountains without a long or steep hike.

Access 🚗	Grading 🚶
Terrain: track, woodland path	Length: 4km
Facilities: toilets, barbecue pits and picnic tables at the riverside meadow	Time: 1hr

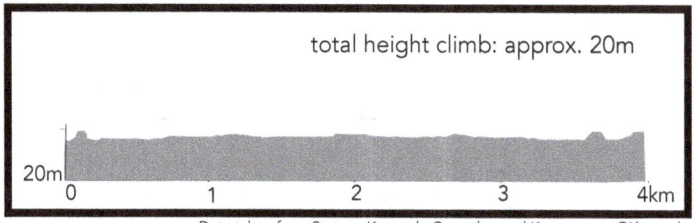

Data taken from Statens Kartverk, Geovekst and Kommunes, ©Kartverket

Shorter Hikes, Stunning Scenery

Hike 7.6 | Røssdalen

To reach the start of the hike:

By car: From Stavanger centre take the Ryfylke tunnel to Solbakk, and turn south along the Rv13 towards the Lysefjord Bridge. After about 19 km, turn left onto the Lysefjord Bridge towards Forsand on the Fv 491. After the bridge, continue to follow Fv 491. After just over 8km, the road will turn left, away from the fjord and up a valley to the lake of Espedalsvatnet. This looks like a left hand turn even though you're remaining on the same road. The car park (parking fee required, via card payment) is on the left hand side of the road, 2km beyond the end of the lake, and 20km beyond the bridge over Lysefjord.

Hike Description

This trail is marked with signposts, red dots and red T-signs.

From the car park, continue along the gravel track (the river will be on your right hand side as you hike). Follow the track around the side of the lake and then through the woods. Approx. 1km beyond the lake, the trees open out and the track continues into a meadow (1).

This is the picnic spot. Here there are barbecue pits, picnic tables and a toilet. A river runs through this meadow, complete with a pool deep enough to swim in, and a large rock to jump from.

Take your time to relax and explore, perhaps following the trail higher into the valley for a little way, before you return the way you came to the parking lot.

© Kartverket

Hike 7.7: Ogna to Brusand

A(nother) world class beach, accessible by train

Brusand is the southernmost beach on the Jaeren coast covered in this book, and one of the finest: it it advertised locally as "Norway's longest and finest beach". Access by train allows for a one-way hike, with many opportunities for picnics and beach fun along the way.

Access 🚆 (or 🚗)	Grading 🚶
Terrain: gravel path, road, coast/beach	Length: 6.9km
Facilities: none	Time: 2hrs

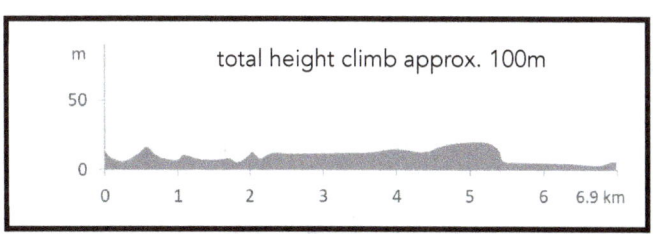

Data taken from Statens Kartverk, Geovekst and Kommunes, ©Kartverket

Shorter Hikes, Stunning Scenery

Hike 7.7 | Ogna to Brusand

To reach the start of the hike:

By train: Take the train from any station to Ogna, and alight there. You will return from the next station north along the line, Brusand. There are regular trains between Stavanger/Sandnes and Egersund that stop at Ogna and Brusand: for current timetables, see www.kolumbus.no

By car: we recommend accessing this walk by train, as the service is good and it allows for a one-way hike. However, if you prefer to travel by car and walk "there and back", there is some parking available at Ogna train station or at Brusand (in which case you will need to take note that the hike directions go the other way, from Ogna to Brusand!). From Stavanger, travel south on the E39 and, after just over 12 km, exit on the Rv444 towards Bryne. After about 6km, take the second exit at the roundabout, on to Rv44 towards Bryne. After 38 km, you will reach Brusand, and the train station is signposted to the left, just before leaving the town. The next town (after about another 4km) is Ogna, and the train station is signposted to the right hand side of the road.

Hike Description

After alighting from the train, you want to be on the side of the train tracks nearest to the sea. Turn north (left) from the train station along Rv44, and take the first left hand turn (Ognaveien), which doubles back and goes underneath the train tracks. You will come to a road junction just after the underpass (1).

Continue straight at this junction: you should be heading towards the sea. Continue on the road as it turns sharp right after 30 metres, and, at the crossroads about 200m further along, turn left, again heading towards the sea. The road ends at the shore, where you will meet two beautiful sandy inlets, and a little sheltered lagoon (Ogna lagunen) (2).

The path leads along the shore to the right. A short traverse over a headland brings you to the little beach of Holmasanden (3). At the end of the beach, turn left along the track and follow it until you reach the long stretch of beach that is Brusand itself on the left. (4). Now you can leave the track and enjoy the glorious stretch of nearly 3 kilometres of sand!

At the end of the beach, there is a little river to cross, via a bridge. Once

Ogna to Brusand | Hike 7.7

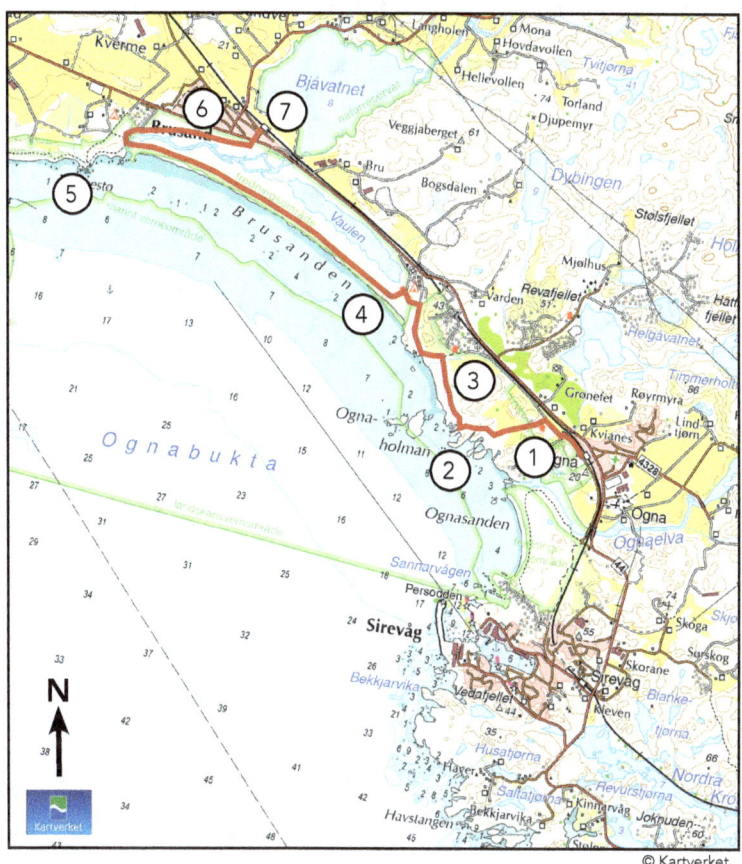

© Kartverket

over, if you are not ready to go home yet and would like a detour, feel free to explore the headland to the left (5). When you are ready, turn right after the bridge and loop back along the side of the river (the river should be on your right hand side). As you draw nearer to the town of Brusand, you may notice a long series of concrete posts sticking up (6). These are locally known as "Hitler's Teeth", because they were erected during the occupation of Norway during the Second World War, to deter any attempt at a land invasion here.

Stay on the path as it bears away from the river and goes towards Brusand. When you reach the main road (the Rv44), look for an underpass to the

Shorter Hikes, Stunning Scenery

Hike 7.7 | Ogna to Brusand

side of "Hitler's Teeth", which will take you safely under the road rather than having to cross it. The underpass leads to a car park: cross this parking area, then cross the road at the pedestrian crossing. Continue turning left into Brusand, then turn right into Auren Road. At the end of this road, turn left into Fuglestadvegen. After about 100m, turn right into Bru Road, signposted towards Brusand train station, where you can catch the train home (7).

Hike 7.8: Frøylandsvatnet
A magical lake, with easy tracks

Frøylandsvatnet lies between Bryne and Sandnes. A gravel track winds through the woods along the northwestern shore. There are almost always birds to see, and in autumn the colours combine with morning mist to give a glorious show. Frøylandsvatnet is well loved locally, and there are playparks for both children and adults along the trail. Access by train allows for a one-way hike.

Access 🚆 (or 🚗)	Grading 🚶
Terrain: gravel path, road	Length: 9.2km
Facilities: none	Time: 2hr 45min

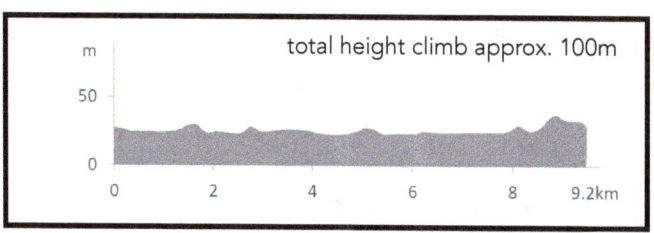

Data taken from Statens Kartverk, Geovekst and Kommunes, ©Kartverket

Shorter Hikes, Stunning Scenery

Hike 7.8 | Frøylandsvatnet

To reach the start of the hike:

By train: Take the train from any station to Bryne, and alight there. You will return from the station two stops north along the line, Øksnavadporten. There are regular trains between Stavanger/Sandnes and Egersund that stop at Bryne and Øksnavadporten: for current timetables, see www.kolumbus.no

By car: We recommend accessing this walk by train, as the service is good and it allows for a one-way hike. However, if you prefer to travel by car and walk "there and back", there is a car park south of Klepp station (in which case you will need to take note that you are starting in the middle of the hike!), at point **(4)** on the map. From Stavanger, travel south on the E39 and, after just over 12 km, exit on the Rv444 towards Bryne. After about 6km, take the second exit at the roundabout, on to Rv44 towards Bryne. After just over 2km, take the first exit at the roundabout, along Øksnevadvegen. Follow Øksnevadvegen for about 2km until you reach a T-junction. Turn right and right again at the junction after 1.8km. Take the next left hand turn, and then turn left again when this road ends in a T-junction. Follow this road until it ends in a T-junction, turn right, and the car park is along a short track immediately to the left.

Hike Description

After alighting from the train, you want to be on the east side of the train tracks (this is the *opposite* side of the train tracks from the bus stops) **(1)**. Depending on which side of the tracks you alight from the train, you may need to go under the underpass to get there.

If you came under the underpass, continue along Hulda Garborgs veg; otherwise, walk ahead with the train tracks on your left hand side, and turn right into Hulda Garborgs veg. At the first junction, turn left into Hetlandsgata, and then continue straight across the Rv506. After just over 100m, the road enters the woods and becomes a track. A further 200m along, take the right hand fork to enjoy a loop around a small peninsula **(2)**. Here you will find frisbee golf and training apparatus.

At the end of the little loop, turn right to continue along the shore of the lake. At the next path junction, turn right to stay close to the lake shore. Continue along, taking the trails closest to the shore for about another 2.6km. Here you will come across an amazing wooden bridge, linking

Frøylandsvatnet | Hike 7.8

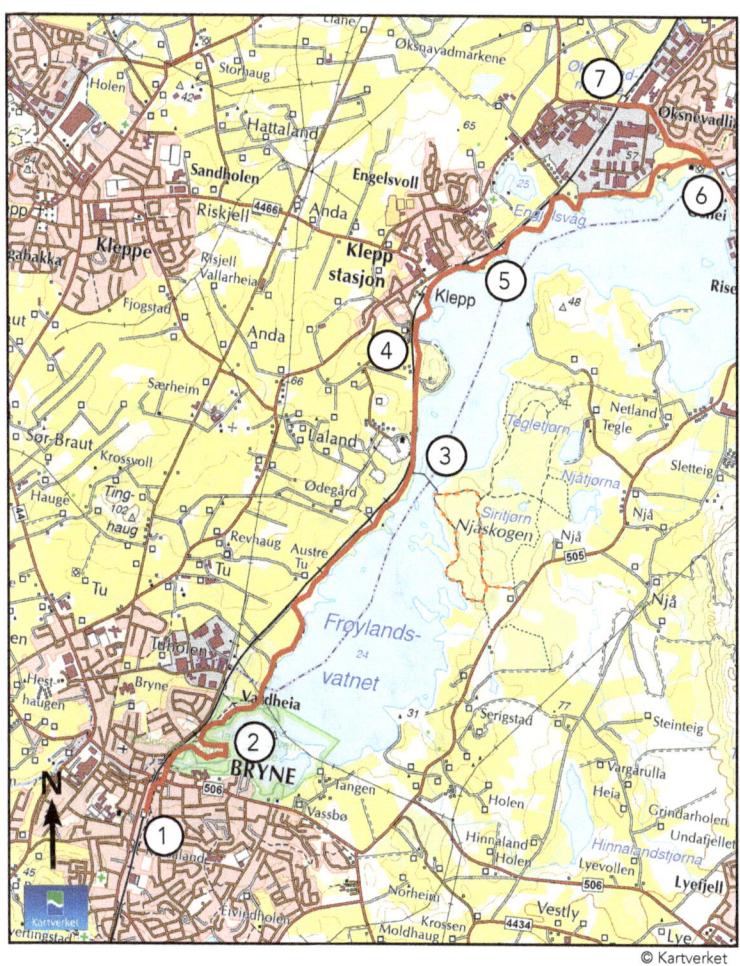

one side of the lake to the other via a small island (Lalandsholmen) in the middle. (3). This bridge provides a link to the lovely woods of Njåskogen on the opposite side, and a useful perch for the birdwatchers observing the inhabitants of these woods. Explore the bridge if you like, and when you are ready return and continue along the shore of Frøylandsvatnet. The track continues past a car park (4).

Hike 7.8 | Frøylandsvatnet

Beyond the car park lies the tiny peninsula of Ytreholmen, and just past this, if you are ready to finish your walk, you can take the left hand fork in the trail (5), and loop back along the road to catch the train home from Klepp Station.

Otherwise, take the right hand fork to continue along the trail as it winds along the north shore of the lake. The trail ends when it meets the Rv505 (6). Turn left here and follow Rv505 to a roundabout. Take the first exit and immediately cross over the road, then turn left into Øksnavadporten Station, where you catch the train home (7).

Synesvarden | Hike 7.9

Hike 7.9: Synesvarden

Atop the High Jaeren, moorland, open skies, and the sculpture Steinkjerringa

On the moors of the High Jaeren, the slopes are gentle, and the views are open for miles in all directions. This walk completes a triangle, taking in the sculpture Steinkjerringa, and the top of Synesvarden.

Access 🚗	Grading 🚶
Terrain: moorland path (sometimes muddy)	Length: 7.6km
Facilities: none	Time: 2hrs

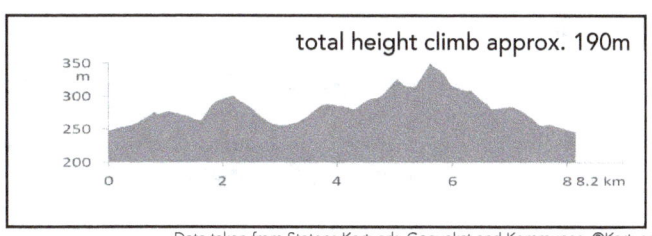

Data taken from Statens Kartverk, Geovekst and Kommunes, ©Kartverket

Shorter Hikes, Stunning Scenery

Hike 7.9 | Synesvarden

To reach the start of the hike:

By car: From Stavanger, travel south on the E39 and, after just over 12 km, exit on the Rv444 towards Bryne. After about 6km, take the second exit at the roundabout, on to Rv44 towards Bryne. Follow Rv44 for just over 26km, then turn left along Rv504. Follow Rv504 through Varhaug, and just over 6km from the junction with Rv44, turn right into Ualand. After about 900m, the road forks. Take the left hand fork along a narrow road. The car park is on the right hand side of the road after about 2.5km, just before the road ends at Holmavatnet Youth Centre.

Hike Description

In the car park, stand facing the little lake (Holmavatnet) and take the trail that leaves the car park on the right hand side. There is a path junction almost immediately (1). Take the right hand fork, along the side of the trees, signposted to Steinkjerringa.

The path meanders a little, but is clear to follow as it gently climbs the moor to the top of Gauleksvarden, at 302 metres above sea level (2). A short downhill stretch leads to a path junction (3). Here, continue straight to see the statue at Steinkjerringa (4).

When you are ready, return the way you came to the path junction at point (3). This time, take the right hand fork, signposted to Synesvarden. Another easily followed track leads to the large cairn at the top of Synesvarden (5). Although there are many higher mountains to the west, Synesvarden is the highest hill in the area, and, on a clear day, there are stunning views both towards the fjords to the west and the farmland and the North Sea to the east.

If you are a collector of tops, you have the option to continue straight from Synesvarden (359m) to the almost as high top of Kartakalven (352m) (6). This detour is marked on the map as a dotted line. If you decide to take in Kartakalven, return to Synesvarden afterwards.

When you are ready to return to the car park from Synesvarden, instead of returning the way you came, take the trail leading away from the hilltop to the northwest, towards Holmavatnet. This trail returns across the moor to the path junction just by the car park.

Synesvarden | Hike 7.9

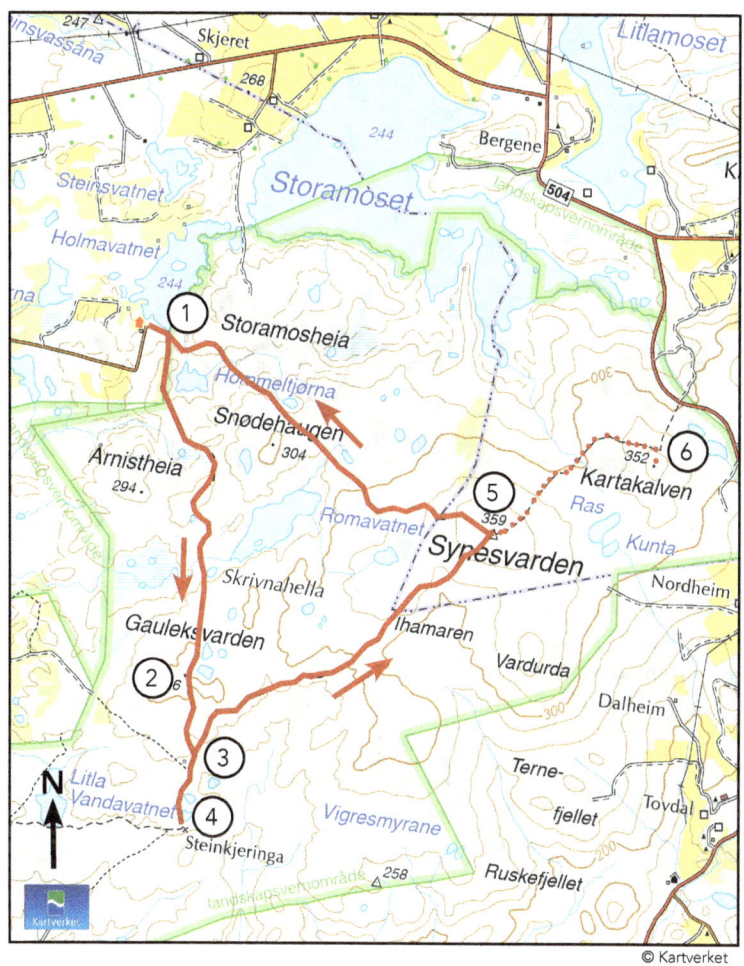

Shorter Hikes, Stunning Scenery

Hike 7.9 | Synesvarden

The history of Steinkjerringa

The statue of the woman at Steinkjerringa was originally sculpted 1898-99 by an artist called Sigurd Sørensen, who went by the stage name S. Neandros. He called the statue "Fortiden", and it was originally intended for Kongsgård school in Stavanger. The plan to display the statue there never came to pass, and instead it gained the nickname "Mother Norway", and languished in Stavanger railway station. In 1924, the statue was purchased for 500 NOK by a group of people from Naerbø and Varhaug in Jaeren. They transported it on a train to Vigrestad, and from there on a lorry to Aniksdal. Then they waited for the winter snow to arrive, before hauling "Mother Norway" on to the moor (in three sections), and lifting it to the boulder top where we see it today.

Chapter 8:
The Way to the Top: Local Hills and Fantastic Views

Our selection of hikes here includes local hills that can be reached in between thirty minutes and one and a half hours by car. They all promise the feeling of being truly on a mountain top, with views that will surprise and delight. These hikes are all graded easy to moderate. They vary in length and elevation to provide for variety and different levels of confidence, but are easy to moderate in difficulty if required. As you climb them and get more familiar with the scenery and the lay of the land, you develop a sense of place and orientation in this magnificent landscape with its rugged topography.

Hike 8.1: Dalsnuten

An easy and popular hike for people of all ages

Dalsnuten is the easiest hike in this hiking area just east of Sandnes, and is a great introduction to hiking. Although the hike is not very strenuous, the views across the Gandsfjord towards Stavanger, the open sea and towards Jæren are very rewarding. Since it is short, it can be done with little preparation, or when the weather forecast is not that great but you still want to get up on a hilltop.

Access 🚗 or 🚌	Grading 🏃
Terrain: track, moorland path	Length: 3.1km
Facilities: Sunday cafe and toilets at the car park	Time: 1hr 45mins

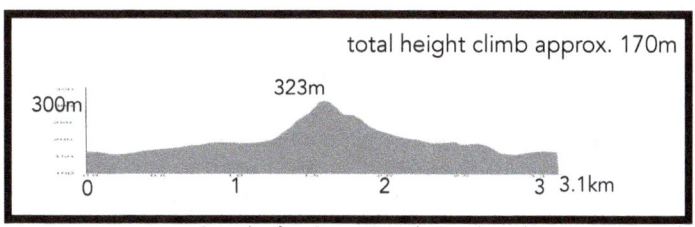

Data taken from Statens Kartverk, Geovekst and Kommunes, ©Kartverket

The Way to the Top: Local Hills and Fantastic Views

Hike 8.1 | Dalsnuten

To reach the start of the hike:

By car: from Stavanger centre take the E 39 south in the direction of Kristiansand for just under 13 km. Take exit 1, Rv 509, towards Sandnes/Sola. Continue downhill on Oalsgata towards Sandnes. Cross the roundabout into Hølandsgata (2 km) and take the 3rd exit at the next roundabout towards Gravarsveien. At the end of this road continue straight at the roundabout into Daleveien (1.2 km).
Follow Daleveien for about 3.6km with the fjord on your left until you reach Daleveien nr 317. Turn right into Fjogstadsveien and continue up the hill (1.6km) until you reach the parking lot. There is ample free parking available, and the cabin of the Stavanger Turistforening is on the opposite side of the road from the parking lot.

By bus: the nearest bus stop is at Stronda on Daleveien and is called Gramstad. From this bus stop, continue uphill along Fjogstadsveien for about 1.6km until you reach the STF cabin and parking lot at Gramstad. Be mindful that this will add the ascent and descent from the Gramstad bus stop to and from the Gramstad car park to your hike (about 20-30 minutes each way). For information on schedules, routes, and tickets, see www.kolumbus.no.

Hike Description

This trail is well marked with signposts, red dots and red T markers.

The hike starts on the opposite side of the road from the parking lot area, just to the left of the Stavanger Turistforening cabin. Initially, the trail goes along a gravel path that leads through a wooded area.

After about 250m, there is a trail junction. Turn right here (1). Continue on this path as it veers towards the northwest and arrives at a small lake called Revholtjørn. Continue along the lake. It might be a bit marshy after rain here. Shortly beyond the lake, the ascent up Dalsnuten begins (2).

This ascent of 130m gives a taste of climbs on other hikes, as it has some steeper rocky sections that can be slippery when wet. At the top of Dalsnuten (3), there are very good panoramic views. Gandsfjord lies below you, and Sandnes is at the end of this fjord. Sola and the open sea are to the west, Stavanger to the northwest and the rolling hills of Jæren to the southwest. Often it can be quite windy up top, so it is best

Dalsnuten | Hike 8.1

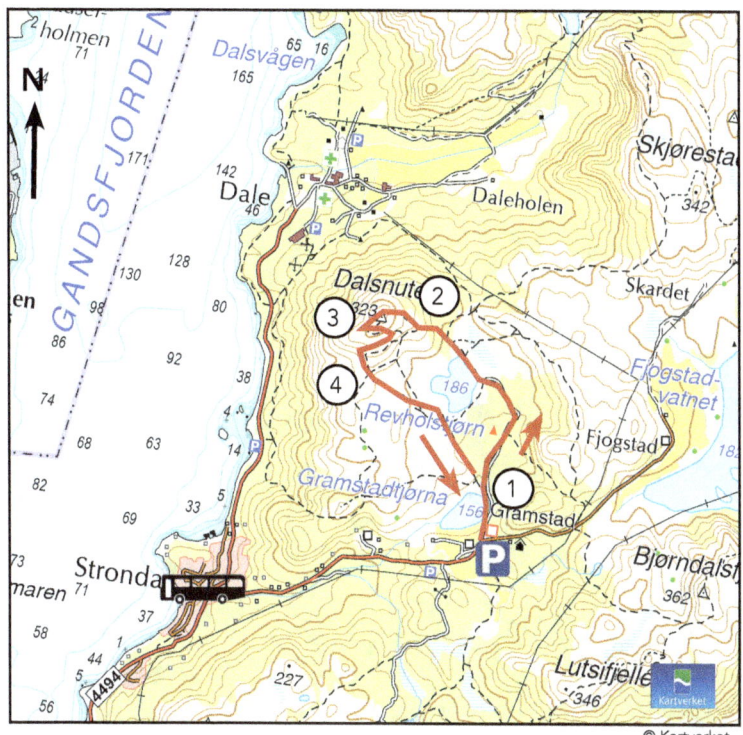

© Kartverket

to descend a few metres to find a sheltered spot if you want to stop for a rest and a picnic.

The route down leaves the summit in a southerly direction, indicated by a signpost. This descent is less steep, and after about 1km the trail reaches a path junction (4). Take the path leading towards the lake, and walk along with the lake on the left. After 2km, you will complete the circle around the lake and arrive at the path junction (1). Here, meet with the gravel path again and turn right to return to the parking area.

Hike 8.1 | Dalsnuten

Vårlivarden | Hike 8.2

Hike 8.2: Vårlivarden

A short hike with stunning vistas from the top of the hill

Although this hike is relatively short, you'll still be rewarded with vistas of Stavanger, the Sandnes hills, Frafjord, Hjelmeland and the north of Rogaland. It's a great place to view the fjords and islands in the area. There is a small amount of fun scrambling, hence the blue rating, but the trail is mostly good underfoot.

Access 🚗	Grading 🚶
Terrain: track, mountain path	Length: 3km
Facilities: none	Time: 1hr 30mins

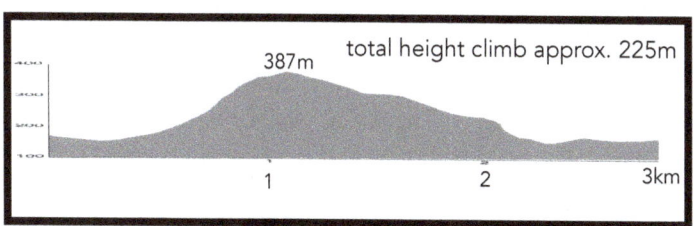

Data taken from Statens Kartverk, Geovekst and Kommunes, ©Kartverket

The Way to the Top: Local Hills and Fantastic Views

Hike 8.2 | Vårlivarden

To reach the start of the hike:

By car: from Stavanger, take the E39 south towards Kristiansand, take exit 27 towards Lauvvik/Hommersåk, and then Rv 516 towards Hommersåk. Continue on the Rv 516 for about 10km, passing the Kronen Gård Hotell, Lake Dybningen on the right and then meeting Lake Lutsivatnet shortly after. 5km before Hommersåk, turn right towards Lauvvik.

Follow this road for approximately 6.5km, until you see a signpost left to Varli. Turn left and follow this narrow road as it winds up a hillside. The road leaves the steeper slope and continues along a valley. Towards the end it turns into a track. The car park is signposted near the end of the road, on the left hand side.

Hike Description

This trail is well marked with signposts, red dots and red T markers.

From the car park, turn left and follow the track until you come to a gate (1). There is a sign that says that the farm (and the remainder of this track) is private. To the right of this sign is a signpost: it shows Vårlivarden both to the right and to the left, because it's a circular walk. For this hike, take the path to the right. Follow the marked trail up the hill. A short way along, there is a track leading to an old farmhouse at Kvelvane (2). *Don't follow the track!* The trail takes a hairpin bend to the left to continue up the steep hillside. As the trail reaches the ridge, there is a path to the right signposted to Bergamot. The trail to the top of Vårlivarden leads in the other direction.

The top of the hill is marked by a large cairn (3). Take the time to stop here and enjoy the panoramas. You may see the city of Stavanger in the distance, looking as though it is built from lego bricks. The islands near to the city are often clearly visible. Towards the south the views are of the Sandnes hills and the fjords towards Forsand.

When you are ready to continue, look carefully for the red trail markings going down the rocks to the north. The trail gradually descends the ridge. At a signed junction (4), take the trail to the left, signposted "Myrland". Be careful here, as there are many small trails in the area around this path junction, and this left turn is very sharp: it may even

Vårlivarden | Hike 8.2

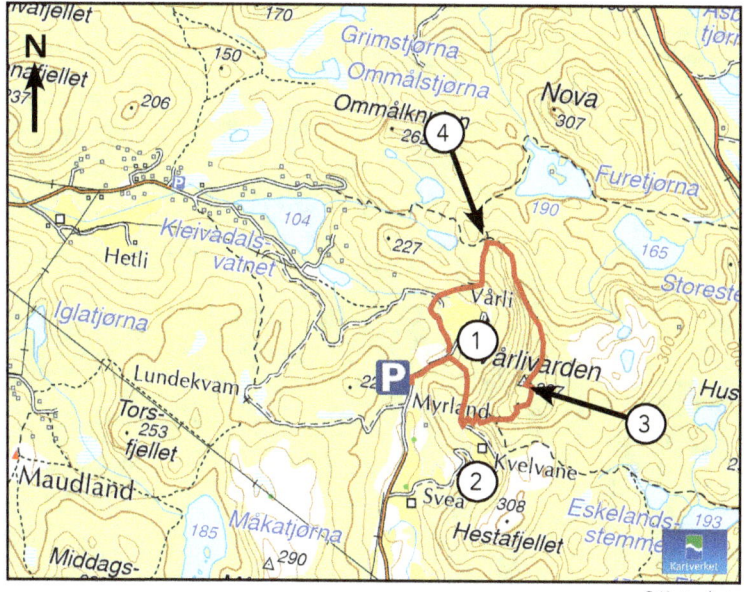

© Kartverket

feel like a U-turn.

The trail continues downhill. Look carefully for red markings on tree trunks and rocks; at the time of writing some of these were rather faint. Lower down the steep slope, watch out for oak trees that are able to thrive in the sheltered, south-facing microclimate here. The trail crosses a little stream, and then follows the outside of the boundary wall of the Vårli farm. Upon reaching the main farm track, turn right to return to the car park at Myrland.

Hike 8.2 | Vårlivarden

Hike 8.3: Skjørestadfjellet and Resasteinen

A superb horseshoe ridge with views over Hommersåk, Storaberget, and Dalsnuten

These hills offer a fine circular ridge walk, with excellent views, and even a plane wreck if you are willing to go on a short detour. There are one or two short rocky sections, but mostly the going is easy, if sometimes rather muddy!

Access 🚗 or 🚌	Grading 🚶
Terrain: track, moorland path	Length: 6.5km
Facilities: kiosk at Dale	Time: 2hrs 30mins

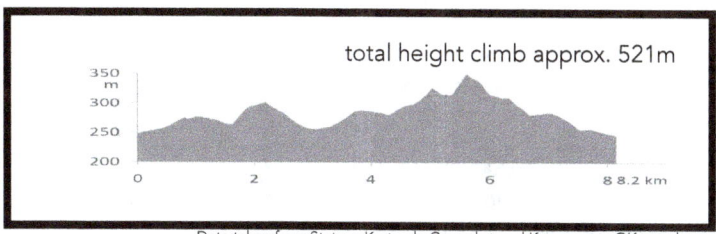

total height climb approx. 521m

Data taken from Statens Kartverk, Geovekst and Kommunes, ©Kartverket

The Way to the Top: Local Hills and Fantastic Views

Hike 8.3 | Skjørestadfjellet and Resasteinen

To reach the start of the hike:

By car: from Stavanger centre take the E39 south in the direction of Kristiansand for just under 13 km. Take exit 1, Rv509, towards Sandnes/Sola. Continue downhill on Oalsgata towards Sandnes. Cross the roundabout into Hølandsgata (2km) and take the 3rd exit at the next roundabout towards Gravarsveien. At the end of this road continue straight at the roundabout into Daleveien.
Follow Daleveien for just under 6km. The road swings to the right in front of the imposing buildings of the former mental hospital. Go past the buildings on your left hand side, and look for the sign for the car parking to the left. Take the signposted track left after you have gone past most of the buildings, and the car park is on the left.

By bus: Buses from Sandnes go to the bus stop at Dale, which is literally at the end of the line: here the bus turns around and goes back towards Sandnes. Alight at the bus stop, which is in front of the main buildings, and continue along Daleveien until you see the sign for the car park to the left. The hike starts at the car park. For current schedules, routes, and prices, see www.kolumbus.no.

Hike Description

This trail is well marked with signposts, red dots and red T markers.

The hike starts from the north east side of the parking lot. Be careful, as there is a second path from the north west of the parking lot. If, after about half a kilometre, you reach a small beach, you have taken the wrong path!

To begin the hike, exit the car park the way you came in, and turn left up the track. After just over 300m, take the path to the right. This farm track can be boggy at times! The track goes through forest then alongside fields before branching to the left for a steep climb through the woods.

The climb tops out at a small dam **(1)**. Turn right and walk across the dam, then continue walking with the lake (Dalevatnet) on your left hand side. After a short stretch along the lake shore, look for the trail markers leading east (to the right) through the trees. Take this trail, and follow it as it turns to climb the hillside. There are some steep sections, but soon you will be on the ridge above the trees and enjoying the views. The first little summit offers a good chance to rest **(2)**.

Skjørestadfjellet and Resasteinen | Hike 8.3

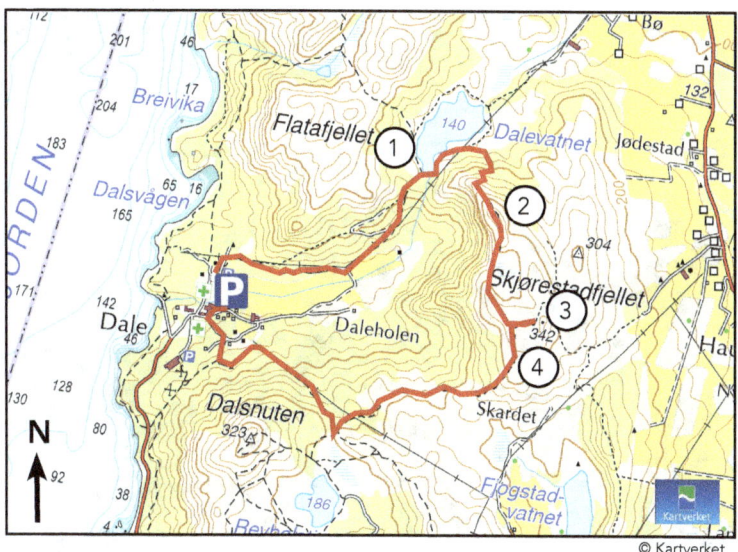

© Kartverket

From here, descend briefly before climbing again to the next plateau. A short (signposted) detour leads to the wreck of a plane from World War II. If you choose to go and see it, there is an information board that describes what happened to the plane whose wreckage lies on the hill.

The final top is Skjørestadfjellet, which is a short way from the main ridge (3). Here is a chance to appreciate the views from the very top one more time before returning to the main path and beginning the descent.

However, the ridge has another spectacular sight to see on the way down, Resasteinen (4) (see box). After Resasteinen, the descent begins in earnest, and is rocky in places. After a short, steep section, you will find yourself traversing a boggy flat and then entering the woods on the side of the hill. At the path junction, turn right to descend the slope alongside the electricity pylons. If you aren't too distracted by the blueberries (when in season), you will soon arrive at a farm. Continue to follow the trail markings (remembering to leave all gates as you find them) until you reach the road. From here, it is a short walk back along the tarmac and past the buildings back to the car park.

Hike 8.3 | Skjørestadfjellet and Resasteinen

Resasteinen

During the ice age, the whole of this area was covered by glaciers. As glaciers inch their way along, they pluck rock from underneath the bottom of the ice and drag it along with them. Sometimes the rocks are small, and are tumbled and rounded into pebbles as they are transported along the bottom of the glacier. However, glaciers have the power to pull huge chunks of bedrock away with them, and Resasteinen is one of these. As the glacier retreated at the end of the ice age, this rock was left standing on top of the ridge. It is well known to local hikers, and may well have provided shelter to generations of adventurers seeking a rest on a windy day!

Hike 8.4: Lifjell

Sweeping views of Stavanger and the "Town Islands" below

Lifjell offers one of the best possible views of Stavanger. Although accessible from Hommersåk, this route from Dale is rather more satisfying, and is accessible by bus. There are some steep sections on the return route, but these may be avoided by returning the way you came instead of completing the round trip.

Access 🚗 or 🚌	Grading 🚶
Terrain: track, moorland path	Length: 6.1km
Facilities: kiosk at Dale	Time: 2hrs 30mins

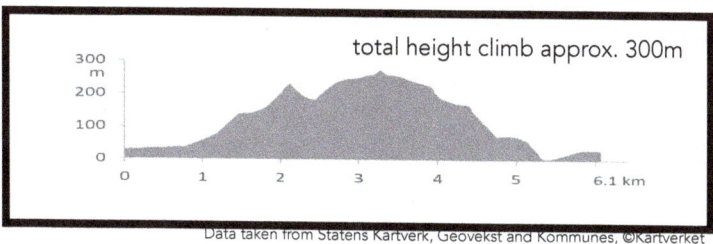

total height climb approx. 300m

Data taken from Statens Kartverk, Geovekst and Kommunes, ©Kartverket

Hike 8.4 | Lifjell

To reach the start of the hike:

By car: from Stavanger centre take the E 39 south in the direction of Kristiansand for just under 13 km. Take exit 1, Rv 509, towards Sandnes/Sola. Continue downhill on Oalsgata towards Sandnes. Cross the roundabout into Hølandsgata (2 km) and take the 3rd exit at the next roundabout towards Gravarsveien. At the end of this road continue straight at the roundabout into Daleveien (1.2 km).
Follow Daleveien for just under 6km. The road swings to the right in front of the imposing buildings of the former mental hospital. Go past the buildings on your left hand side, and look for the sign for the car parking to the left. Take the signposted track left after you have gone past most of the buildings, and the car park is on the left.

By bus: Buses from Sandnes go to the bus stop at Dale, which is literally at the end of the line: here the bus turns around and goes back towards Sandnes. Alight at the bus stop, which is in front of the main buildings, and continue along Daleveien until you see the sign for the car park to the left. The hike starts at the car park. For current schedules, routes, and prices, see www.kolumbus.no.

Hike Description

This trail is well marked with signposts, red dots and red T markers.

The hike starts from the north east side of the parking lot. Be careful, as there is a second path from the north west of the parking lot, which is the path you will return on. If, after about half a kilometre, you reach a small beach, you have taken the wrong path!

To begin the hike, exit the car park the way you came in, and turn left up the track. After just over 300m, take the path to the right. This farm track can be boggy at times! The track goes through forest then alongside fields before branching to the left for a steep climb through the woods.

The climb tops out at a small dam (1). A path crosses the dam, but you need to bear to the left and continue with the little lake (Dalevatnet) on your right hand side. Just under 400m from the dam, turn left up the hill, away from the lake. The trail is well marked as it climbs away from Dalevatnet, over a saddle, and drops slightly into a valley. Near the middle of the valley is a path junction (2). Turn right, signposted Lifjell.

Lifjell | Hike 8.4

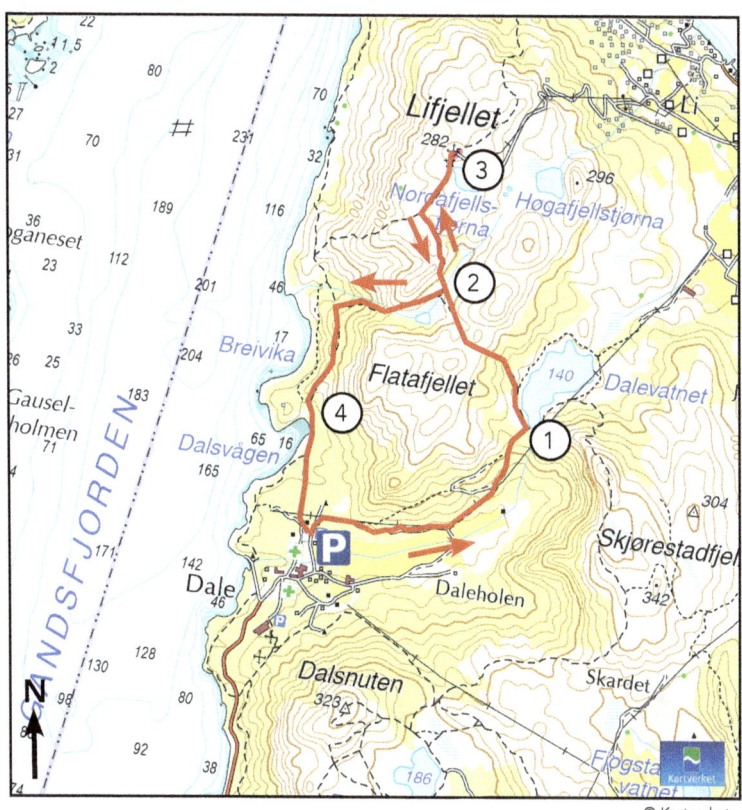

© Kartverket

The trail is well marked and continues up past some scrubby trees and on to a higher, more rocky section. At the top of the hill is the large radio mast that can be clearly seen from Stavanger (3).

Enjoy the views in the other direction, towards the city: Storhaug and the small "town islands" are visible from here, and the opposite side of Gandsfjord seems very close. On a clear day, it is also possible to see across to Hjemeland. There is a large summit cairn a short distance from the radio mast that may provide good shelter for a break if it is a very windy day.

When you are ready to leave the summit, return the way you came to the valley at point (2), and turn right towards Gandsfjord. At the lip of the

The Way to the Top: Local Hills and Fantastic Views

Hike 8.4 | Lifjell

valley, the trail descends steeply through trees before turning towards the south along the steep bank of Gandsfjord. This section of the trail is quite rocky, and can be slippery when wet. If the weather is very wet, this section can be avoided by turning left at point (2) and returning to the car park the way you came.

After the rocky sections, the trail descends to Dalsvågen (4). Here you will be well rewarded for your exertions, with a delightful little beach tucked away by the fjord-side. Here is surely a place to relax and enjoy!

Beyond Dalsvågen, it is a short (and well-trodden) distance back to the parking area.

Hike 8.5: Bjørndalsfjellet

An airy ridge hike with fabulous views

This wonderful round trip hike goes up the highest peak in the recreational hiking area around Gramstad. The hike offers an opportunity to ascend a ridge and enjoy the airy feeling of scenery to either side. There are vistas all around, but the views into Sandnes County and Lake Lutsivatnet, with its scattered islands, are stunning.

Access 🚗 (or 🚌)	Grading 🚶
Terrain: forest, moorland, mountain path	Length: 4.1km
Facilities: STF seasonal Sunday cafe at the car park, toilets	Time: 2hrs

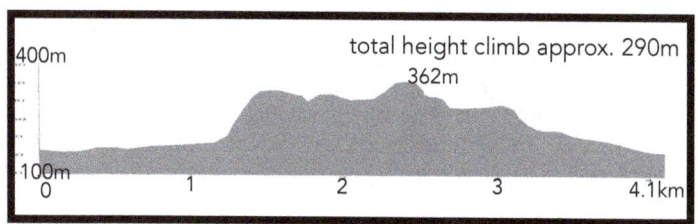

Data taken from Statens Kartverk, Geovekst and Kommunes, ©Kartverket

Hike 8.5 | Bjørndalsfjellet

To reach the start of the hike:

By car: from Stavanger centre take the E 39 south towards Kristiansand for just under 13 km. Take exit 1, Rv 509, towards Sandnes/Sola. Continue downhill on Oalsgata towards Sandnes. Cross the roundabout into Hølandsgata (2 km) and take the 3rd exit at the next roundabout towards Gravarsveien. At the end of this road continue straight at the roundabout into Daleveien (1.2 km).

Follow Daleveien for about 3.6km with the fjord on your left until you reach Daleveien nr 317. Turn right into Fjogstadsveien and continue up the hill (1.6km) until you reach the parking lot. There is ample free parking available, and the cabin of the Stavanger Turistforening is on the opposite side of the road from the parking lot.

By bus: the nearest bus stop is at Stronda on Daleveien and is called Gramstad. From this bus stop, continue uphill along Fjogstadsveien for about 1.6km until you reach the STF cabin and parking lot at Gramstad. Be mindful that this will add the ascent and descent from the Gramstad bus stop to and from the Gramstad car park to your hike (about 20-30 minutes each way). For information on schedules, routes, and prices, see kolumbus.no

Hike Description

This trail is well marked with signposts, red dots and red T-markers.

The hike starts at the far right (south west) corner of the large parking lot. There is a stile after only a few metres. The path starts out wide, and the first 'T' markers are visible. The terrain is fairly open and flat with a marshy meadow on the right. After around 350m, the trail passes under some powerlines (1). Just after this, the path veers towards the west and moves gently uphill.

You may encounter horses or sheep on the path in this area. As you proceed the path narrows and becomes rockier underfoot. The gentle ascent levels out: in the subsequent flat area hold generally towards the left hand side (do not veer off on a path towards the right). Passing a subtle saddle, the path descends towards a stile that goes to the left over a fence (2). Follow the rocky path, keeping the marshy meadow on the right.

Bjørndalsfjellet | Hike 8.5

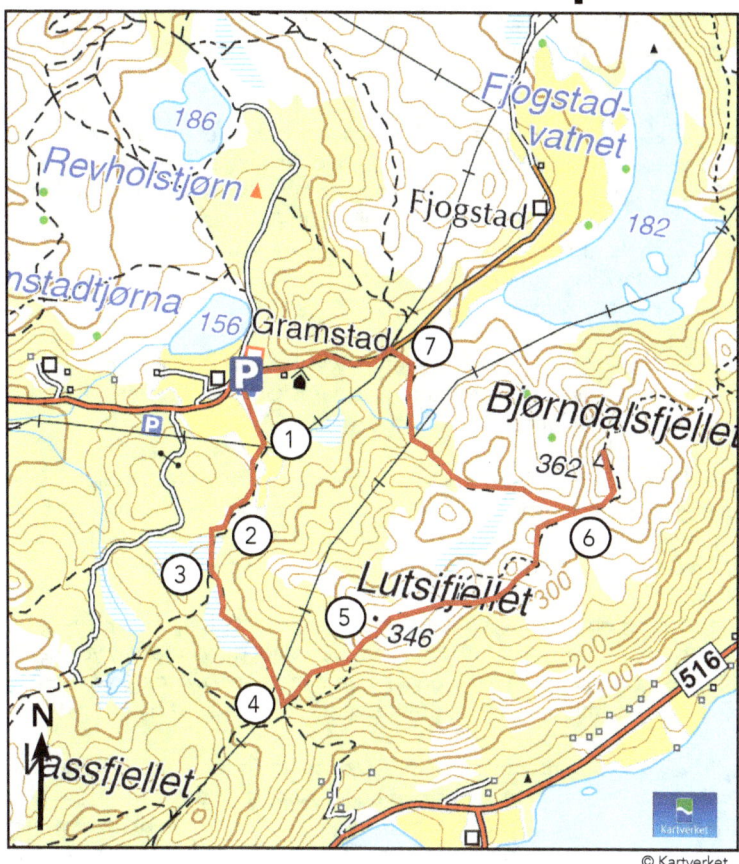

© Kartverket

At the end of the meadow the path turns a sharp left and up on a short ascent with some large boulders on the right. The trail reaches a signpost (3) showing Bjørndalsfjellet to the left; other directions are Kubbetjørn/Lutsi to the right. Once more, the path goes beside a meadow. It crosses under another powerline, and over a gravel road at Paradisskaret (4), where a signpost signals the way.

The steep ascent begins here. Soon after, the trail emerges from the forest and climbs a steep ridge. The ascent is likely to take your breath away in more than one way as the views open up towards Lutsivatnet Lake. As this ridge levels out, the path hangs to the left into the trees

Hike 8.5 | Bjørndalsfjellet

on the west side. The respite from the climb is short, as the path turns right and up a rocky path between the trees, until it arrives at the top of the ridge.

This is about 2.5km into the hike, and at a height of about 325m. You can choose to do a little detour to conquer two peaks in one hike by climbing up the last few metres of Mattirudlå (signposted towards the left) (5). Looking ahead Bjørndalsfjellet is the highest top and is in clear view with its high cairn. The trail is now very straightforward to follow, with the familiar T-markers showing the way. The path proceeds with some up and downs along the ridge.

Just before the final ascent, the return way to Gramstad is signposted to the left (6). It is here that you turn towards Gramstad for the way back to complete the loop.

The final ascent is through rocky terrain and above the treeline, with ever more views opening up. Towards the north is the township of Hommersåk, with Storaberget Mountain (Hike 8.6) and the extensive Lake Lutsivatnet to the east and south. Stavanger is to the west.

Depending on weather conditions, a more or less long break seems in order. Once you are ready to descend, backtrack down the way you came to the small valley below the peak, where the sign towards Gramstad (6) appears. As with the ascent, the descent too is steep at times.

Midway, as you enter into the forest, once again there is a fence with a wooden stile and powerlines overhead. Almost at the end of the hike there is a marshy section, which might require some balancing and stepping on wooden planks to keep feet dry. There is one last wooden stile onto the road (7). From here, it is a left turn and 500m walking downhill on the road to reach the parking area and the end of the hike.

Storaberget | Hike 8.6

Hike 8.6: Storaberget

Enjoy a "big mountain" feeling, at just 342m

Storaberget is one of those mountains that will quickly gain "favourite" status. Literally translated, Storaberget means 'the big mountain'. Indeed, it does tower imposingly over lake Lutsivatnet and looks like an impressive climb from down below. It gives the hiker a good climb, while not being too long, rewarding with 360-degree views. The area also has some historical remnants of the Second World War.

Access 🚗, or 🚆 + 🚌	Grading 🚶
Terrain: forest, boggy moorland	Length: 5.5km
Facilities: none	Time: 2hrs

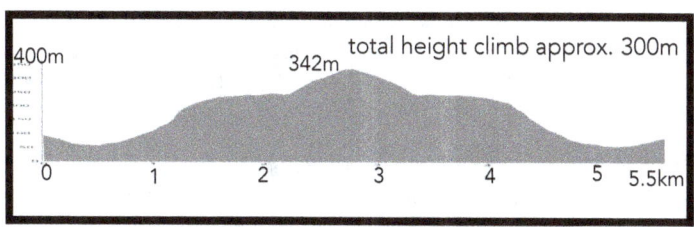

Data taken from Statens Kartverk, Geovekst and Kommunes, ©Kartverket

The Way to the Top: Local Hills and Fantastic Views

Hike 8.6 | Storaberget

To reach the start of the hike:

By car: from Stavanger, take the E39 south towards Kristiansand, and leave at exit 27 towards Lauvvik/Hommersåk. Continue towards Lauvvik/Hommersåk/Austrått, passing through the Austråtunnel, then go straight at the Hana roundabout. Continue past the Kronen Gård Hotell, with Lake Dybningen on the right, and then meeting Lake Lutsivatnet shortly after. Stay on the Rv 516 towards Hommersåk until you reach Hogstad.

No signpost for the parking area is available, but, at the height of Hogstad, there is a street sign to the right with numbers 400-416, numbering the houses on the road. On busy weekends it is best to park close to the road. Otherwise, turn right down the gravel road towards the farm. There is space for about four cars by the farm buildings, where there is also an overview map of the hiking area. You may park here if you are not obstructing the farm entrance. It is courteous to ask the farmer for permission if you see him around.

By public transport: There is a regular bus service between Sandnes and Hommersåk that stops at Hogstad Nord, and a regular train service between Stavanger and Sandnes Station. For details of schedules and fares see www.kolumbus.no

At the bus stop, you will see the street sign with numbers 400-416, numbering the houses along the road. Follow the description in the "by car" section above from this point.

Hike Description

This trail is well marked with signposts and red dots.

The walk starts by the information board next to the small parking facility. Proceed down a gravel path with a small quarry by the side. Beware during weekdays, as big trucks might be exiting or entering the site. The path goes downhill to a gate, which you leave as you find it, just as with all other gates on hikes in Norway (1). Proceed to the left past the gate along the path, with the fence on the left hand side. There will likely be sheep or cows grazing on the pasture, so be careful as you pass.

As the path veers to the right, some old bunkers from the Second World War come into view. Soon a signpost comes up: follow the sign towards Storaberget (2). The well-formed path ascends through shady woods

Storaberget | Hike 8.6

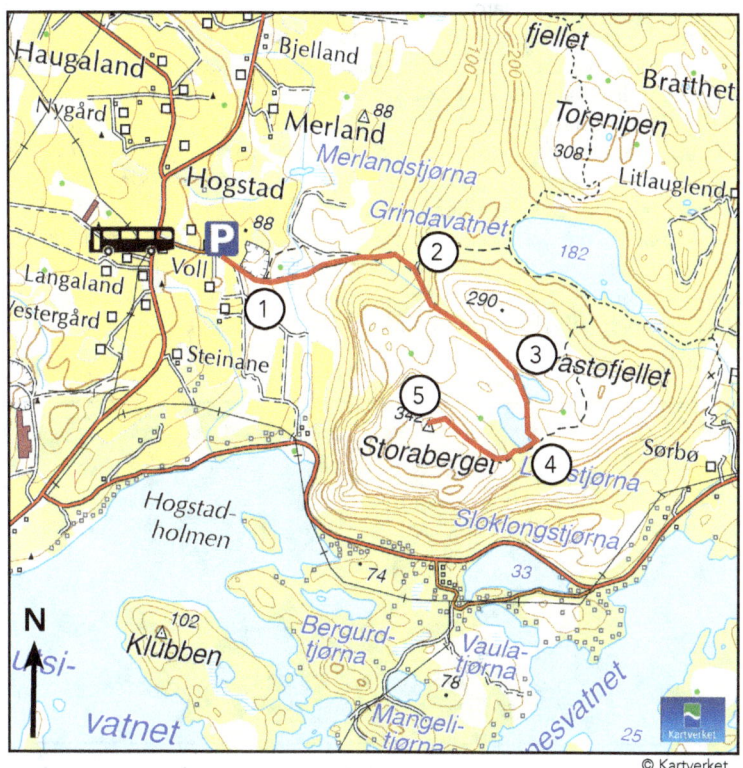

© Kartverket

as it makes its way up towards a dam (3). The dam was built by the Germans during the Second World War as additional water supply. On windy days with strong gusts, spray can make you very wet; on sunny days with a breeze, the mist can be a welcome cool down. During the winter months, beware of icy conditions here on the ledge.

At the other side of the dam the path hugs the rock face and a short scramble is needed. The path flattens out and follows the lake, before veering away into a small wooded area. It then goes past a second, much smaller dam that opens up to lake Lomstjørna (4), with charming views across the water. The narrow path can be quite damp here. Soon, another signpost announces the direction towards either Grindavatnet or Storaberget.

The Way to the Top: Local Hills and Fantastic Views

Hike 8.6 | Storaberget

Following the sign towards Storaberget, you find yourself on the ascent again. The path here can be wet and muddy after rain. Indeed, the path can become a small stream and the hiker might need to navigate between dry patches and soggy marshes. The ascent from 200 to 300 metres is fairly steep, then the trail levels out towards the top. Storaberget's cairn (5) soon comes into view (approaching the top this way, in a counter-clockwise direction, makes for an easier descent). The magnificent outlook includes the village of Hommersåk to the north, Dalsnuten to the west, and, most spectacularly, the lake and islands of Lutsivatnet under you to the south-west. This gem of a mountain is generally not very busy, but gets a steady stream of visitors. Enjoy a well-deserved break, before heading down the same way back to the car park.

Behave appropriately around cows: you cannot outrun an angry bovine!

Most people will stay out of the way of bulls, but fewer realise that cows too can become agitated and therefore dangerous. As placid as they look, they can move fast and due to their size could inflict considerable damage. Stay alert yet move calmly and, if possible, walk around a herd rather than through it. Dogs can be perceived as a threat by cows and more often than not, cow-related incidents have involved dogs. If your dog acts aggressively and a cow is charging towards you it is vital to let go of your dog. Attempting to hold onto and protect your dog may be fatal. The dog can generally easily outrun a bovine, but you would likely not.

Hike 8.7: Eikefjellet

Beautiful, varied terrain along a gradual ascent to the top

This hike gives great views over farms, hills and lakes right from the start. It follows a variety of terrain climbing up meadows, through different wooded areas and reaches the top with mountain views of the surroundings. The hike builds stamina, as it has a long, gradual ascent, while the descent back towards the parking area is much shorter.

Access 🚗	Grading 🚶
Terrain: forest, moorland	Length: 6.2km
Facilities: none	Time: 2hrs 30 mins

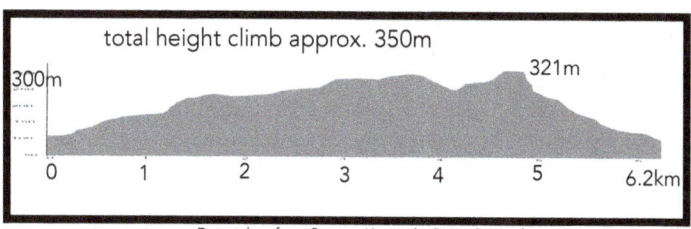

Data taken from Statens Kartverk, Geovekst and Kommunes, ©Kartverket

Hike 8.7 | Eikefjellet

To reach the start of the hike:

By car: from Stavanger, take the E39 south towards Kristiansand. After passing the town of Ålgård (after approx. 28 km), turn left along the Rv450 towards Sirdal. After 4.0km, at the sign for Gjesdal church, turn right into Våglandsvegen. The start of the hike is just some 50m further to the left, but parking is not allowed here. Therefore, continue along the lake for another 0.9 km. Drive over the 'ferist' (cattle grid), and the parking area is signposted on the right by the lake shortly afterwards. The hike ends opposite this spot by the gate and the signpost.

Hike Description

This trail is unmarked at the beginning, but is marked with blue dots after crossing the stone bridge (near point 4 on the map). However, some of the blue dots were mounted on posts that had fallen over at the time of writing.

To start the hike, walk back along the road you arrived on towards the farmhouse just after the turn off into Våglandsvegen (this is about a 10 min walk back along the road). Open the gate on the right (1) that has a sign saying 'lukk grinda' (lock the gate) in faint lettering, and start walking on the farm path uphill. You soon arrive at the next gate and a stile that needs to be climbed.

Starting from here, the views towards the surrounding farmland and back towards the lake begin to open up. Continuing along the old tractor path there is a 3rd gate and stepladder (2) as the track moves towards the left. Climb the stepladder and proceed up the grassy hill. Although unmarked, a clear path is visible. Further up, the path turns east, new vistas open and the path reaches an open meadow (3). Looking back, it is possible to see Gjesdal church, with its modest white building and church tower.

Stay towards the right of the meadow for a few minutes, and soon there is a lake in front, and a rocky promontory in the otherwise grassy meadow. Continue towards the left of the promontory to a small stream, which is crossed by a bridge made from a large slab of stone (4). Cross the bridge and proceed into the wooded pine area. Climb over a stepladder, beyond which the woods continue.

From here onwards, the path is marked with blue markings on poles,

Eikefjellet | Hike 8.7

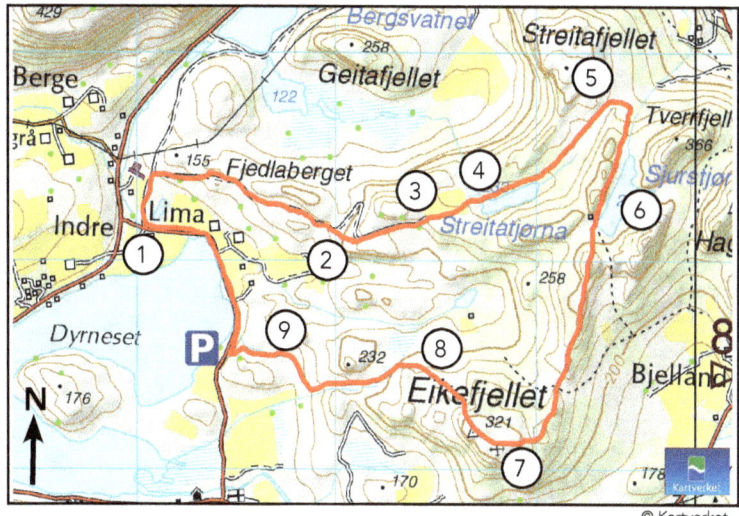

rocks or trees, although be aware that some of the poles may have fallen! After a short ascent, the path leads to a saddle (5) with great views towards mountain farms below and tops above. Look out for the blue pole markers to the right as they cross the meadow down rather steeply, while a tractor path continues straight. This meadow descent can be quite slippery in wet conditions.

At the bottom of the meadow yet another stile awaits. Go over it and proceed upwards on the other side of this small valley where the blue markings appear soon. The trail leads to a lake (6) after about 150m, with the impossible name of Sjurstjørnet. Follow the lake shore, towards the hut of the Ålgård scouts. The trail opens up again into a meadow. After crossing this meadow the path goes up and down, through woods and meadows, along a ridge towards the Eikefjell mountain

Continue following the trail to the top of Eikefjell (7), with its tell-tale mast. Many boulders that have been deposited by glaciers as they moved across the tops of these mountains can be seen here.

After enjoying the views, begin the initial descent. This is steep, and goes through a beech forest before emerging onto more gentle meadows (8). From here, the meandering path follows another older farm track down to the car park (9).

The Way to the Top: Local Hills and Fantastic Views

Hike 8.7 | Eikefjellet

Øykjafjellet | Hike 8.8

Hike 8.8: Øykjafjellet

A fun ascent to a peak that towers like a sentinel above Lake Lutsivatnet

The start and finish of the Øykjafjellet hike is very close to the Alsvik Natursenter with its various recreational facilities. It is a great option for a group of people with different abilities and interests: some might do the hike, while others enjoy the day here. Although not very long, this hike is not easy as the terrain is quite steep. On days with good weather, there are fabulous views over the Lutsivatnet area.

Access 🚗	Grading 🚶
Terrain: forest, moorland	Length: 5.5km
Facilities: Nature Centre at Alsvik	Time: 2hrs 30 mins

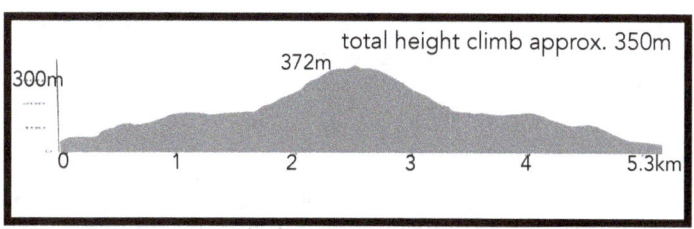

Data taken from Statens Kartverk, Geovekst and Kommunes, ©Kartverket

The Way to the Top: Local Hills and Fantastic Views

Hike 8.8 | Øykjafjellet

To reach the start of the hike:

By car: from Stavanger, take the E39 south towards Kristiansand, and leave the motorway at exit 27 towards Lauvvik/Hommersåk. Continue until you have gone through the Austråtunnel, and at the next roundabout (the Hana Roundabout), go straight towards Ims/Hommersåk on Rv516. After passing Lake Dybnigen, turn right towards Furenes/Alsvik along Furenesveien. Follow the windy, small road over two bridges. In just under 3km there is a sign towards Alsvik. Turn right here onto the narrow road. The car park for the Alsvik Naturesenter is 700m along this road. The parking area is spacious, and the "natursenter" area is just another 200m further on foot.

Hike Description

This trail has very faded blue markings at the start, with red markings, red dots and signposts later

The hike starts at the Aslvik Natursenter information board. This can be seen to the left of the gravel path that leads from the car park. There is an older looking sign saying 'Tursti': turn left here, up the hill, on a grassy path. The path enters a pine forest, then comes out of it but continues along the edge of the woods for a while. It arrives at a stile **(1)**: don't cross!! Instead, take a right turn walking along the fence and uphill into the woods.

Soon, pass (and ignore) a second stile. There are some faded blue markings on rocks and trees along the path. A steep ascent takes you out of the woods onto a rocky outcrop. Turn left on this ridge and veer right after about 20 metres. Look for a cairn, and turn right there, where the rocks are covered in vegetation again. The track here goes downhill, but is hard to see as a birch tree obstructs the view! As you scramble down along the rocks here, you may notice some faded blue markings. Keep left going up this valley. Pass (and ignore) a fallen stepladder. Stay on the right here, crossing up and over the next ridge, again with some blue markings visible. Keep the old stone fence on your left until you reach a drop-off. It's easier to go down the rocks about 10 metres further right (west) of the fence line.

At this point, you meet the path that you will later take back to Alsvik (on the right hand side) when you return. But, for now, turn left (east) where the path comes to yet another stile, this time with blue and red

Øykjafjellet | Hike 8.8

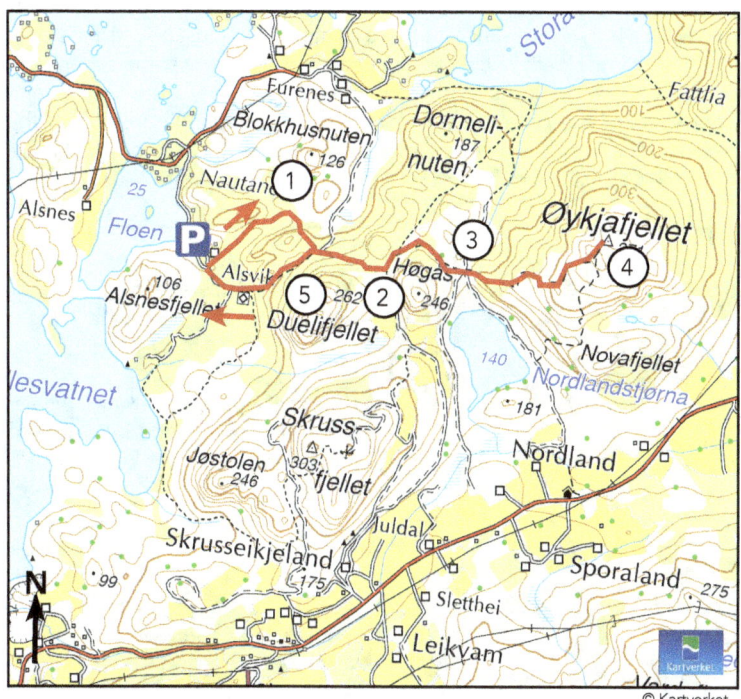

© Kartverket

markings. Cross this stile. From now on the hike follows the red marks. Initially the path is quite flat through beech woods. As you proceed you come to a path junction. A post and the red marks lead you up the hill on a wide path that emerges into a meadow. Some 200 metres further, you meet up with a large signpost and stile. Climb the stile over the fence (2) and continue left, with the fence on your left, still following the red markings. The ground underfoot here can be quite wet. The well-marked trail now leads you up over several ridges alternating woods and meadows as you proceed. It crosses a fence gap and track (3), before beginning the ascent up the final ridge.

On good weather days there are views onto the lake of Lutsivatnet and the mountains beyond that open on the higher slopes. There are a few "false" tops to scale before the summit of Øykjafjellet is reached at 372 metres (4).

The Way to the Top: Local Hills and Fantastic Views

Hike 8.8 | Øykjafjellet

For the return to Alsvik Naturesenter, follow the red markings all the way down. This is a slightly different route to the ascent. Just beyond the path junction (5), the path becomes quite steep and there is some scrambling over large size boulders. The red marks alternate between the left and right sides of the valley. Just before reaching Alsvik Naturesenter, the path leads through a pine forest and into the picnic area of Alsvik. The car park is some 300m further back down the gravel path.

Alsvik Natursenter

Alsvik Natursenter is a large recreational area with basic toilet facilities, several barbecue pits, a volleyball court, a sheltered picnic area with several large wooden tables and areas for playing ball or other games. The Natursenter can be booked in advance for larger parties for a maximum of two days via an online booking system. For more information (in Norwegian) see www.sandnes.kommune.no and search for Alsvik Natursenter.

Undeknuten | Hike 8.9

Hike 8.9: Undeknuten

A hidden gem, with lovely views along a horseshoe walk

Undeknuten is in the middle of the Sandnes hills. This horseshoe ridge allows you to be up in the surrounding tops, but without spending an entire day on the trip. If the weather is clear, there are glimpses of the Lysefjord bridge, plus Selvigstakken, Bynuten, and the mountains to the east.

Access 🚗 or 🚌	Grading 🚶
Terrain: track, moorland path	Length: 7.7km
Facilities: none	Time: 2hrs 30mins

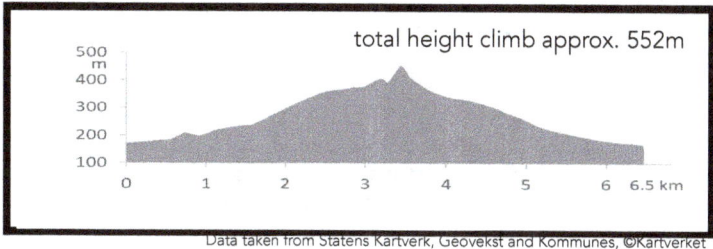

total height climb approx. 552m

Data taken from Statens Kartverk, Geovekst and Kommunes, ©Kartverket

The Way to the Top: Local Hills and Fantastic Views

Hike 8.9 | Undeknuten

To reach the start of the hike:

By car: from Stavanger centre take the E 39 south in the direction of Kristiansand for about 16km. Exit on Rv506, towards Hommersåk. The road goes through a short tunnel, then, at the next roundabout (about 3km from the E39), take the third exit (Noredalsveien) towards Høle. After about 13km, you should see the lake of Tengesdalsvatnet on the left hand side. The car park is at the far end of the lake, about 15km from the roundabout, on the left hand side of the road.

By bus: Buses from Sandnes go to the bus stop at Hommelend, which is further along Høleveien from the car park. Alight at the bus stop, then turn back along Høleveien towards Tengedalsvatnet, and look for the farm track on the left hand side of the road after about 350m. Turn left into the track to join the hike at point (1). If you reach the car park by the lake, you have gone too far. For bus schedules, routes, and prices, see www.kolumbus.no.

Hike Description

This trail is well marked with signposts, red dots and red T markers.

The hike is described in a clockwise direction: we recommend completing the circuit in this direction partly because the navigation is more straightforward, and partly because it offers an easier descent mostly on a farm track at the end of the hike, when one tends to be more fatigued.

To begin the hike, leave the car park and cross the road. On the other side is a track that begins parallel to the road, but quickly turns right to join a farm track just beyond point (1). Turn right along the farm track, and after about 250 metres, look for a marked trail leading to the left (2). Take this trail, and follow it up the (quite steep) valley side. The trail crosses a saddle and then descends gently as it turns towards the south. It traverses a small ridge, before entering a wooded area.

Continue following the marked trail as it joins a larger track and turns to the right, uphill. The track eases the steepness of the slope via a couple of zig-zags. Just as the track stops climbing, look for the marked path on the right hand side (3). Take this path (if you reach the end of the track, you have gone too far).

Undeknuten | Hike 8.9

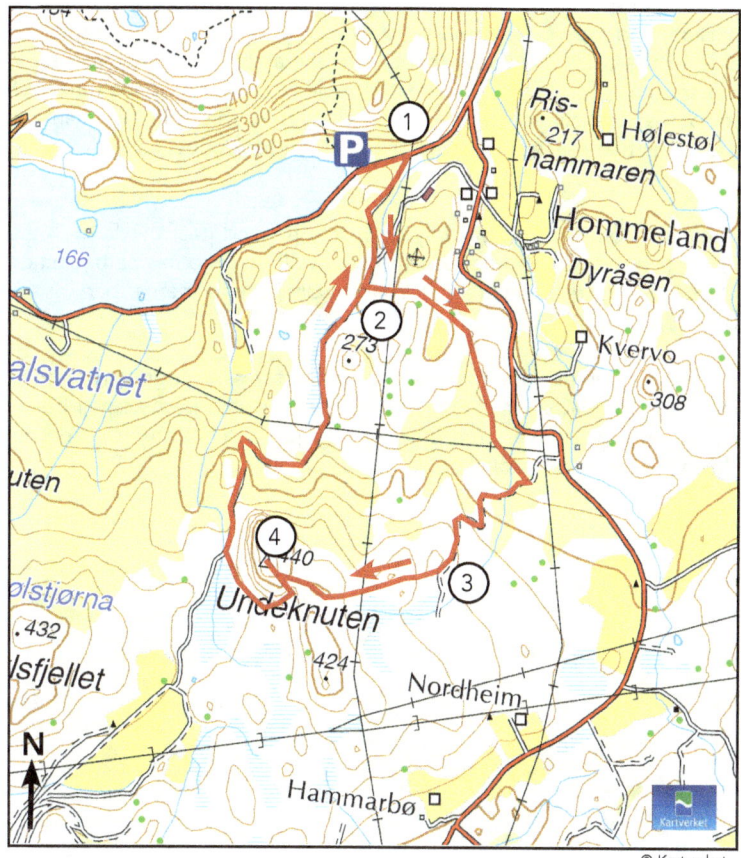

Now you are above the treeline, and can enjoy the views as you walk westwards and climb over a ridge. The trail dips a little way to a saddle before taking you on the final climb to the summit of Undeknuten (4). If the weather is fine, do stop a while to appreciate the views.

When you are ready to move on, it's important to turn back the way you came: this hill has dangerous crags on its north and west sides. However, you need only retrace your steps for a short way down the rocky hillside, before turning off on the (marked) trail down a steep valley to the right.

Hike 8.9 | Undeknuten

As the slope eases, the trail contours around the bottom of the craggy hillside, and crosses a meadow (which is marshy in places!). At the far side of the marsh, the trail meets a well-maintained farm track. Join this track as you continue down; it provides easy walking. Do turn back to look at the hill you have just climbed: from this side, you can see the crags that make the top of Undeknuten look spectacular from this direction.

The track continues all the way down the hill and past the farm in the bottom of the valley. After the farm you will return to the path junction at point (2), and from here is it a short walk back to the car park or the bus stop.

On a fine summer's day, the lake beside the car park, Tegnesdalsvatnet, is a very popular swimming spot, as it combines a pretty small beach with a refreshing lake. You may want to join the swimmers, and cool down after your exertions!

Rennesøy Hodet | Hike 8.10

Hike 8.10: Rennesøy Hodet
A popular hike in the Ryfylke archipelago

Since this is one of the highest points in the Ryfylke archipelago, there are marvellous views over the beautiful inlets and islands. With its lush farmland and abundant, shallow coastline, one can see why Rennesøy is home to one of the oldest places of human habitation in Norway. At the start of this hike is a pretty picnic area by a lake, allowing for some people to stay and enjoy while others do the hike.

Access 🚗	Grading 🚶
Terrain: forest, boggy moorland, gravel path	Length: 5.5km
Facilities: many picnic tables along the way	Time: 2hrs 30 mins

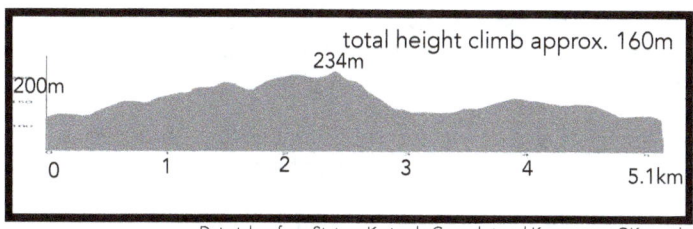

Data taken from Statens Kartverk, Geovekst and Kommunes, ©Kartverket

The Way to the Top: Local Hills and Fantastic Views

Hike 8.10 | Rennesøy Hodet

To reach the start of the hike:

By car: from Stavanger, take the E39 north towards Bergen. Passing Randaberg, the road soon reaches the Byfjord tunnel. The highway comes up to ground level briefly, and enters a second tunnel, this time under the Mastrafjord. Immediately after emerging from this second tunnel, take the exit towards Vikevåg. Follow the signs for 'Sentrum' turning left at the roundabout and proceed towards the harbour. Here keep left into Daleveien (signposted Dale).

The road follows the coastline, becoming a much smaller road as you climb it. Follow Daleveien for 2.2 km and then keep left, up the hill following Selsveien. Selsveien goes 700m further along the hill in a series of narrow turns, and ends at the parking lot where the hike starts. The parking lot is initially hidden from view; it is to the right of the farm gate. A parking fee applies, payable either through an app or by honesty box.

Hike Description

This trail is well marked by signposts, red dots and red T-signs

From the parking lot, continue along the track. It reaches Dalestemmen lake and picnic area after a few hundred metres. The dammed lake was used as a reservoir for two mills in Vik until after the First World War. Cross the dam on a narrow ledge. At the end of the dam go straight up the slope (1), following the well-worn path with red markers up a gentle hill.

This terrain is one of the oldest coastal heather landscapes in Rogaland, having been deforested about 4000 years ago by bronze-age people. At about 300m the path forks: follow the right fork to Rennesøyhodet (2). The return loop rejoins this path here. On the next gentle slope, there are views towards Mosterøy with the Utstein Cloister bay clearly visible. The path has recently been upgraded and wooden planks have been placed over some particularly wet sections. There is a stile crossing over a fence that uses ancient stone uprights.

Next there is a short steep section going through a small valley and up on the other side. Some wooden planks have been attached to the rock opposite, to help against sliding off the slippery slope. In winter and in icy conditions this might not be enough, and it may be advisable to

Rennesøy Hodet | Hike 8.10

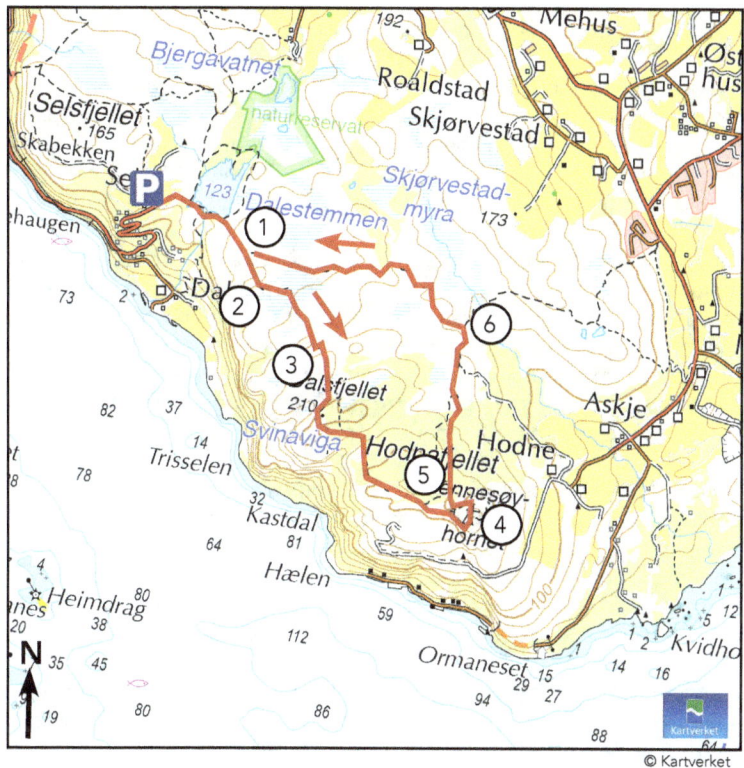

© Kartverket

follow the valley some 15-30 metres down in order to find an alternative way up the other side.

The path continues gently up, before descending into a valley just before a forested hill top. The path forks in the valley. Ignore the right fork and cross the stile on the left. The trail is almost always muddy here, and a good test for footwear. Soon you encounter a second stile over a stone fence as the path proceeds through the woods. From a clearing, the forested top of Dalehodet can be seen.

The trail descends into a dark pine forest that could come straight out of a Grimm's fairy tale. Emerging from the forest, there are sweeping views opening up to the south. After another stile over a fence, the path skirts the forest along the fence to the top of a ridge. From here, the cairn on top of Rennesøyhodet and two telecommunication towers are

Hike 8.10 | Rennesøy Hodet

visible. The path moves across the meadows, passing some beautifully positioned picnic tables that might tempt you to linger.

Moving along, you reach a stile. It is here that you will turn left on the return, but, for now, turn right, up the final ascent on the rocky path. From the top **(4)**, you will have fabulous 360 degree views. During the Iron Age, a fort stood here that was used to protect the farmers and provide shelter in case of danger.

As you survey the view from up high, the Ryfylke basin dotted with its many islands can be seen all around, and on clear days it is possible to see the mountains towards the east. From autumn to late spring they may be covered in snow. Stavanger can be seen to the south; the telecommunications-mast on Ullandhaug hill is a great point of reference. There is sometimes a rig or other large installation being serviced in the wharfs in Randaberg or Dusavik.

Descend from the peak the same way you came up. Alternatively, you could scramble down on the northern side of the top. In both cases you end up at the stile signposted towards Sel **(5)**. Climb over and follow the path alongside the stone wall and fence. As the path descends gently into the valley, the stones of the wall become ever more covered in moss. The path has red pole markings at regular intervals.

Down the valley, the forest ends at a picnic area. Turn left here over a stile and you will emerge from the woods into open meadows dotted with some beech trees. The trail from here becomes gravel underfoot. It continues meandering along the hill, signposted **(6)** to Sel (1.9km). Turn left here uphill along the gravel path until you reach and cross yet another stile. From here, it is a pleasant stroll across open meadows. Soon you will see Dalestemmen lake appearing. The path leads back to the lake and from there to the parking lot of Sel, with the farm houses of Sel in the background.

Hike 8.11: Vårlivarden (longer route)

Another approach to enjoying this classic hill, slightly longer than hike 8.2

This hike approaches the summit of Vårlivarden from a different direction to hike 8.2. The slightly longer route allows more time to enjoy the scenery, and also offers the possibility of access by bus from Hommersåk. As with hike 8.2, there is a small amount of fun scrambling, but the trail is generally good underfoot.

Access 🚗 or 🚌	Grading 🚶
Terrain: track, mountain path	Length: 5.2km
Facilities: none	Time: 2hr 30mins

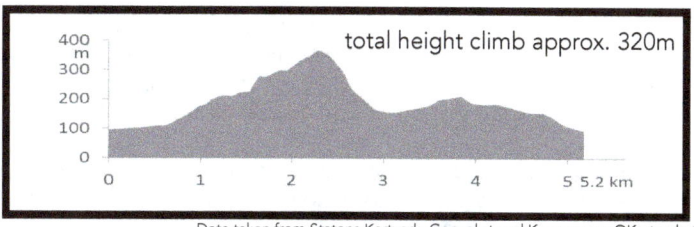

Data taken from Statens Kartverk, Geovekst and Kommunes, ©Kartverket

Hike 8.11 | Vårlivarden (longer route)

To reach the start of the hike:

By car: from Stavanger, take the E39 south towards Kristiansand, take exit 27 towards Lauvvik/Hommersåk, and then Rv 516 towards Hommersåk. Continue on the Rv 516 into Hommersåk, and in the town turn right into Berselveien, about 13.5km from where you left the E39 (if you reach the harbour, you have gone too far). After 750m, turn right into Kleivadalveien. The car park is on the left hand side of the road after 2km.

By bus: Buses from Sandnes service this area. The nearest bus stop is at the junction of Bergaselveien and Kleivadalveien, however if you are prepared to walk the extra 750m, the bus stop "Lineveien" in Hommersåk has a more frequent service. If you alight at Lineveien, walk along Bersagelveien to meet the bust stop at Kleivadalveien, then walk 2km along Kleivadalveien to the car park at the start of the hike. For bus schedules, routes, and prices, see www.kolumbus.no.

Hike Description

This trail is well marked with signposts, red dots and red T markers.

From the car park, turn left along the road. After just a few metres, there is a junction. Take the road on the left hand side. This is an access road for the cabins along the left hand side of the lake, which should be on your right. Just beyond the lake, a signposted trail leaves this road on the right hand side. Follow the trail (which can be muddy at times) as it climbs up a valley alongside a stream. The trail levels out a little as it passes a small lake on your right hand side, shortly after which you reach a busy path junction (1). The junction is well signposted: take the path straight ahead towards Vårlivarden. If you find yourself going downhill, you have taken the wrong turn!

The path leads up and on to the main ridge of Vårlivarden. You may have to look carefully for the red dots in one or two places, as the going is quite rocky here. As you climb higher, the spectacular views open out. Continue on to the summit (2), which is marked with a large cairn.

When you are ready to descend, be careful over the direction you take! There is a large signpost just below the summit cairn: you want to leave heading south towards Myrland/Kvelvane. At first, the descent is

Vårlivarden (longer route) | Hike 8.11

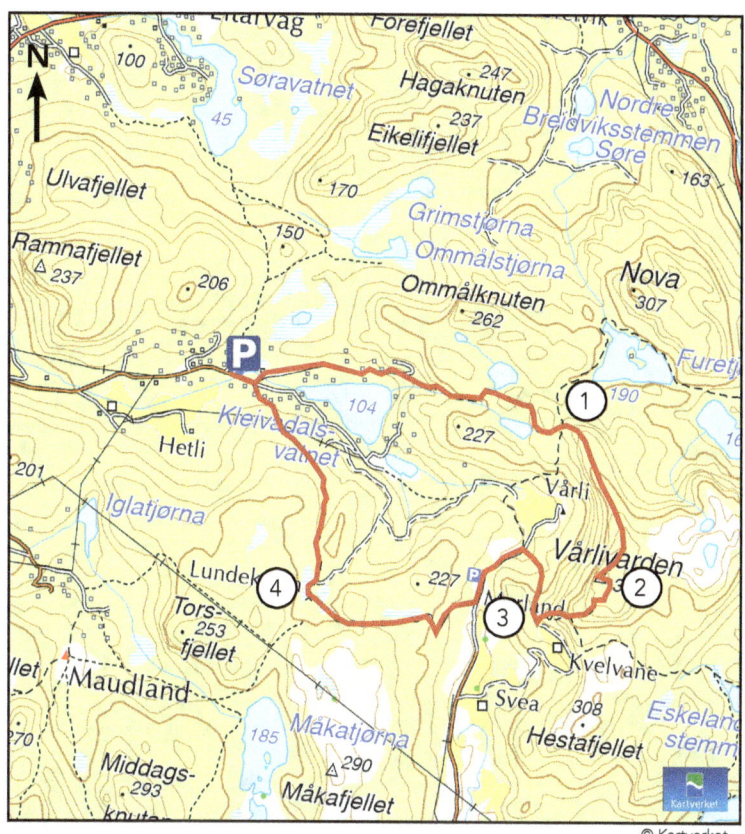

© Kartverket

gentle, but soon you will be scrambling down steeper sections of the hill. Continue straight past the track to Bersagel, and down to turn right along the farm track to Kvelvane. This track goes steeply down to a junction with the road to the hill farm of Vårli (3). The path crosses the road, but here you leave the path and turn left along the road. Go past the car park at Myrland, and, once past it, look for the marked trail that leaves the road on the right hand side and crosses a field.

Take this path (and be aware that there are often cows in this field!) up a very gentle hill to a marshy flat. Cross over a saddle to another marshy flat, where the trail forks (4). Take the left hand fork (which is a trail rather than a track), and follow it gently down the hill and past some cabins to the road. Turn left here to return to the car park or the bus stop.

The Way to the Top: Local Hills and Fantastic Views

Hike 8.11 | Vårlivarden (longer route)

Chapter 9:
Longer Days and Overnight Adventures

The hikes in this chapter are considered difficult. This can be due to different factors, such as the steepness and elevation that needs to be climbed, the length of the hike or the terrain. The rewards will be views of truly magnificent Norwegian panoramas. On days with good weather, views can extend to 50km, whilst on misty days they may be mysterious, giving just short glimpses of other-worldly landscapes.

We have included three hikes to mountain cabins (9.7, 9.9, and 9.10). While these hikes make great day hikes, stopping for a break at the cabin before continuing, it is also possible to stay the night and enjoy "cabin-life". Let yourself be charmed by the wonderful location of these mountain cabins, their basic yet splendidly-thought out facilities and the companionship of fellow hikers.

Hike 9.1: Reinaknuten
Half of Rogaland at your feet

This hike has some of the most spectacular views possible anywhere in Rogaland. With its height of 787m, Reinaknuten is one of its highest peaks and being so close to the coast it provides for truly magic vistas into the islands of Ryfylke. Half of Rogaland is literally at your feet once you reach the top.

Access 🚗	Grading 🚶
Terrain: forest, moorland, mountain	Length: 10.9km
Facilities: none	Time: 4hrs 30mins

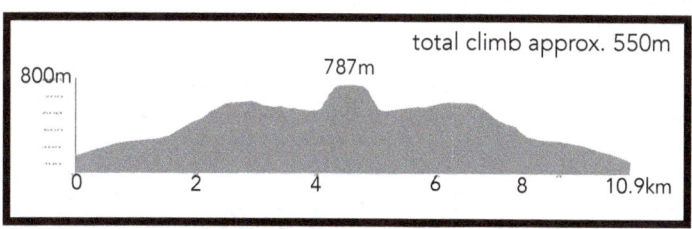

Data taken from Statens Kartverk, Geovekst and Kommunes, ©Kartverket

Longer Days and Overnight Adventures

Hike 9.1 | Reinaknuten

To reach the start of the hike:

By car: Starting from the E39 in Stavanger, take the Hundvåg and Ryfylke tunnels to Solbakk. As you exit, you meet with the Rv13. Turn north towards Tau/Røldal, and, at the roundabout in Tau, turn right, continuing along Rv13 towards Hjelmeland. 7km after the roundabout, and just past a short lake on the right hand side of the road, turn right, signposted Bjørheimsheia (the turnoff is easy to miss: look for workshops either side of the road, and a parking lot, just after driving over a small bridge). On Leitevegen road, a faded sign shows the direction to Bjørheimsheia. The road winds up a hill, at times becoming a gravel track, as it goes through dense forest. After 3.5km there is a signpost to Bjørnheimsheia (left turn). Follow the (at times) steep gravel road uphill. The parking lot is at the end of the road. There is ample parking available. Parking was still free at the time of writing, but this might change.

Hike Description

This trail is marked with signposts and red dots

The hike starts at the cabin area parking lot, and is signposted together with a number of other hikes in the area. It is an old, wide sheep trail that initially goes through light forest of pine, and later birch. A few paths run parallel over the first few hundred metres, and some venture off to cabins on the left. After about 300m there is a fork, with a path to Longabergdalen signposted to the right. This path leads to a few lakes, which offer lovely picnic and swimming opportunities on a summer day. The lakes are situated just below point (1) on the map. It could be an enticing area for the younger hikers in your party, while others do the main hike.

For Reinaknuten, stay on the trail going straight ahead. Keeping the cabins on the left, slowly move out of the forest into the more open heather country (1). Here the terrain is relatively flat.

The first climb (2), goes up to a saddle through another wooded area. From there, continue upwards until the trail passes the top of Krossen to the left.

As you proceed, the path descends to a group of lakes. This might be a great opportunity for a break. The scenery is beautiful, and also these

Reinaknuten | Hike 9.1

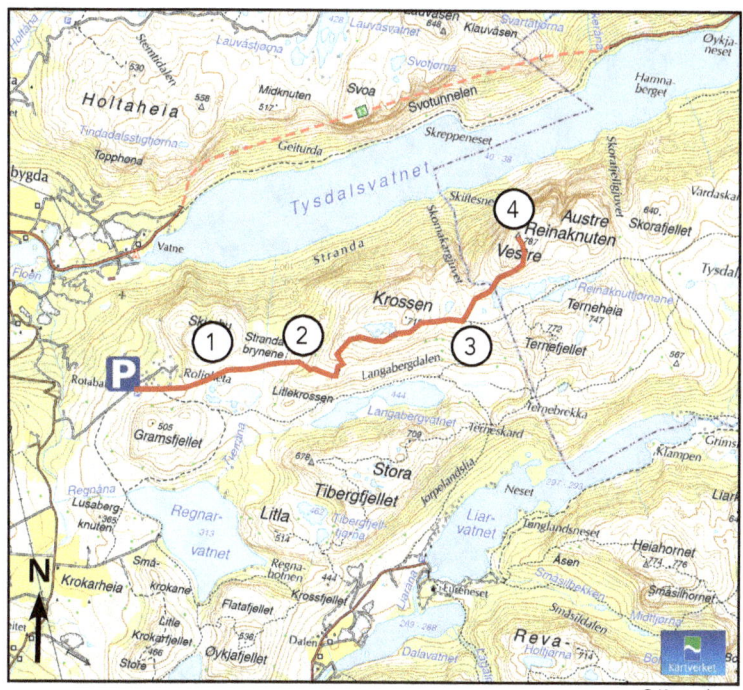

© Kartverket

lakes could be inviting enough for a swim in the summer or an extended picnic.

Beyond the lakes, at the bottom of the valley, there is a path junction. Reinaknuten is signposted from here (3). Towards the end of the valley, the final ascent begins. This is guaranteed to get your heart rate up, but at the end of the climb comes the summit (4)!

Enjoy the magnificent 360 degree views that open up quite unexpectedly. No matter which way you turn it will be difficult to peel your eyes away. Straight below you is Tysdalsvatnet; beware of the sheer drop though. To the west is the city of Stavanger. To the northwest are the Sjernarøyene, a set of beautiful little islands best explored by bike, but that's maybe for another day. Don't forget the inland views with barren and rugged mountain tops. A truly magnificent all-round panorama.

The way back goes down the same way that you came up, but as so

Hike 9.1 | Reinaknuten

often with these walks it will seem quite different in this direction. No reason to be disappointed because it is not a circular walk, especially as you will be enjoying the views as you descend.

Hike 9.2: Storaberget (longer route)

A hike with a wonderful opportunity for a swim on a summer's day

Storaberget towers imposingly over lake Lutsivatnet and looks like an impressive climb from down below. Including Grindavatnet on this hike provides the opportunity for a summer swim. It would also suit a group that wants to split up, one staying at Grindavatnet, which is a 2.2km walk with a mild ascent only, the other doing the complete walk and joining later.

Access 🚗 , or 🚆 + 🚌	Grading 🚶
Terrain: forest, moorland, lakes	Length: 8km
Facilities: swimming, picnic area	Time: 3hrs

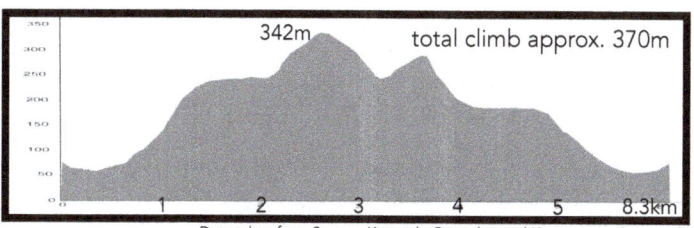

Data taken from Statens Kartverk, Geovekst and Kommunes, ©Kartverket

Longer Days and Overnight Adventures

Hike 9.2 | Storaberget (longer route)

To reach the start of the hike:

By car: from Stavanger, take the E39 south towards Kristiansand, and leave at exit 27 towards Lauvvik/Hommersåk. Continue towards Lauvvik/Hommersåk/Austrått, passing through the Austråtunnel, then go straight at the Hana roundabout. Continue past the Kronen Gård Hotell, with Lake Dybningen on the right, and then meeting Lake Lutsivatnet shortly after. Stay on the Rv 516 towards Hommersåk until you reach Hogstad.

No signpost for the parking area is available, but, at the height of Hogstad, there is a street sign to the right with numbers 400-416, numbering the houses on the road. On busy weekends it is best to park close to the road. Otherwise, turn right down the gravel road towards the farm. There is space for about four cars by the farm buildings, where there is also an overview map of the hiking area. You may park here if you are not obstructing the farm entrance. It is courteous to ask the farmer for permission if you see him around.

By public transport: There is a regular bus service between Sandnes and Hommersåk that stops at Hogstad Nord, and a regular train service between Stavanger and Sandnes Station. For details of schedules and fares see www.kolumbus.no

At the bus stop, you will see the street sign with numbers 400-416, numbering the houses along the road. Follow the description in the "by car" section above from this point.

Hike Description

This trail is marked with older, but still clearly visible, red markings

The hike starts by the information board next to the small parking facility at the farm. Walk down the gravel path that has a small quarry by the side. Beware during weekdays, as big trucks might be exiting/entering the site. Proceed downhill to a gate, which you leave as you find it. Past the gate continue along the path, keeping the fence on the left hand side (1). There may be sheep or cows grazing on the pasture.

Following the path as it steepens and veers to the right, some old bunkers come into view. After this a multiple signpost comes up (2). Grindavatnet is signposted here. If you are with a group that is going

Storaberget (longer route) | Hike 9.2

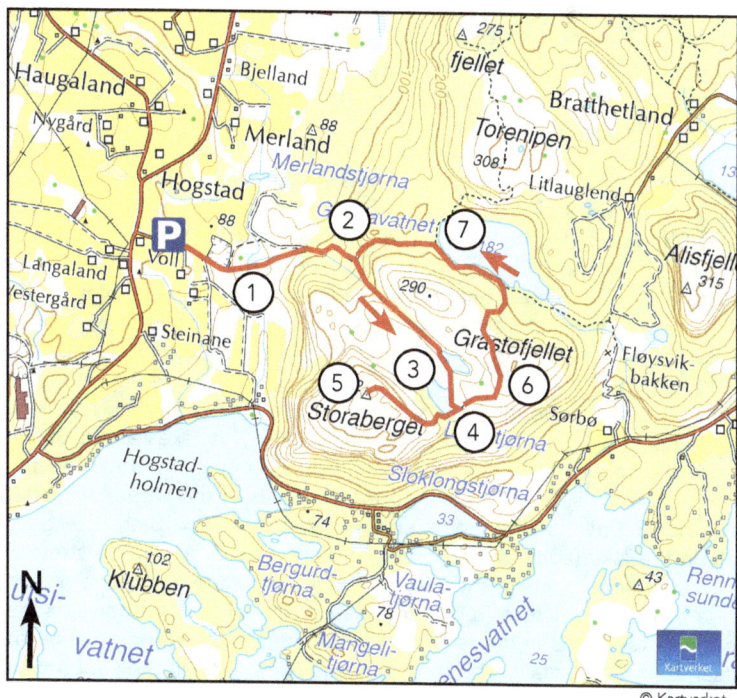

© Kartverket

to divide up and meet at the lake later, here is where the group splits. For those going directly to Grindavatnet the track continues on a slight ascent before levelling off. A short walk through the woods (about 500m) leads to the lake.

The other path goes towards Storaberget. This old road ascends through shady woods as it makes its way up towards the dam (3). The dam was built by the German occupying forces during World War II as an additional water reservoir. Cross the dam. At the other side of the ledge, the path hugs the rock face for a short scramble of a few metres. It then flattens out and follows the lake. Next it veers away into a small wooded area, past a second much smaller dam, which opens up to Lake Lomstjørna with charming views across the water. The narrow path can be quite damp here. Soon another signpost announces the direction towards either Grindavatnet or Storaberget (4). For now, follow the path towards Storaberget, past the dam of Lomstjørna lake.

Longer Days and Overnight Adventures

Hike 9.2 | Storaberget (longer route)

The path begins to ascend again. Along this stretch it can be wet and muddy after rain. Indeed, the path can become a small stream and the hiker might need to navigate between dry patches. The ascent from 200 to 300m is fairly steep, with a few steps of scrambling, then levelling out towards the top.

Here Storaberget's cairn soon comes into view (5). The magnificent outlook includes the village of Hommersåk to the north, Dalsnuten and Bjørndalsfjellet to the west, and, most spectacularly, the lake and islands of Lutsivatnet below to the south-west. This gem of a mountain is generally not very busy, but gets a steady stream of visitors. Enjoy a well-deserved break, before heading down. Return the same way back to Lake Lomstjørna, and from there follow the sign to Grindavatnet at (4).

This will take you up the bare rocks until the path levels off and ascends on a ridge towards the top of Grastofjellet (6). It takes about 30min from the top of Storaberget to this point. Continuing down on the north-westerly side, descend into the coolness of the wood, and after another 300m the trail meets Grindavatnet lake. The path now goes along the lake (again the path can be quite muddy along this stretch). Shortly before reaching the swimming spot, you arrive at the remnants of a concrete structure. Turn right towards the lake, or left towards the car park. Just above, there is a fairly flat area in the woods that lends itself to make a small camp or picnic area. Take a dip in the cool waters of the lake, or just relax (7).

Heading back towards the car park will be an easy, mostly downhill, 2km hike.

Hike 9.3: Bynuten

A collector's top: the highest point in Sandnes

There's no place higher than Bynuten in Sandnes County! That in itself is motivation enough for many to climb this top. It makes for a fine day in the hills, and the rewards are 360 degree views, with all the 'lesser' tops of Sandnes down below.

To reach the start of the hike:

Access 🚗	Grading 🚶
Terrain: forest, boggy moor, mountain	Length: 11.8km
Facilities: none	Time: 5hrs 45min

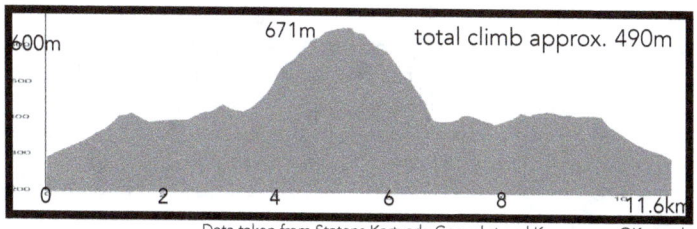

Data taken from Statens Kartverk, Geovekst and Kommunes, ©Kartverket

Longer Days and Overnight Adventures

Hike 9.3 | Bynuten

By car: From Stavanger, take the E39 south towards Kristiansand. Leave the motorway at exit number 27 towards Lauvvik/Hommersåk. Follow towards Lauvvik/Hommersåk/Austrått until you pass through the Austråtunnel. At the following roundabout at Hana, turn right towards Lauvvik at Noredalsveien and Høleveien. Continue for about 11km, and then take a sharp right turn onto the Rv 508 towards Søredalen/Oltedal. Two parking lots come into view after 2.3km, one on each side of the road.

Hike Description

This trail is marked with signposts and red dots

The hike starts from the parking area on the east side of the road (this is the one with the information panel). In the beginning, follow the wide gravel road that runs across a paddock. This gravel road is part of 'Lyseveien' and was built to facilitate the construction of the high voltage electricity masts that transport the hydroelectric power across the Høgsfjord from Forsand power station. In summer cows might be present on the paddocks and very much on the path itself (see hike 8.6 for advice on how to behave around cows).

The path ascends slowly, arriving at a gate. From here it is still wide, but a bit rockier. Soon there will be electricity lines overhead. After about a kilometre, at the top of the path's rise, the way to Bynuten is signposted towards the right (1). Here you leave the easily walkable, but somehow uninteresting gravel path for a more natural path turning towards the southeast. It passes Blommetjørn, a small lake on the left, and then ascends towards a set of power masts. Here the northern tip of lake Trollabaertjørna comes into view. This is the largest of the many picturesque mountain lakes visited on this hike.

The path now follows the forest at the lake's shoreline for a few hundred metres, at times quite close to the water. As the lake widens, the path turns away from the shoreline and upwards. It emerges from the forest onto a rocky meadow (2). Here is the first view of Bynuten, high up on the left with its cairn and impressive rock face. Leaving Trollabaertjørna behind, the path makes a sharp turn to the left (north, signposted), and Lake Storatjørn comes into view. The path goes high above the northern shore of the lake, towards the steep valley of Svartedalen directly ahead.

Bynuten | Hike 9.3

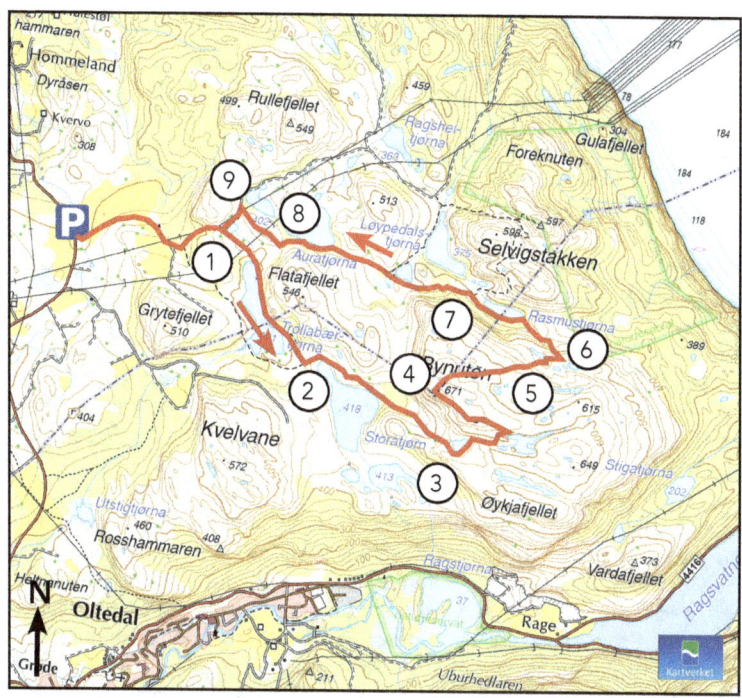

© Kartverket

The ascent in the valley above lake Storatjørn is gradual at first, then becomes quite steep (3). The last few metres are a scramble past a lovely little waterfall: an ideal spot for a break. The waterfall runs down from a lake set in a bowl of mountain ridges all around. The path follows a track around the southern shore of the lake towards the remainder of the steep climb out of Svartedalen.

Once on the ridge, another lake comes into view ahead, but this time continue towards and through the gully on the left, finally ascending onto the ridge that leads to the top of Bynuten. Take a moment to turn around and view the lakes at your feet and Øykjafjellet mountain behind. The route now turns back towards the west, gently ascending for about 600m through undulating higher mountain vegetation of low grass and rocky surfaces. The top of Bynuten with its impressively high cairn can be seen with 200m left to walk (4). This is the highest top in the area, as well as the half-way point of the hike.

Longer Days and Overnight Adventures

Hike 9.3 | Bynuten

You can only continue down from here, and the path initially goes northwards, then turns towards the east, on a steady descent between two small lakes, then up another ridge. Lovely views across Høgsfjord and into Espedal open up during the gradual but steady descent towards yet another set of little lakes (5). The path is clearly visible on the shallow ridge across from the lakes. Continuing onto that ridge, the spectacular bridge over the Lysefjord comes into view, but the path turns sharply away towards the Rasmus lake (6).

The descent towards Lake Rasmustjørna is steep and care needs to be taken especially during wet conditions. On the way down, beech trees appear that may provide some support. After the steep descent, the path seems to split, but both branches come together again very shortly. Follow the red dot markings straight to the lake. Once at the lake, most of the descent from Bynuten is over. Pass to the left of Rasmustjørna Lake, and continue to the path junction where a path from Selvigstakken (Hike 9.4) joins (7).

The path continues with some ups and downs in a westerly direction, passes a southern arm of lake Løypedalstjørna, a second turn-off to Selvigstakken (which is an alternative route to that described in hike 9.4) and then undulates towards lake Auratjørna for a last scramble over rocks, wet roots and muddy puddles. It is probably with some relief that you note the path ascending away from Auratjørna Lake, steadily going up until passing under a set of electricity pylons (8). From there it is a short distance to Lyseveien, the gravel road (9). Turn left, and go past the original turn-off to Bynuten (1). The hike finishes with a gentle stroll towards the parking lot, where the last bit of initially tedious gravel road may now strike you as very comforting.

Selvigstakken | Hike 9.4

Hike 9.4: Selvigstakken

The best view into Lysefjord and its bridge

The views from Selvigstakken are unrivalled in Sandnes. From almost 600m high, you look into the opening of the Lysefjord. The elegance of the Lysefjord Bridge as it spans across can best be appreciated from here. On a summer day it can be mesmerising to watch the ferries, sailing yachts and pleasure boats moving as toys along the Høgsfjord and Lyseford and into the Frafjord.

Access 🚗	Grading 🏃
Terrain: forest, boggy moor, mountain	Length: 10.8km
Facilities: none	Time: 5hrs 30min

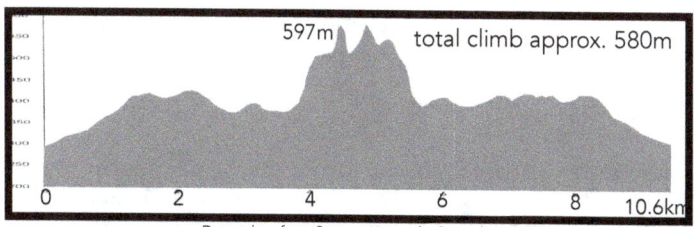

Data taken from Statens Kartverk, Geovekst and Kommunes, ©Kartverket

Longer Days and Overnight Adventures

Hike 9.4 | Selvigstakken

To reach the start of the hike:

By car: From Stavanger, take the E39 south towards Kristiansand. Leave the motorway at exit 27 towards Lauvvik/Hommersåk. Follow towards Lauvvik/Hommersåk/Austrått until you pass through the Austråttunnel. At the following roundabout at Hana, turn right towards Lauvvik at Noredalsveien and Høleveien. Continue for about 11km, and then take a *sharp* right turn onto the Rv 508 towards Søredalen/Oltedal. Two parking lots come into view after 2.3km, one on each side of the road.

Hike Description

This trail is marked with signs and red dots

The hike starts from the parking area on the east side of the road (this is the one with the information panel). Go through the gate and follow the wide gravel road that moves across the paddock. In summer, take caution as cows might be present in this field and actually very much on the path itself (see hike 8.6 for advice on how to behave around cows).

The path ascends slowly and soon there will be electricity lines overhead. After about a kilometre, the way to Bynuten is signposted towards the right (1), but for Selvigstakken, continue along the path towards the northwest. There will still be overhead electricity lines for another 500m or thereabouts. During this part of the walk, they come in and out of view numerous times, and are very much the reason for the path. Forsand County on the other side or the fjord is a major hydroelectricity provider for the Stavanger region, and this path ("Lyseveien") was constructed for building and maintaining the installations.

Soon after the Bynuten path junction, there is a path junction, with Selvigstakken signposted to the right (2). For now, *ignore the signpost*, and continue to follow the track to the left. The return route rejoins this path here. Soon there will be a small lake on the right: this part of the hike goes through the valley as it skirts around the hill to the right. About 1.3km beyond point (2), the path swings from a northeasterly to a more easterly direction (3). The ascent towards Selvigstakken comes into view here.

As you pass a local cabin on your left hand side, pay special attention. The Lyseveien will turn left, descending gently. Some 15-20m after the left turn there is a grass track to the right, marked with a wooden sign

Selvigstakken | Hike 9.4

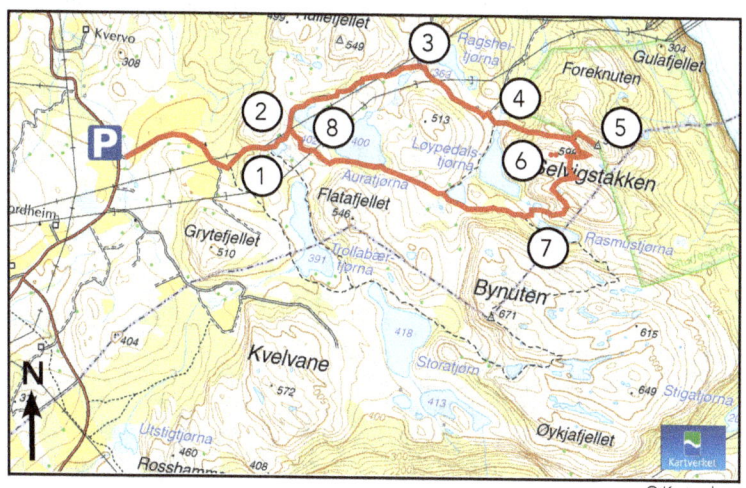

© Kartverket

saying "Selvigstakken". Turn off the main track and follow this path down the meadow towards the stream at the valley bottom. Follow this trail, keeping eastwards. Cross the stream, continuing east. After crossing over the small stream that runs down from Løpedalstjørna the ascent begins in earnest (4).

The steep and sometimes narrow 200m ascent first scrambles up the forested valley side, up into a gulley. From there, turn left and continue steeply up the zig-zag path to the top. This last section is not for those who suffer from vertigo! The ascent does not give much of the view away until the summit is reached (5). The sense of the unexpected just adds to the astounding feeling the view creates as it opens up in front of you. It is a narrow top, but truly the most spectacular one in Sandnes County. There are three fjords: the Høgsfjord just underneath, with the Lysefjord opposite and Frafjord a little towards the east. The mountains on the other side of the fjords are crisscrossed with many more hiking paths, which are connected by mountain huts to make multiday adventures possible.

Once you decide to move on, return the way you came down the steep

Hike 9.4 | Selvigstakken

zig-zag path to where you turned left up the hill. Instead of retracing your steps all the way back to the car park, turn left here and continue south east. The trail climbs gently, before crossing over a spur. Here, there is a second top to visit if you wish. Selvikstakken has a "twin" that is just a metre higher and can be "collected" on the way. By the time you are about to begin descending the spur, you are almost all the way there. The way to the second top can be seen from the main path as a small detour (6). The views are not quite as spectacular, but the top is not as narrow as Selvigstakken itself, so there is much more space from which to enjoy them.

From this top, the next kilometre is a steep descent that goes to a small lake, Rasmustjørna (7). Follow the stepping stones across the stream below Rasmustjørna, and continue straight up the side of the valley a short way to join the path that comes down from Bynuten (hike 9.3). Turn right, and enjoy this trail as it passes alongside two more lakes. Once again, the trail comes upon some electricity masts overhead (8). Shortly after this is the fork of the path that leads back towards the start of the walk (2). Turn left here and return to the car park along the same route.

Hiking Lysefjord and beyond: day trips in the Stavanger Region

Hike 9.5: Vådlandsknuten

An accessible mountain with marvellous views and varied terrain

Boasting 811 metres in height, this top towers over its surroundings. It rewards with stunning views all around hinting at Høgsfjord and Lysefjord in northerly direction and the beaches and farmland of Jæren to the west. The walk is great for building stamina and gaining confidence in the higher mountains, while not being overly steep or difficult to navigate.

Access 🚗	Grading 🏃
Terrain: forest, boggy moor, mountain	Length: 11.6km
Facilities: toilet at the car park	Time: 5hrs 45min

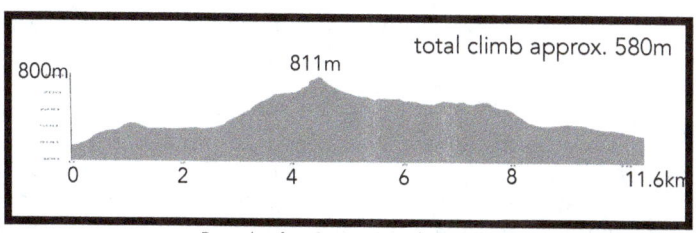

Data taken from Statens Kartverk, Geovekst and Kommunes, ©Kartverket

Hike 9.5 | Vådlandsknuten

To reach the start of the hike:

By car: From Stavanger take the E39 south towards Kristiansand. After passing the town of Ålgård (after approximately 28 km), turn left along the Rv 450 towards Sirdal. After 8.1km turn right into Rv 287 towards Madland and Brekko. After 3.1 km the road meets Rv 286. Turn left here, again towards Madland, and follow the road to the very end. A signpost warns not to park here as it is a turning area for the public bus (unfortunately, this bus comes only once a day, and so is not practical for day hikers). Follow through the gate (leaving it as you find it: open or closed) and continue up the hill for 1.1 km. You'll pass two more gates before you arrive at a sizeable parking lot on your right, with a little toilet block. There is a charge for the car park to help with the cost of maintaining the facilities, payable via mobile phone app. At the time of writing, this app was Vipps, which requires both a Norwegian phone number and a Norwegian ID to use.

Hike Description

This trail is well marked with signposts and red T-markers

Start the hike form the lower section of the parking lot, by crossing the small bridge over the stream. There is a second path starting at the upper end of the parking lot, both join after some 150m. The path goes directly up the valley for the first kilometre, gaining about 100m in height. At first the stream is to the left, then the trail crosses over a bridge to the other side. The valley opens up as the trail ascends. It passes by a cabin belonging to the local Scouts (1), and continues climbing out of the valley.

The trail crosses over a saddle, then descends through beech trees towards an elongated lake, called Fisketjørna (2). It's really two lakes, with a small connecting stream. There is an old, rusted 1960's signpost at the stream, dating from the time when this began to be a very popular cross country skiing area. The sign is in the middle of the river which freezes in winter. Later in the walk, you will see more of these signs, perched on boulders in the middle of streams. A newer signpost on the lake shore points to Fisketjornbu across the lake. Ignore this and continue along the shore, with the lake on your left hand side. The path follows the shoreline close to the edge almost towards the end of the lake. This is naturally a rather flat stretch. At the end of the lake the path leads up the valley again, with a stream on the left. Some nice flat stones

Vådlandsknuten | Hike 9.5

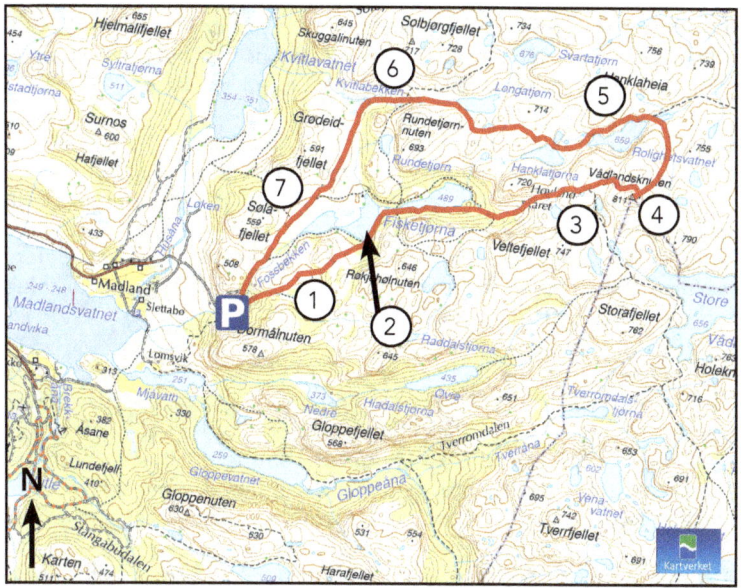

© Kartverket

offer a great spot to relax on a warm day.

At this point, the trail climbs above the treeline and towards the highlands. The path levels out for a short section, then ascends steeply out of the valley and towards a pass on the left. At the pass height, it enters a 'bowl' with a number of lakes. Vådlandsknuten is ahead. Keep to the left as another trail heads down to the right (3). The path ascends first towards the left to a saddle; the return path is visible, looking north, on the far shore of the Lake Rolighetsvatnet far below (5). First however, turn sharply to the right and keep climbing to a pass height between the two peaks of Vådlandsknuten.

Note the signpost here for the way back. At the time of writing it was new, but not very well secured, so keep an eye out for the well-marked red 'T's. The marked (but strangely not signposted) path for the final ascent takes you in northerly direction at first and around the peak, where it is climbed from the east (4). This makes the ascent far less steep than from the west. In good weather, you are the "King of the Castle" with views all around. Towards the west the mountains give way to the rolling hills, farmland and beaches of Jæren county; to the north

Longer Days and Overnight Adventures

Hike 9.5 | Vådlandsknuten

the steep slopes towards the Høgsfjord and Lysefjord can be made out. All around is the high plateau of the mountains that bear the flattened features so characteristic of landscapes sculpted by glaciers.

The way back begins by descending back the way you came towards the signpost, then heading down northwards into the valley before you. The path back is generally very well marked. It goes on a roundabout way towards Lake Rolighetsvatnet, descending from the mountain in a northerly direction, which makes for a slightly less steep descent. Before reaching Rolighetsvatnet, cross over a field of boulders, one of three such crossings on the way back.

You proceed along the northern shore of the lake (5), only to descend further to another lake called Hanklatjørna. At this lake, the path leaves the lake shore and veers off and up to the right. The trail continues in a westerly direction with Lake Longatjørn on the right side. It crosses another boulder field before starting a steep descent into the valley of Kvitlabekken (6), going around Rundetjørnnuten along its northern side.

At the bottom of the descent, there is a stream to cross (with plenty of stepping stones). The path continues in southerly direction, gently up and down, through a lovely valley with marshes alongside, heather, scattered beech trees, flowers and blueberries (when in season) – a truly lovely stroll (7). The final descent goes along a well-trodden and easy path along the Fossbekken valley. At its end you reach the upper parking lot, from where it is a short two minutes to the starting point.

While the hike has been described here counter clockwise, it is perfectly possible to do it the other way around. The ascent will then be less steep and longer, meaning that once at the top of Vådlandsknuten you are more than half way. The descent is shorter and steeper. If you wish to do the hike in clockwise direction proceed to the upper half of the carpark and start from there. The red 'T' marks can be seen just as well from this direction.

Hike 9.6: Månafossen and Månavatnet

Beyond Månafossen waterfall to mountain meadows and a lake, Månavatnet

The waterfall at Månafossen, and the via ferrata to reach the viewpoint, are highlights of the region. Beyond the waterfall (and most of the tourists) lies a mountain meadow and, higher up the valley, Månavatnet, a lake with steep forests on either side.

Access 🚗	Grading 🚶
Terrain: forest, moorland, "via ferrata": rocks with chains to hold on to	Length: 12km (easy to shorten)
Facilities: Cabin (with toilets) at Mån	Time: 4hrs

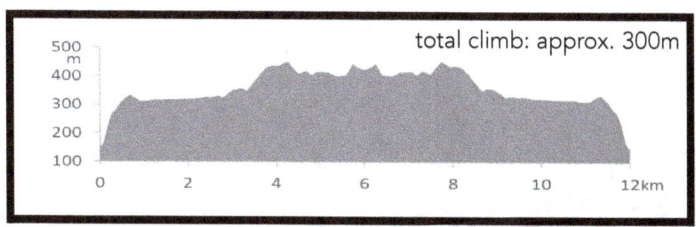

Data taken from Statens Kartverk, Geovekst and Kommunes, ©Kartverket

Hike 9.6 | Månafossen and Månavatnet

To reach the start of the hike:

By car: From Stavanger, travel south on the E39. Just after leaving Ålgard, turn left onto the Rv 450, signposted to Sirdal. Continue along the Rv 450 past Oltedal and through the tunnel to Dirdal. About 6km after exiting the tunnel turn left on to the Rv 4414, towards Frafjord. Continue straight through the tunnel as soon as you leave the Rv 450 (if you find yourself zig-zagging up a mountainside, you have missed the tunnel and need to turn around when you can). The tunnel ends in Frafjord: continue straight on the Rv 4414 towards Eikeskog. The road climbs a short hill, and the car park is at the end of the road (payment required).

Hike Description

This trail is marked with signposts, red T-markers and red dots

The trail begins at the far end of the car park, and almost as soon as you begin the walk, you will encounter the "via ferrata", as the trail turns steeply up rocks with chains to hold on to. Steep climbing makes for a rapid ascent though, and if you don't have to wait for too long for your turn using the chains, you'll soon be at the first Månafossen viewpoint **(1)**.

Take your time to enjoy the sight of the water crashing down, before continuing uphill through woods and around in a large curve. The climb leads to the top of the waterfall, where there is a labyrinth of paths to allow you to explore the views of the plunge pools from the top. Afterwards, find your way back to the main trail. A short distance along is the "Friluftsgarden" (literally: "fresh-air farm") at Mån **(2)**. The building was originally a hill farm, but has been converted to a nature centre.

Månafossen and Månavatnet | Hike 9.6

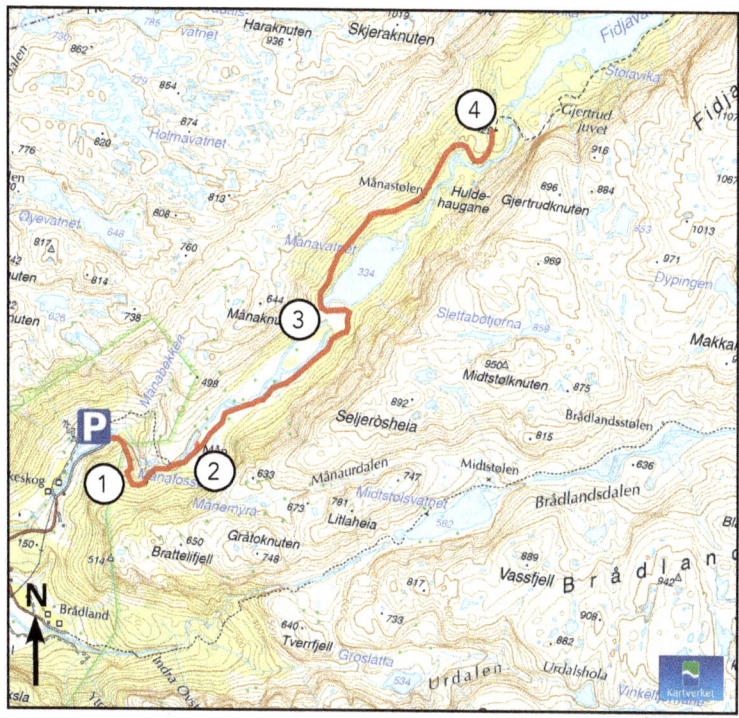

© Kartverket

After the nature centre at Mån, the trail becomes quieter, and traverses a serene meadow. The going is reasonably level, through grassy areas, berry bushes, and some trees. Just before the lake at Månavatnet, the path turns sharply to the left across a boulder field (3).

CAUTION: When the river is in spate, which is when the snow is melting in the spring and after any period of heavy rain, the river surges over the boulder field and the crossing here becomes unsafe. Please look at the conditions when you are here and judge whether or not it is safe to cross, remembering that the river level could have risen a little by the time you return if it is either a hot sunny day in spring, or if there has been recent heavy rain!

Provided that the boulder field is safe to cross, the path turns to the right afterwards. Now you are in the forest, climbing through the trees on the steep mountain side, with the lake below. At the head of the lake, the

Longer Days and Overnight Adventures

Hike 9.6 | Månafossen and Månavatnet

trail returns to the riverside, and climbs a little knoll (4). Here is a good place to stop and return the way you came, enjoying the views back down the Mån valley as they open up below you.

If you don't want to stop here, the path continues for a full 14km from the car park at the beginning of the hike to the mountain cabin at Blåfjellenden, and you can stop and turn back at any point you like. Be aware though, that there is another river crossing higher up the trail that also becomes impassable when the river is in spate. Although all the way to Blåfjellenden and back would make for an extremely long day hike, there is of course the possibility of staying overnight at the cabin and even hiking further into the mountains from there for a multi-day adventure.

The "Friluftsgarden" at Mån

This nature centre is owned and operated by Jaeren Friluftsråd, who also operate the "Friluftshuset" at Orre beach. There is a "warming room" in the cellar that is open all year round, where you can not only warm up, but find out more about the history of this former mountain farm. There is also space for you to eat your packed lunches here, but you are asked to tidy up afterwards and contribute a daily visit fee to help with maintenance of the site. At the time of writing, this was payable via Vipps, an app that requires both a Norwegian phone number and bank account. If you would like to stay overnight at the centre, rooms are also bookable in advance. For more details, see www.jarenfri.no

Viglesdalen | Hike 9.7

Hike 9.7: Viglesdalen

Stunning valley scenery in the Hjelmeland mountains

Viglesdalen is one of the most beautiful valleys in the area. The trail rises along a cascade of waterfalls to a spectacular lake and beyond. The valley has been a farm for centuries; the remaining buildings remind us of those who lived here.

Access 🚗	Grading 🚶
Terrain: forest, moorland	Length: 13.3km
Facilities: STF Cabin at Viglesdalen	Time: 4hrs 30mins

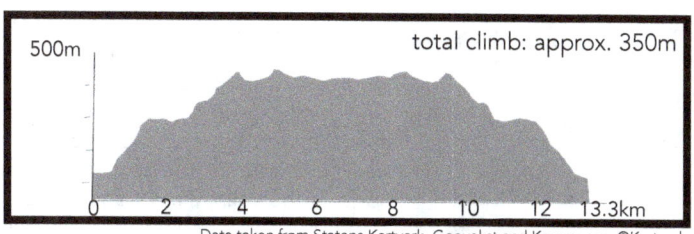

Data taken from Statens Kartverk, Geovekst and Kommunes, ©Kartverket

Longer Days and Overnight Adventures

Hike 9.7 | Viglesdalen

To reach the start of the hike:

By car: Starting from the E39 in Stavanger, take the Hundvåg and Ryfylke tunnels to Solbakk. As you exit, you meet with the Rv13. Turn towards Tau, and, at the roundabout in Tau, turn right, continuing along Rv13 towards Hjelmeland. About 22km from the roundabout, turn sharp left along the Fv 661, signposted to Nes. This is a sharp turn near the bottom of a steep hill (If you reach the village of Årdal, you have gone too far). After 2km, Fv 661 turns right, but you need to proceed straight along Fv 638 for another kilometre, until it ends in a T-junction. Turn right along Fv 633 (signposted Nes). The car park is at the end of the road after 4km.

Hike Description

This trail is marked with signposts, red T-markers and red dots

Follow the T-markers from the car park across the bridge and left around the farmyard at Nes. Look for T-markers on the gates. Past the farmyard, the trail follows a rough stone track (more of this later) uphill. In the first kilometre, there are two path junctions. At both of them, stay on the main trail continuing uphill, signposted "Viglesdalen". Soon after the second junction, the effort of the climbing is rewarded by the first view of a waterfall: below the trail the Sendingfossen tumbles, deep into a gorge (1). It makes for a memorable picnic spot.

Above Sendingfossen, the trail continues up a cascade of rapids. Across the river, the abandoned hill farm of Hia is visible on the opposite hill. Beyond Hia, the trail climbs to cross a saddle, and the lake of Viglesdalsvatnet comes into view.

At two points on the climb, a signpost will invite you to take a 0.5km detour (2). The detour involves a steeper ascent (or descent, if you do it in the reverse direction on the way back to the car park) than the rest of the path, but you will be well rewarded. At the top of a narrow ridge in the valley lie a perfectly round kettle-hole and a boulder, deposited in a

Viglesdalen | Hike 9.7

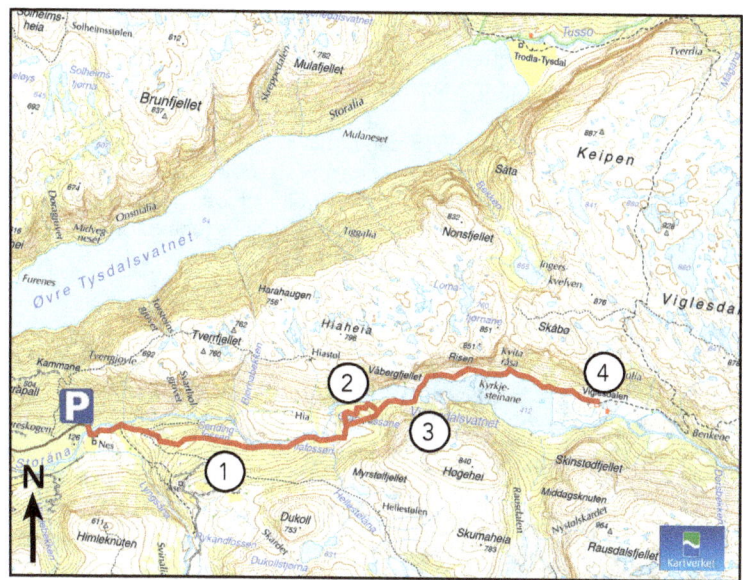

© Kartverket

crack by a glacier, and now firmly lodged there, just like its larger cousin Kjeragbolten (see hike 10.9). Looking down the valley, the view of the rapids is stunning. Whichever direction you take the detour in, the path goes under the "bolt" and continues. It is well marked with red dots, and rejoins the main path after about half a kilometre.

Descend on the main path to the stone bridge that crosses the water at a narrow point (3). After the bridge the stony track is similar to the one at the very beginning of the hike. It is part of a drove road built using Swedish labour in 1907-12. The drove road continues along the lake to the STF Cabin and farm buildings at Viglesdalen (4).

When you are ready, return to the car park along the same track (perhaps

Longer Days and Overnight Adventures 209

Hike 9.7 | Viglesdalen

taking the detour to the "bolt" and kettle-hole if you haven't already). The views in this direction are no less stunning as you descend the mountain valley back to the farm at Nes.

This hike goes as far as the STF cabin at Viglesdalen before returning, but you don't have to stop there. From Viglesdalen, there are marked trails to Trodlå-Tysdal (be aware that this trail includes a steep descent), and also to the STF cabin at Stakken, giving options for exploring further into the mountains and multi-day adventures.

The track to Viglesdalen
Originally, the only way for the villagers from the local area to reach the summer pastures at Viglesdalen was via a treacherous boat crossing across the lake Viglesdalsvatnet. The current track was built by Swedish labourers between 1907 and 1912. The original plan was to extend the track further into the mountains, but it was stopped at Viglesdalen after much of the land beyond had been sold off as hunting grounds.

Vinjakula | Hike 9.8

Hike 9.8: Vinjakula

The highest point in Bjerkreim, with U-shaped valleys all around

The top of Vinjakula boasts spectacular views in all directions: steep-sided U-shaped valleys to the north, east, and south, and the south of the Jaeren to the west. The climb is long, but generally steady, although there are one or two "scrambly" sections.

Access 🚗	Grading 🚶
Terrain: forest, moorland, mountain	Length: 14.4km
Facilities: none	Time: 6hrs

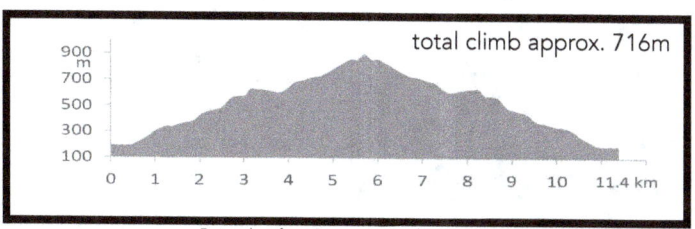

total climb approx. 716m

Data taken from Statens Kartverk, Geovekst and Kommunes, ©Kartverket

Longer Days and Overnight Adventures

Hike 9.8 | Vinjakula

To reach the start of the hike:

By car: Starting from the E39 in Stavanger, travel south through Ålgard and onwards to Vikeså. Just after descending the hill into Vikeså, turn left on the Rv 509 towards Byrkjedal. The road twists and winds, and becomes narrow in places. After passing three lakes, and just over 19km from Vikeså, the parking area is on the right hand side of the road (payment required). If you reach a tunnel, you have gone too far, and will need to turn around after exiting the tunnel.

Hike Description

This trail is marked with signposts and red dots

From the car park, face the road and turn left along it for a few metres before turning left again along a farm track. Follow the marked track past the farm (please stay on the marked trail and leave all gates as you find them). About 360m after leaving the Rv 503, cross the river on the left hand side via the bridge (1). Go past a large farm building on the left hand side, and, just after it, look for a track on the left hand side. Take this track.

As the track loops around to the right, it leaves the farm behind and begins to climb the wooded side of the valley. Soon the trees become more sparse, the track narrows to a trail, swings to the left and enters

the narrow valley of Mjådal (2). Continue up the valley: at the head of the valley, there is a delightful little lake that might provide a good spot for resting and refreshments.

Just beyond the lakes, the path swings to the left (3) and continues to climb in earnest. The views begin to open out here, and before too long you will be passing the lake of Stemmatjørn below and to the right. A slightly steeper section of climb beckons just after Stemmatjørn, but soon you are climbing steadily up more

Vinjakula | Hike 9.8

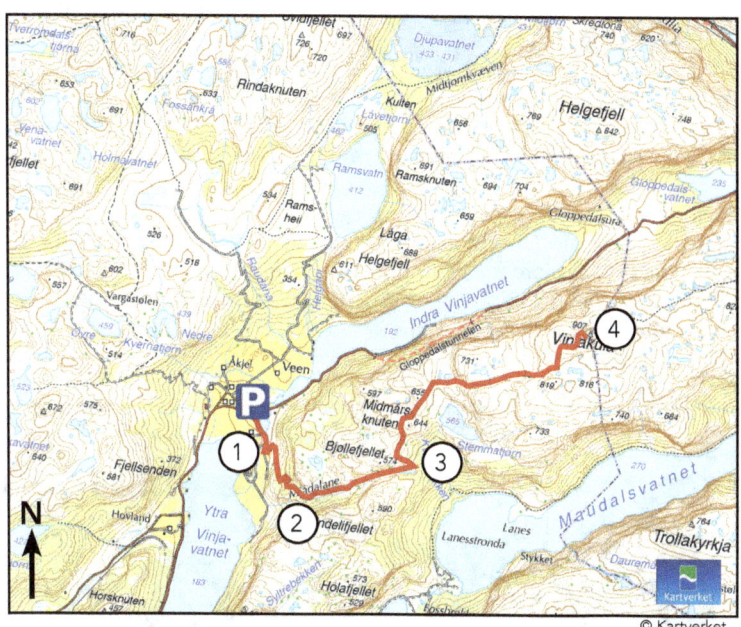

© Kartverket

of a plateau. The reward is the summit (4), and its views, marked by a large cairn.

You are now at the highest point in Norway's Magma Geopark. The rocks you just climbed are ancient gneisses, that once formed the base of a huge mountain chain. Those mountains have now eroded away over the eons, leaving the base exposed. Glaciers in the (relatively) recent ice ages carved out the huge U-shaped valleys that you see in all directions from here.

When you are ready to descend, be careful to return the way you came. There is a second trail leaving the summit of Vinjakula that goes in the opposite direction; if you descend the wrong way, you'll need help to return to your car! Check using your compass that you are descending to the southwest, not towards the northeast! Take care also at point (2), where it is easy to go straight instead of turning right along the track you came up.

Although you return the way you came, you'll enjoy different views in this direction, and, with the sun (if it is a clear day) having moved while you

Longer Days and Overnight Adventures

Hike 9.8 | Vinjakula

have been climbing, the lakes and narrow valley will look very different on the way down.

If, after you have returned to your car, you would like to travel back to the Stavanger area via a different route and a short stop at one of the area's finest sights, instead of returning back the way you came, turn right along Rv503 and go through the tunnel. Shortly after leaving the tunnel, you will come to the car park for Gloppedalslura. The best way to appreciate Gloppedalslura is to see it, so do take the time to park here and explore for a few minutes, before you continue along the Rv503 down the hill into Byrkjedal. Here you turn left along the Rv450 and return to Ålgard via Oltedal.

Gloppedalslura

At Gloppedalslura, a huge rockfall fell from the steep sides of the valley. This was more than a trickle of scree: boulders the size of mountain cabins fell from the cliffs above, totally blocking the valley and diverting the course of the river from Hunnedalen to the northwest.

The boulders are so huge that, during the Second World War, the local resistance movement used Gloppedalslura as a hideout.

Hike 9.9: Kvitlen

Out into pristine forests and ancient mountain farms

Kvitlen cabin was opened in 2015 and lies in a remote valley that was used for mountain farming for hundreds of years. You approach on the old road that is clearly visible at times. The first ascent up against the side of the river takes you through some of the most pristine mountain forest this region has to offer. All you are likely to hear is the sound of water in its many variations, birds singing, your footsteps and the occasional bell of a sheep.

Access 🚗 about 90km from Stavanger	Grading 🚶
Terrain: forest, moorland	Length: 11km
Facilities: toilet, STF cabin	Time: 5hrs

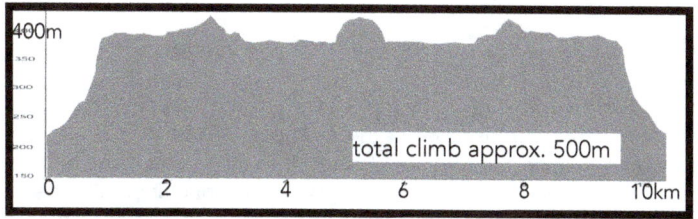

Data taken from Statens Kartverk, Geovekst and Kommunes, ©Kartverket

Longer Days and Overnight Adventures

Hike 9.9 | Kvitlen

To reach the start of the hike:

By car: From Stavanger take the E39 south towards Kristiansand until you reach Vikeså (after approx. 50km). Turn left into Rv 503 towards Stavtjørn and then after about 13km turn right into Fv 117 towards Ørdsdalen/Stavtjørn. Beyond Stavtjørn, the road enters a narrow tunnel. Just as you exit the tunnel, there is a car park on the left hand side of the road, with a signpost for a walking route to Kvitlen. This is Eikkebekka, the car park for one end of the one-way walk (see below). After the tunnel, the road descends dramatically into Ørdsdalen. At the bottom of the valley, just before the bridge, turn left towards Bjordal. The parking area is on the right hand side of the road after another 6km, just before Bjordal.

Hike Description

This trail is well marked with signposts and red T-markers

The start of the hike is signposted opposite the lake and parking area. It begins with a small scramble over some large boulders and leads to a grassy area by the river. Here the stream needs to be crossed, and there are T-markers leading again over some boulders, this time across the water. The first hour up towards Brattebø is steep, scaling boulders, generally moving uphill by the side of the roaring river. At times, the scramble is assisted by chains (1). Smaller streams and waterfalls are regularly crossed as the trail proceeds.

Getting closer to Brattebø the valley flattens out, and opens up into a bowl (2). A large meadow intersected by beech trees lies in the bowl, surrounded by high mountains and bordering the river. The excellent signage points in the direction of Kvitlen, and turning the corner Kvitlen valley opens up in a wide open view. The cabin is visible in the distance in good weather. It is reached in another 1.5km of mostly flat terrain. Only the last 10 minutes are again steep, as the last stream is crossed via a new metal bridge. The mountain cabin is beyond the bridge (3).

To return to the car park, retrace your steps in the opposite direction.

Kvitlen can be visited as a day trip, but offers much more. You can sleep over and return via Eikkebekka the next day (10km), You could stay a day longer and do the Kvitledalen roundtrip (8km) that starts and ends at the mountain hut, or you have the option of continuing on to the next mountain hut, Støle that is either 10 or 12.5km away depending on the

Kvitlen | Hike 9.9

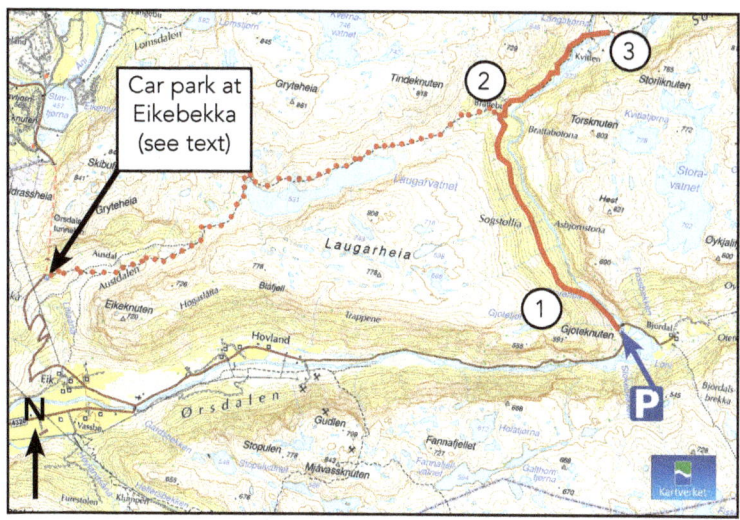

© Kartverket

route you take (see below).

Whatever your choice, the beauty and wilderness of the area as well as the human spirit that has made it a home is likely to impress.

Alternative: one-way hike to Kvitlen

If you are fortunate enough to be able to organise transport to/from the car park at Eikebekka in addition to the car park at the start of the hike, it is possible to complete a one-way hike to Kvitlen. The section of the hike from Eikebekka to Brattebø (point (2) on the map) is around 10km long. Thus there is the possibility to hike from Eikebekka to Ørsdalen via Kvitlen, either as a day hike or with an overnight stop at Kvitlen, or begin in Ørsdalen and climb to Brattebø before continuing to Eikebekka (although there is no need to detour to Kvitlen, it would surely be a shame to miss out on this beautiful valley and the views from Kvitlen!).

Hike 9.9 | Kvitlen

Onwards from Kvitlen

The sketch below gives some of the possibilities of hikes onwards from Kvitlen, if you are able to stay overnight at the Kvitlen cabin:

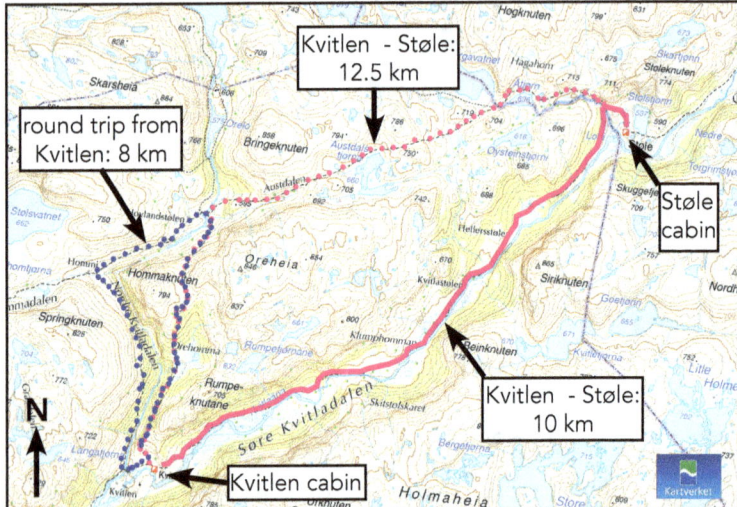

Hike 9.10: Tomannsbu

A lofty traverse across the mountains to Tomannsbu cabin

This high-level traverse leads to the STF cabin at Tomannsbu. It makes for an easily-accessible day trip high into the hills, an overnight trip with a stay at the cabin or the beginning of a longer adventure in the wilderness. It is graded "difficult" due to length and one or two rocky sections, but these are short and most of the trail, while boggy, is not overly demanding.

Access 🚗	Grading 🚶
Terrain: boggy moor, mountain	Length: 12km
Facilities: toilet at the car park, STF cabin at Tomannsbu	Time: 6hrs

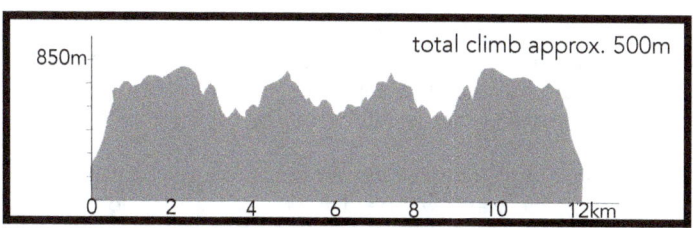

Data taken from Statens Kartverk, Geovekst and Kommunes, ©Kartverket

Longer Days and Overnight Adventures

Hike 9.10 | Tomannsbu

To reach the start of the hike:

By car: From Stavanger take the E39 south towards Kristiansand. After passing the town of Ålgård (after about 28 km), turn left along the Fv 450 towards Sirdal. Follow Fv 450 to Byrkjedal, where the road begins the ascent up Hunnedalen. The car park for Tomannsbu is signposted on the right hand side of the Fv 450 approximately 20km beyond Byrkjedal. There is ample parking space available, although this does fill up on busy days.

Hike Description

This trail is well marked with signposts and red T-markers

From the car park, stand with your back to the road and look to the left: the trail leads from this side of the car park, across a narrow bridge and south up the steep side of the valley. Follow the T-markers up the slope. Unless the weather has been unusually dry for a long time, there will be a little waterfall cascading down the hill on the right hand side.

This steep section of the trail is quite short, and after just over half a kilometre, the slope lessens and the traverse across the moor begins (1). Continue past a weather station (2), and begin to descend about 700m later as the trail bends to the left. This section of the trail goes over a section of bare rock: use care on the wet sections, as they can be slippery (3). At the bottom of the slope, cross over the stream at the bridge, and go past a cabin on your left hand side (4).

Just beyond the cabin, a sign points along the track to Tomannsbu. Enjoy the short stretch along the side of Store Øyevatn and the little valley just beyond, before beginning the final hill. The T-markers show the way up a little gulley and over a saddle (5). On a clear day, it is possible to see other mountain tops miles away from here.

The trail dips slightly, and then turns right to ford a river (there are stepping stones in place). The STF cabin by the shore of Djupevatn is visible from here (6). Stay and enjoy the area for as long as you like. It is possible to use the facilities at the cabin by paying a fee for day use.

When you are ready, return to the car park the way you came. On the return journey, the views will be different (you will be looking north, towards Hunnedalen and the mountains beyond), and, if it is sunny, the

Tomannsbu | Hike 9.10

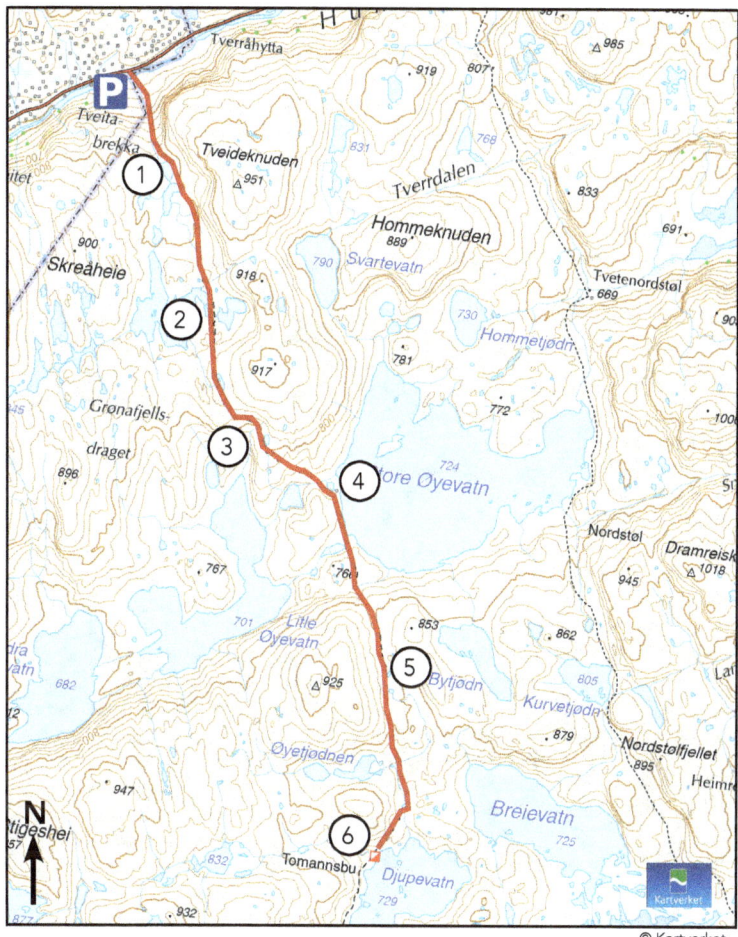

shadows will have shifted.

If you are interested in overnight or multi-day adventures, there are marked trails from Tomannsbu to other STF cabins at Støle and Kvitlen (see hike 9.9).

Longer Days and Overnight Adventures

Hike 9.10 | Tomannsbu

Chapter 10:
Around the Lysefjord

Preikestolen, as it hovers above the magnificent Lysefjord, will be a "bucket list" destination for most people living in or travelling to Southern Norway. The trek to the top of this "Pulpit Rock" was 'discovered' in 1889. With the help of a couple of local farmers' boys, two hikers from Stavanger scaled it for the first time. Nowadays, it is one of the most iconic hikes in the country.

There are many more hikes around the beautiful and glorious landscapes of the fjord, none of them as busy as Preikestolen, with views that will enchant and surprise you. This chapter takes you 'around' the Lysefjord in a series of hikes of varying length and difficulty. As a visitor you could easily spend a week exploring them, and if you live nearby no doubt they will become favourites.

Preikestolen | Hike 10.1

Hike 10.1: Preikestolen

Experience Norway's most international hike as you climb to this famous landmark

Preikestolen, the "pulpit rock" has been a popular hike for more than a century. It is easy to see why as you stand on this rock formation that balances over the Lysefjord, 604m below. The views from the pulpit are unique in this landscape that has been sculptured by glaciers. Of the three 'vertigo' hikes in the region, it is the most accessible and can be reached by anyone with a reasonable level of fitness.

Access 🚗 OR 🚌	Grading 🚶
Terrain: forest, rocky moorland	Length: 7.6km
Facilities: toilet, cafe, restaurant, hostel, camping, and hotel at main car park	Time: 4hrs

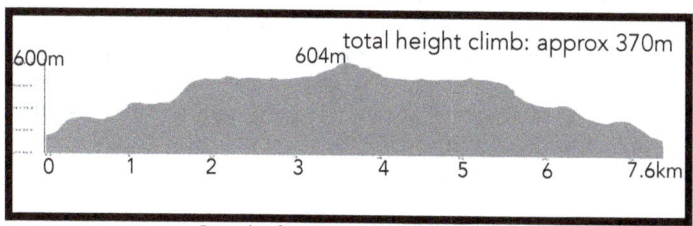

Data taken from Statens Kartverk, Geovekst and Kommunes, ©Kartverket

Around the Lysefjord

Hike 10.1 | Preikestolen

To reach the start of the hike:

By car: From the E39 in Stavanger take the Hundvåg and Ryfylke tunnels to Solbakk. As you exit you will meet the Rv13. Follow the Rv13 (Ryfylkevegen) towards Jørpeland; after about 11 km, turn left into Preikestolvegen (signposted). Follow Preikestolvegen for 5.1km until you reach the parking area, at the end of the road. Note that you must use the "pay" area unless you are staying overnight at the Preikestolen BaseCamp.

In peak times, an 'overflow' parking area will be opened, further back up the road towards the Rv 13. If you have to use this car park, you will need to walk along the road to reach the Preikestolen BaseCamp area, which is where the hike starts.

Neither of the car parks is free! If you use the main car park, you will have to pay at the exit barrier before you leave. If you are directed to the overflow car park, the parking fee will be collected as you enter the car park.

By bus: During the summer season, there are a number of bus companies that offer services directly to the Preikestolen mountain hut, at the start of this hike. See the Appendix for more information. During spring and autumn, when the summer buses direct to Preikestolen do not run, take a bus to the town of Jørpeland, and from there a taxi for the final 9km to the Preikestolen mountain hut and the start of the hike.

Hike Description

Note: more than 250 000 people climb Preikestolen each year, making it one of Norway's biggest tourist attractions. This means that if you do not want to share the hike with thousands, you will need to be an early bird or hike later in the day. Luckily summer time brings almost 20 hours of daylight and/or twilight, giving time and light enough for hiking at both ends of the day. In recent years, Preikestolen has become a year-round destination. Be aware that conditions on this hike will vary drastically outside of the summer season. For more information, see www.preikestolen365.com

Preikestolen | Hike 10.1

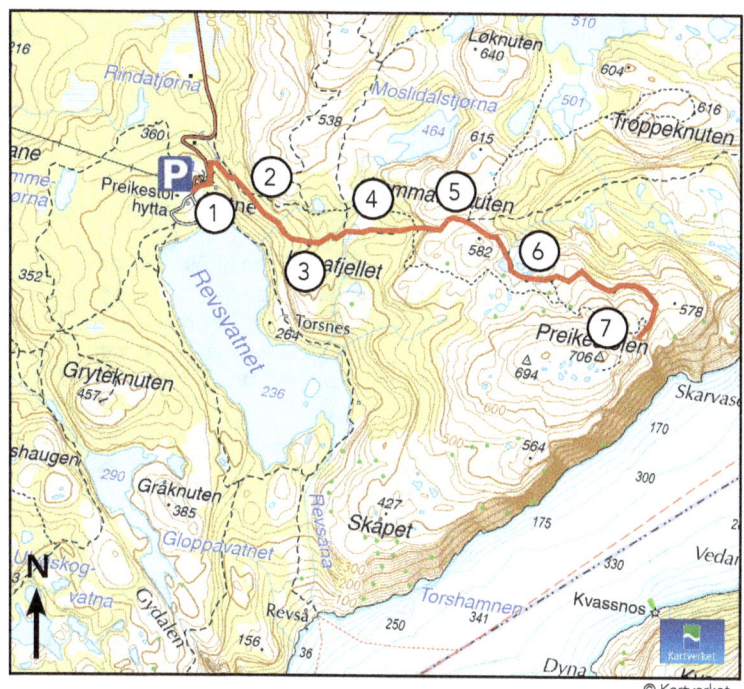

This trail is very well marked by signposts and red T-signs

The start of the hike is reached from the main car park by walking towards the hiker's cafe and rental gear shop that can be seen from here. It starts in the open space between these two and follows a path that goes immediately uphill (1). The first viewpoint is at 350m, after about 0.5km. If it is a busy summer's day and you had to park in the overflow car park, the start of the hike is on a forest path, is less steep and arrives at this viewpoint too.

This plateau gives a view towards the mountain hut and Lake Revsvatnet, and a chance to catch your breath (2). The pine trees here are one of the first tree species to arrive in Norway after the last ice age.

Continuing, the well-marked path is at times surrounded by big boulders. These were deposited by the retreating Lysefjord glacier only about ten thousand years ago. In former days, it was necessary

Hike 10.1 | Preikestolen

to scramble over them, but these days a path has been constructed to cope with the number of visitors. The next viewpoint is reached after a relatively short climb (3). On a clear day it is possible to see the view towards the Boknafjord, with Stavanger in the distance.

Continuing on, the trail crosses the marshlands of Krogebekkmyra (4), 1.5km into the hike. The bog is crossed on a wooden causeway, which has been constructed to protect the delicate environment. Next, the trail climbs the Neverdal pass (5), through scree that was deposited by the glacier (2km from the start of the hike). At the higher elevations, the pine forest has retreated and birch is now the most common species. Above the steep section of the trail, the lakes at Tjødnane await (2.5km from the start of the hike). Depending on the season and weather, there might be ice, eerie fog or lots of people in and around these lakes (6).

From here, the trail leaves the tree line below. There are two bridges on the edge of the Neverdal valley. The final ascent is on rock, and along the ridge before Preikestolen, the trail suddenly faces Lysefjord. Soon after this you arrive at the pulpit rock (7). This plateau of 25 x 25 metres seems to be suspended above the fjord. There are no barriers and the fjord is 604m below. On a clear day it is possible to see all the way towards Lysebotn, the start of the fjord, and the old mountain farms on the left hand side. Opposite is the high mountain area of Frafjord, with peaks that are in the 1000m range. No matter how many fellow hikers you have to share the view with, it remains impressive and spectacular. Once ready to leave, you descend the same route back to the car park.

Preikestolen BaseCamp (www.preikestolenbasecamp.com) offers different accommodation options and is an excellent base for visitors who might like to explore the surrounding hikes and water based activities in the area. In our book we present four hikes: Gryteknuten (Hike 10.4), Preikestolen (Hike 10.1), Moslifjellet (Hike 10.3), and Fantapytten (Hike 10.2) – all four start and/or finish close to the hiker's cafe.

Hike 10.2: Fantapytten

A new classic! Hike into the Lysefjord from Høllesheia to Preikestolen BaseCamp

This is a stunning hike into the Lysefjord. Awesome views await as you walk high above the fjord and look down and into it. The icing on the cake is a minuscule but very photogenic pond, that looks like an infinity pool. Since this hike is more demanding than hiking Preikestolen, the number of people will be much reduced and the views no less spectacular. It does have a few exposed sections and scrambles.

Access 🚌 (or 🚗 possible)	Grading 🚶
Terrain: forest, mountain, moorland, some very short exposed sections	Length: 8.9km
Facilities: Preikestolen BaseCamp with cafe, toilets, lodge, camping at the end	Time: 5 - 6hrs

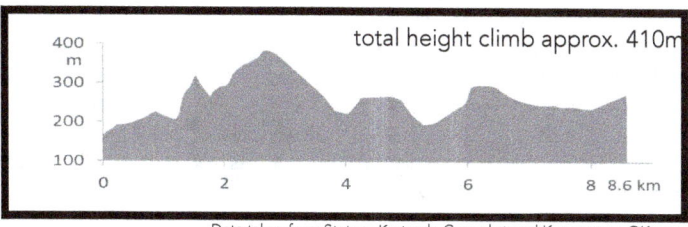

Data taken from Statens Kartverk, Geovekst and Kommunes, ©Kartverket

Around the Lysefjord

Hike 10.2 | Fantapytten

To reach the start of the hike:

By car: This hike is best accessed by bus. If you come by car, you will need to go back to the start of the hike to retrieve it after you have finished, since this is a one-way hike. If you still prefer to come by car: from Stavanger take the E39 and go through the Hundvåg and Ryfylke tunnels towards Solbakk. Take the Rv 523 past Jørpeland and continue towards Oanes/Forsand. Just 200m before the Høllesli tunnel turn left onto the parking area of Høllesli and 'The Bolder Sky lodges'. Parking is open between 6am and 10pm and overnight stays are not allowed.

By bus: Take any public bus from Stavanger to Jørpeland bus station (which is at the harbour in Jørpeland). Although there is no bus stop near the start of the hike, the Kolumbus bus service between Jørpeland and Forsand (121 at the time of writing), will stop near the parking lot, on the road, if you ask the driver. GPS coordinates are: 58.94986 N, 6.10339 E. At the end of the hike, take a bus from Preikestolen Base Camp back to Stavanger. This will not be a public service bus, but one operated by a different private company. See the Appendix for more information, and www.kolumbus.no for "regular" public bus schedules, prices, and routes.

Hike Description

This trail is well marked by signposts and red T-markers.

From the parking lot, walk uphill past the Schlagbaum, and you will soon see a signpost with directions to Preikestolen BaseCamp and Fantapytten among others. The track descends into the forest and is well marked. After a few minutes it crosses a very marshy area. Some stepping stones have been placed here, but depending on recent weather they might be under water too, in which case a small scramble up the side will be needed. Continue on the T-marked path, ignoring the other signposts (a hand with outstretched digit, this belongs to a small circuit starting from the sky lodges). A gentle ascent takes you towards the fjord and the first of many, many viewpoints along this hike (1). Here you can admire the entrance to the Lysefjord, the bridge across it and some of the islands below, while looking into the fjord as you turn around. Many more opportunities await as you move forward.

Fantapytten | Hike 10.2

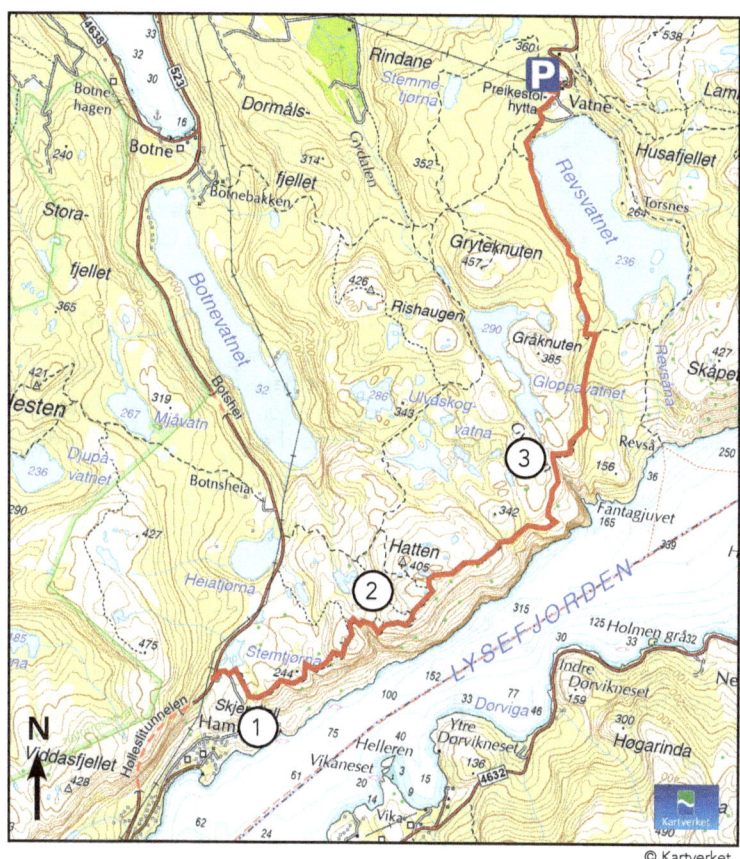

© Kartverket

For the next 4km, the path will head in and out of the forest, above and below the treeline all the way to Fantapytten. The descents and ascents are steep, often muddy and wet. In some instances you will be aided by metal stairs and rods that have been mounted into the rock. To protect marshlands from erosion wooden planks or walkovers have been laid in places. Every time you come up and out from the woods you will be greeted with a new perspective on the Lysefjord as you slowly move inland. They are all breathtaking and spectacular.

At 2.1km into the hike you reach the small escarpment at Skjerajuvet (2). The trail is very steep here. At Skjerajuvet, while you have no sweeping

Around the Lysefjord

Hike 10.2 | Fantapytten

views into the fjord there is one that goes a long way down!

Continue steeply uphill once more towards the top at Hatten. The top itself is a 1.4km detour from this hike, if you are minded to "collect" it. Continuing through this mountainous terrain, you eventually reach Fantapytten (3). The view from here into the Lysefjord is nothing short of spectacular and the highlight of the hike. It is a great place for a picnic, weather permitting. The pond is very shallow and there is a lot of silt in the water. Nevertheless viewed from the right angle it looks like a most incredible infinity pool over the Lysefjord.

Once you are ready to leave, the trail starts to turn away from the fjord, heading inland. Progress here will be much faster than the first part of the hike as the trail becomes less steep. It passes through marshes and goes through lush forest. At a T-junction you meet up with the trails around Revsvatnet lake and down towards the Revså quay on the fjord itself.

Go left here uphill towards Preikestolen BaseCamp. Soon you get the first glimpses of the hut as well as the lake. A short while later you might be tempted to take a cooling dip in the lake. There are various options from rocky outcrops to minuscule sandy beaches. As you reach Revsvatnet be aware that there is a Frisbee Golf Course here. People might be playing, beware of flying objects! The hike continues past Revsvatnet and finishes onto a gravel road at Preikestolen BaseCamp.

Facilities here are extensive and include a cafe, restaurant, lodge, camping, rental gear and transport back to Jørpeland, Stavanger and Sandnes. If you have left your car at the start of the hike, local taxi firms will (for a fee) drive you back around to the start, or, alternatively, take any public bus to Jørpeland and either take a taxi from there, or take the regular bus service between Jørpeland and Forsand and ask the driver to drop you off at the car park.

Hike 10.3: Moslifjellet

A fine hill in the Preikestolen area, with stunning views on the descent

If this hike were in another area of Rogaland, it would most likely be much more popular. A moderate climb leads to an open plateau summit and excellent views. Although it lives in the shadow of its more famous neighbour, Preikestolen, it is still a fine hike.

Access 🚗 or 🚌	Grading 🚶
Terrain: forest, moorland, mountain	Length: 5.8km
Facilities: toilets, cafe, restaurant, hostel, camping, and hotel at the main car park	Time: 2hrs 30mins

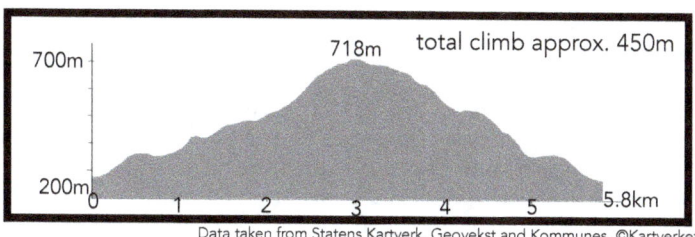

Data taken from Statens Kartverk, Geovekst and Kommunes, ©Kartverket

Hike 10.3 | Moslifjellet

To reach the start of the hike:

By car: From the E39 in Stavanger take the Hundvåg and Ryfylke tunnels to Solbakk. As you exit you will meet the Rv13. Follow the Rv13 (Ryfylkevegen) towards Jørpeland; after about 11 km, turn left into Preikestolvegen (signposted). Follow Preikestolvegen for 5.1km until you reach the parking area, at the end of the road. Note that you must use the "pay" area unless you are staying overnight at the Preikestolen BaseCamp.
In peak times, an 'overflow' parking area will be opened, further back up the road towards the Rv 13. If you have to use this car park, you will need to walk along the road to reach the Preikestolen BaseCamp, which is where the hike starts.
Neither of the car parks is free! If you use the main car park, you will have to pay at the exit barrier before you leave. If you are directed to the overflow car park, the parking fee will be collected as you enter the car park.

By bus: During the summer season, there are a number of bus companies that offer services directly to the Preikestolen mountain hut, at the start of this hike. See the Appendix for more information. During spring and autumn, when the summer buses direct to Preikestolen do not run, take a bus to the town of Jørpeland, and from there a taxi for the final 9km to the Preikestolen mountain hut and the start of the hike. For more information on bus schedules, routes, and prices, see www.kolumbus.no

Hike Description

This trail is marked with signposts, red dots and red T-markers

From either of the car parks, follow the main Preikestolen trail for just over a kilometre. It goes past the top of the first plateau, and shortly after this, the trail to Moslifjellet is signposted to the left **(1)**. As you leave the main Preikestolen trail, you will pass a large "Stop" sign, with a warning. Continue past this, as it is intended for hikers climbing Preikestolen.

The trail is marked with red dots as it climbs to a moor and turns slightly to the right along the side of a steep slope. After approximately 1.3km, there is a path junction in a steep valley, with a knoll to the right and a steep slope to the left **(2)**. If you begin to go downhill, you have gone too far.

Moslifjellet | Hike 10.3

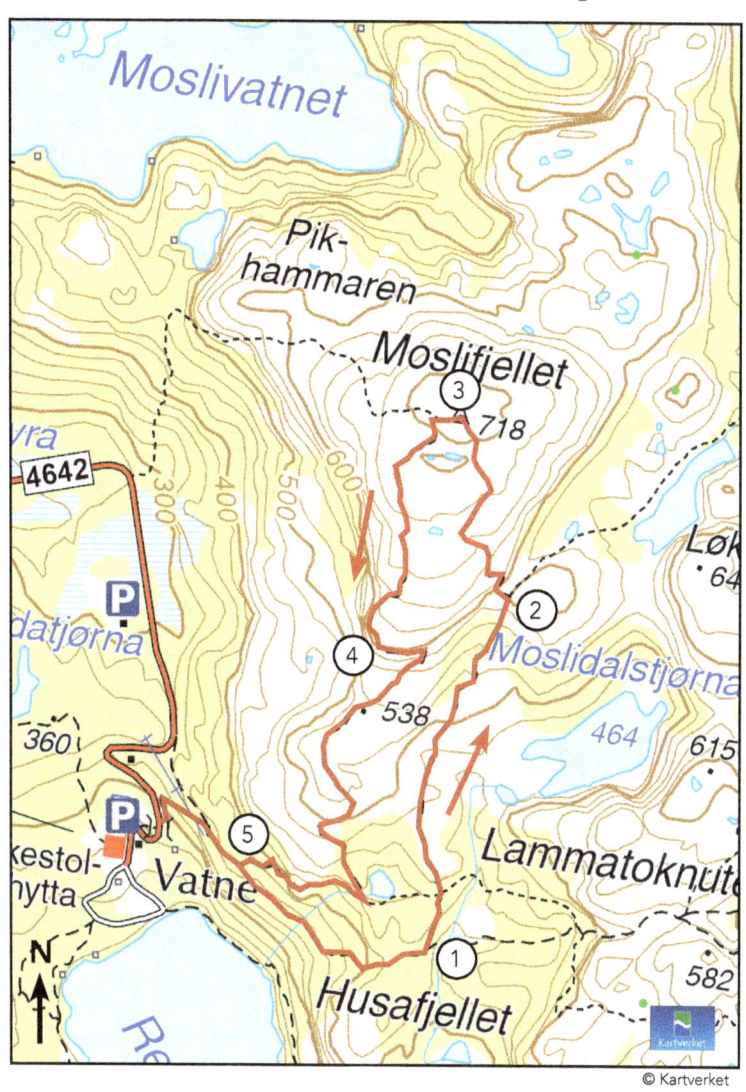

© Kartverket

Take the trail up the steep slope to the left, which leads to a plateau. Here the trail turns right up a gentle slope to the main summit, which is marked by a cairn and a weather station (3).

Hike 10.3 | Moslifjellet

The return path leads away from the summit to the south west. Follow the red dots as it veers to the south and makes its way down a spur. If the weather is clear, there are views towards the town of Jørpeland and beyond, towards Stavanger. Take care as the trail veers to the left after the end of the spur **(4)**. Continue into the forest and follow the trail downhill until it meets the main Preikestolen path again **(5)**. Follow the main Preikestolen path down to the main parking area to finish the hike.

If you are parked in the "overflow" car park and don't require the facilities at the main car park, return the way you came directly to your car.

Hike 10.4: Gryteknuten

Escape the Preikestolen crowds and enjoy this easy hill with fine views from the top

Gryteknuten is often neglected, because it is not nearly as spectacular as neighbouring Preikestolen. That said, it is a very pleasant wooded walk, with nice views from the top. It is a good choice for anyone who would like to avoid the tourist crowds while still enjoying the amenities of the area, prefers a less strenuous hike than the higher hills nearby, or wants to explore the area.

Access 🚗 or 🚌	Grading 🚶
Terrain: forest trail, marsh	Length: 4.7km
Facilities: toilets, cafe, restaurant, hostel, camping, and hotel at the main car park	Time: 2hrs

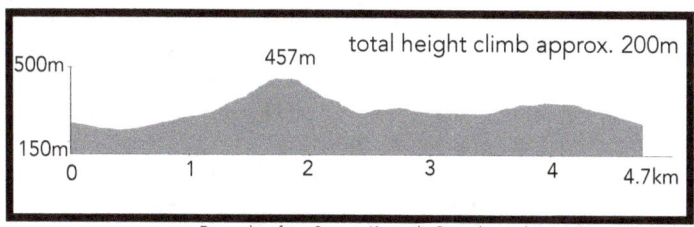

Data taken from Statens Kartverk, Geovekst and Kommunes, ©Kartverket

Around the Lysefjord

Hike 10.4 | Gryteknuten

To reach the start of the hike:

By car: From the E39 in Stavanger, take the Hundvåg and Ryfykke tunnels to Solbakk. As you exit the tunnel follow the Rv 13 towards Jørpeland. After about 11 km turn left into Preikestolvegen (signposted). Follow Preikestolvegen for 5.1km to the parking area, at the end of the road. Note that you must use the "pay" area unless you are staying overnight at Preikestolen BaseCamp.

In peak times, an 'overflow' parking area will be opened, further back up the road towards the Rv 13. If you have to use this car park, you will need to walk along the road to reach Preikestolen BaseCamp, which is where the hike starts.

Neither of the car parks is free! At the main car park, payment is at the exit barrier upon leaving. At the overflow car park, the parking fee is collected at the entrance.

By bus: During the summer season, there are a number of buses that offer services directly to the Preikestolen mountain hut, at the start of this hike. See the Appendix for more information. During spring and autumn, when the summer buses direct to Preikestolen do not run, take a bus to the town of Jørpeland, and from there a taxi for the final 9km to the Preikestolen mountain hut and the start of the hike. For more information on schedules, routes, and prices, see www.kolumbus.no

Hike Description

This trail is marked with signposts, red dots and red T markers.

Start from the hikers cafe adjacent to the main car park (from the overflow car park, go to the car park entrance, turn right and walk down the road to reach the kiosk). Cross the small car park that is reserved for guests at Preikestolen BaseCamp, and take the track past the bunkhouse (Preikestolhytta). The trail to Gryteknuten is signposted to the right off the track, just before the track bends to the left (1). For the first few hundred metres, the trail goes through the frisbee golf course, so beware of flying objects and pay attention to the red dots and trail markings: there are many trails leading to the different "holes" of the

Gryteknuten | Hike 10.4

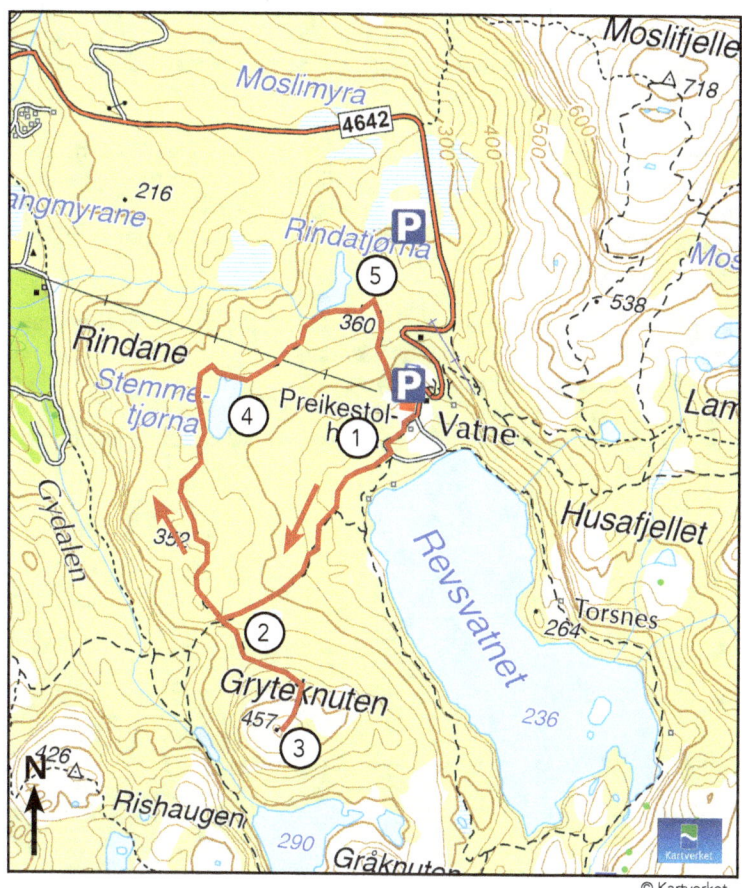

© Kartverket

frisbee golf course, potentially confusing the hiker.
Follow the trail, which is marked with (sometimes faded) red dots, through the forest for approximately 200m to a path junction. Gryteknuten is signposted to the right. If you reach the lakeshore, you have taken the wrong trail!

Take the Gryteknuten trail up a rather marshy slope. The trail is marked with red dots, and after approximately 750m there is a path junction. Turn left, signposted "Gryteknuten" (2).

Around the Lysefjord

Hike 10.4 | Gryteknuten

From here, the trail gets rather steeper as it climbs the flank of the hill. In the final 100m, the trail rises above the treeline. On a clear day there are views to the west, towards Stavanger, and glimpses of the Lysefjord and its bridge towards the south. The summit is marked with a cairn (3).

To return to the car park, follow the trail back down the hill to the path junction at (2). From here, either turn right and return to the car park the same way, or continue straight and follow the pleasant trail through the forest around the little lake of Stemmetjørna (4), and over the top of Rindatjørna.

If you choose the Stemmetjørna route, follow the trail around the lake and onwards up the gentle climb to Rindatjørna. Just past the top, look for a signpost towards Preikestolhytta to the right (5). Take this steep path back down the hill to the car park, which will guide you through the trees as you descend. The trail ends in at the RV car park, just behind the main car park.

Sokkaknuten | Hike 10.5

Hike 10.5: Sokkaknuten

Few hills offer such stunning panoramas

A relatively short (although, in places, steep) hike to this top gives views both into Lysefjord, and also across the water to the Sandnes hills in the west. This is a particularly satisfying hike when the higher hills are under snow and ice.

Access 🚗 or 🚌 + 🚂	Grading 🚶
Terrain: forest, mountain, moorland, some steep sections	Length: 4.2km
Facilities: none	Time: 2hrs 30mins

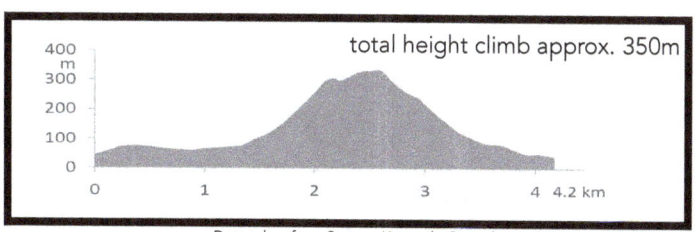

total height climb approx. 350m

Data taken from Statens Kartverk, Geovekst and Kommunes, ©Kartverket

Around the Lysefjord

Hike 10.5 | Sokkaknuten

To reach the start of the hike:

By car: from Stavanger take the E39 and go through the Hundvåg and Ryfylke tunnels towards Solbakk. Take the Rv 523 past Jørpeland and continue towards Oanes. You will pass the Lysefjord bridge on your left. About 1.8km after the Lysefjord bridge, turn right at the roundabout into Fv495. After another 530m, turn right into the cabin area. The car park is beside the service building for the cabins at Lysefjord Hyttegrend, Leivikvegen 13 (a fee is payable).

By bus/ferry: This hike can also be accesses from the Oanes ferry terminal. There are two ways to get there by public transport:

1. From Sandnes bus station, take the bus to the bus stop just before the ferry terminal at Lauvvik, Selvikveien. From the bus stop, walk about 750m up the road to the ferry terminal, and take the ferry to Oanes as a foot passenger.

2. From Stavanger, take the 100 bus to Jørpeland. Alight at Strand Rådhus and then take bus 120 towards Forsand, and alight at the Oanes ferry terminal.

From the Oanes ferry terminal, walk along the side of the road (Rv523) until you reach a roundabout (about 870m from the ferry terminal). Turn left along this road to join the hike in another 530m, where the lane to the cabins joins the Fv495.

For bus routes, prices, and schedules, see www.kolumbus.no. At the time of writing, the Lauvvik/Oanes ferry runs as a shuttle service, approx every 40mins in each direction. Note that neither of these options runs frequently, and so careful planning will be needed, however this hike is well worth the effort!

Hike Description

This trail is well marked by signposts and red T-markers.

On foot (if you arrived by car), continue uphill on the Fv 495 until you see a sign for Sokkaknuten. The sign is located next to a gate and a stile. Take this path, which begins slightly downhill. To the right,

Sokkaknuten | Hike 10.5

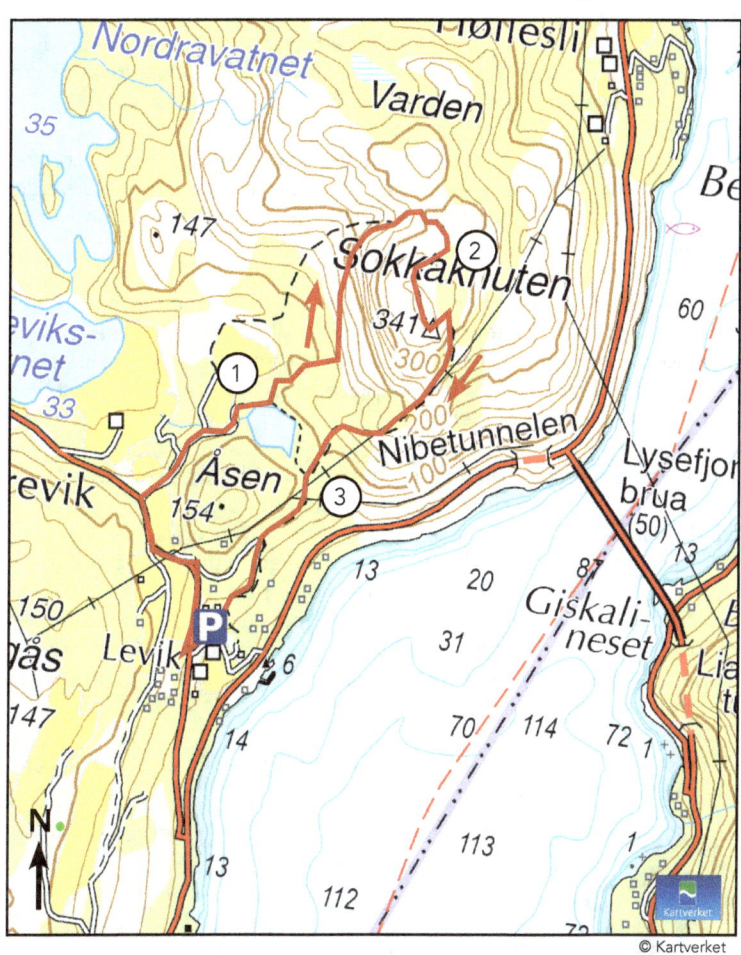

© Kartverket

there is a small house and some stables. The trail soon meets a wide gravel path. Follow the gravel path until you come to a signpost for Sokkaknuten, Levikåsen, and Eikeltjørna (1). If your group includes small children, Eikeltjørna lake could be a great place to set up "camp" and explore with the little ones, while others could continue to the summit. At Eikeltjorna, the gravel path turns left, and continues on to a small path into the woods.

Follow the red dots, keeping slight left. The ascent begins gradually,

Around the Lysefjord

Hike 10.5 | Sokkaknuten

with the steep mountain face to the right and open views out to the fjord on the left. Soon, the path becomes narrower and steeper as it moves up a gulley. Towards the top of the gulley, the trail turns towards the south, and levels out somewhat.

Here you need to look carefully for the trail that leads to your right, up the side of Sokkaknuten (2). There is a path that continues over this saddle and descends, so it is possible to bypass the top and inadvertently miss the views!

The path to the summit takes you up one last steep climb, which brings you to the summit plateau. By now you will be enjoying views in all directions. The summit itself is towards the south end of the plateau, and is marked by a cairn. This is a place to spend some time, and take some photos, if the weather permits.

When you are ready, continue on the trail, which takes you down from the summit, first towards the east, and then doubling back towards the southwest. This trail is steep in places, and if you prefer to avoid this kind of excitement, there's no reason not to return the way you came. If you don't mind the steep trail, continue down the side of the mouth of Lysefjord. As the slope becomes less steep, you will see the lovely lake of Eikelitjørna on the right (3). If you would like to detour and spend some quality time by the side of the lake, there is a track that will take you there and back.

To finish the walk, continue along the path, past the little hill of Åsen and back to the car park at the cabin area.

Hike 10.6: Uburen

See the mouth of Lysefjord from above

Seen from Oanes, the sheer cliffs of Uburen tower menacingly over Høgsfjord. From the gentler east side, a very achievable trail winds up the hill and along the west ridge to a viewpoint. From there, the views of Høgsfjord and the mouth of Lysefjord are truly stunning.

Access 🚗	Grading 🚶
Terrain: forest, mountain trail	Length: 5.2km
Facilities: none	Time: 2hrs 30mins

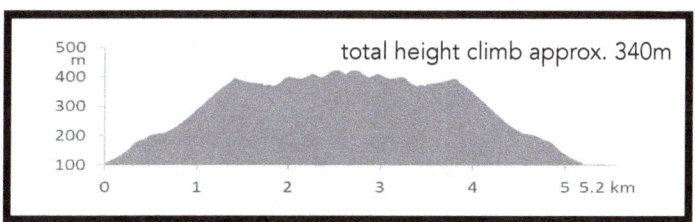

total height climb approx. 340m

Data taken from Statens Kartverk, Geovekst and Kommunes, ©Kartverket

Hike 10.6 | Uburen

To reach the start of the hike:

By car: from Stavanger take the E39 and go through the Hundvåg and Ryfylke tunnels towards Solbakk. Take the Rv 523 past Jørpeland and continue towards Oanes. About 20km beyond Solbakk, turn left across the Lysefjord bridge on Fv491. Fv491 takes you to Forsand, where, about 3km after turning off Rv523, you need to turn left (still on Fv491). The car park is on the right hand side of the road after about another 3.6km.

Hike Description

This trail is well marked by signposts and red T-markers.

From the car park, take the signposted track that leads away from the car park and then turns to the right as it begins to climb the hill. This track was originally constructed by the hydroelectric company, when they were building the power lines and pylons that you will meet nearer the top of the hill. The track has one hairpin bend, and then meets with a path on the right hand side just before it begins to descend again (1). Look carefully for where the path leaves the track, as the path doubles back away from the track as it continues to climb.

If you find yourself going downhill on the track, you have gone too far, and need to turn around and look for the path.

Just past a little knoll, the path begins to climb in earnest. You may notice that you cross under some power lines. There is another hairpin turn quite close to the top of the tree line (and underneath another power line), then the trail emerges from the trees and begins to contour around the south of the summit.

Now the views are opening up! The trail meanders past a small tarn on the right hand side, then continues along a ridge. There are a couple of ups and downs before reaching the final viewpoint at the end of the ridge (2).

From here, you are looking over the steep cliffs of Uburen into Høgsfjord and the entrance to Lysefjord. There are few finer places from which to see not just Lysefjord, but all of the hills in Sandnes county to the west.

Uburen | Hike 10.6

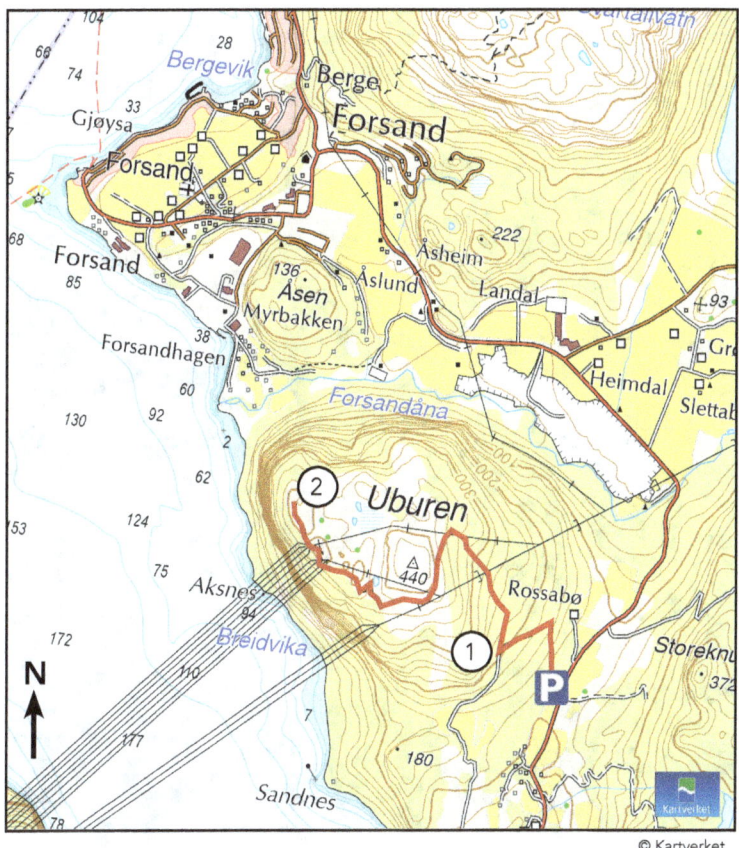

© Kartverket

When you are ready to leave, follow the trail back the way you came: as you walk back along the ridge, you will be able to enjoy the fine views to the south. The small tarn at the end of the ridge (now on your left hand side) also provides a good place to relax; since it is still above the tree line, it enjoys fine views.

Beyond the tarn, return the way you came to the car park, taking care to turn left at point (1) to return to the car park!

Around the Lysefjord

Hike 10.6 | Uburen

Looking north from Uburen

Hike 10.7: Sollifjellet

View Lysefjord and Preikestolen from this hill to the south of the fjord

Sollifjellet is a fantastic hike on the 'other side' of Lysefjord from Preikestolen. Preikestolen can be admired from across the fjord with binoculars. Whilst there will probably be hundreds of people perched on Preikestolen, you may have the view to yourself on Sollifjellet. The hike is rated as moderate due to the steepness in some shorter sections, otherwise it is easy.

Access	Grading
Terrain: mountain, boggy moorland	Length: 4.2km
Facilities: picnic table and toilet at the car park	Time: 2hrs

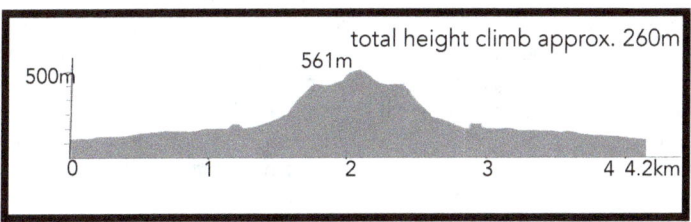

Data taken from Statens Kartverk, Geovekst and Kommunes, ©Kartverket

Hike 10.7 | Sollifjellet

To reach the start of the hike:

By car: Starting from the E39 in Stavanger, take the Hundvåg and Ryfylke tunnels to Solbakk. As you exit, you meet with the Rv523. Turn right here, towards Jørpeland. Continue through Jørpeland, and about 12.6km beyond Jørpeland, turn left onto the Lysefjord Bridge. The bridge is followed by a tunnel and as you emerge, turn sharp right onto the Fv 496 to Fossmark. The road is very, very narrow for the first kilometre or two. It goes past Dørvika beach. After the hamlet of Eiane the road steers away from the Lysefjord, passing a lake and continues steeply up the mountain towards Fossmark. The parking lot at Skrøyla is signposted to the right. Turn right here and continue up the mountain. The road ends at the parking area (13 km after the turn-off for Fv 496).

Hike Description

This trail is marked by signposts and red dots.

The parking lot is closed off by a gate. To begin the hike, go back through the gate and turn left along an old access road. Follow this for some time, until it reaches a small dam, and shortly after its feeding stream. A little further along is a signpost. Sollifjellet is in the direction of a small path veering left, which soon crosses the brook via a small bridge (1).

From here the path is well marked by red dots on boulders or trees. It traverses the south-facing side of a wide valley, therefore on warm summer days it can be quite hot here. A slow ascent begins mainly over wide boulders and little vegetation, and a second signpost appears pointing uphill. After a while the trail passes into an area of trees, with birches and small pines. The path underfoot tends to become earthier and muddy after rain. There are some short, steep sections here.

After this ascent you reach Sollitjørn, a small charming lake. In late summer there might be some cloudberries around this area (2), if they have not already been harvested by those who know exactly when they are due to be ripe for picking (please remember not to pick cloudberries before they are ripe as this damages the plants!). The last stretch of the ascent is quite short and again well marked. The path ends at a small cairn on the top of Sollifjellet (3) with amazing views over the Lysefjord. It might be possible to see the flashes of photography from Preikestolen itself. Fossmork farmstead can be seen just below towards the west, as

Sollifjellet | Hike 10.7

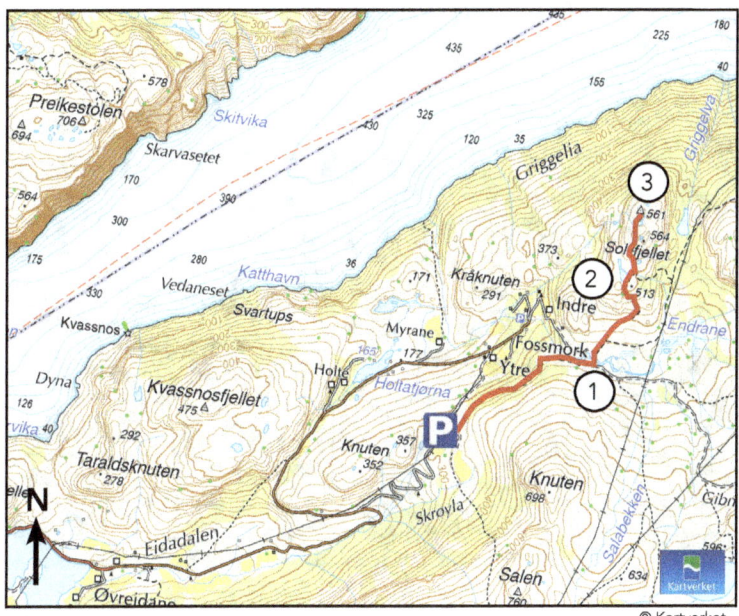

© Kartverket

well as the waterfall of Hengjane on the opposite side and the old farms of Brattlia and Songesand.

The descent goes back the same way in the opposite direction. The red dots appear at regular intervals and lead back to the bridge. Take the service road back towards the parking area. There is a picnic table at the parking lot, if you wish to sit down and enjoy the view towards Preikestolen some more.

Hike 10.7 | Sollifjellet

Along the way up Sollifjellet

Hike 10.8: The Flørli Steps

Climb the side of Lysefjord via 4,444 steps: the longest wooden staircase in the world!

This hike is one of the classic challenges in Rogaland: it climbs the side of the fjord via a wooden staircase built alongside pipes from a disused hydroelectric power plant. The climb is exciting, and the return route is nearly as steep, past the old hill farm of Flørlistølen and back to Flørli again. If you suffer from vertigo or have knee problems, this is not your hike, but otherwise it is one of the most Norwegian of adventures, accessible in a day from Stavanger.

Access 🚢 OR 🚶	Grading 🚶
Terrain: wooden steps, forest, mountain	Length: 4.7km
Facilities: toilet, cafe, hostel and STF cabin at Flørli	Time: 3-4hrs

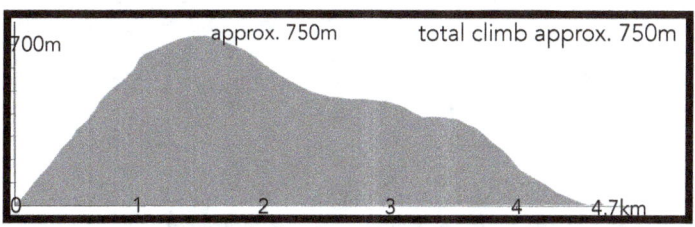

Data taken from Statens Kartverk, Geovekst and Kommunes, ©Kartverket

Hike 10.8 | The Flørli Steps

To reach the start of the hike:

Flørli is an isolated hamlet on the side of Lysefjord. It has no roads in and out: getting there is part of the adventure!

This hike is not accessible by car. Flørli is served by a ferry operated by Kolumbus all year round. This ferry takes up to 10 cars, plus passengers and bikes, and stops at a number of places along Lysefjord. For cars, and during the busy summer season, pre-booking is recommended. Tickets can be booked on the kolumbus website, which is also where current timetables and fares are to be found (www.kolumbus.no). It is also possible to bring your own boat: the quay has room for guest tie-ups, although, again, it is worth phoning ahead during busy times (www.flørli.no).

During the summer, Flørli is also served by various tourist ferries and package day excursions from Stavanger or Sandnes: see the Appendix for details of tour operators.

Another way to access this hike is on foot: long distance trails lead to and from Flørli and STF cabins at Skåpet and Langavatn. There is also an STF cabin at Flørli itself, so the steps can be climbed as part of a "Round Lysefjord" long distance hike.

Hike Description

This trail is very well marked with signposts and red dots

From the boat quay, turn right along the gravel track by the side of the fjord. The steps begin on the left hand side, just before the large white building, the former hydroelectric works (1). The staircase is quite steep for most of the way, and there is a handrail to hold. Steps are numbered every 500 steps, to help keep track of progress. Several platforms have been built to allow people to take breaks and enjoy the view: one of these is at the building that contains the former control room. Much of the machinery for winching the tram wagons is still there: it is worth looking in, even if you don't need a rest.

Near the top of the staircase, the gradient lessens, and the staircase ends at the dam at Ternevatnet (2). This little lake was used by the

The Flørli Steps | Hike 10.8

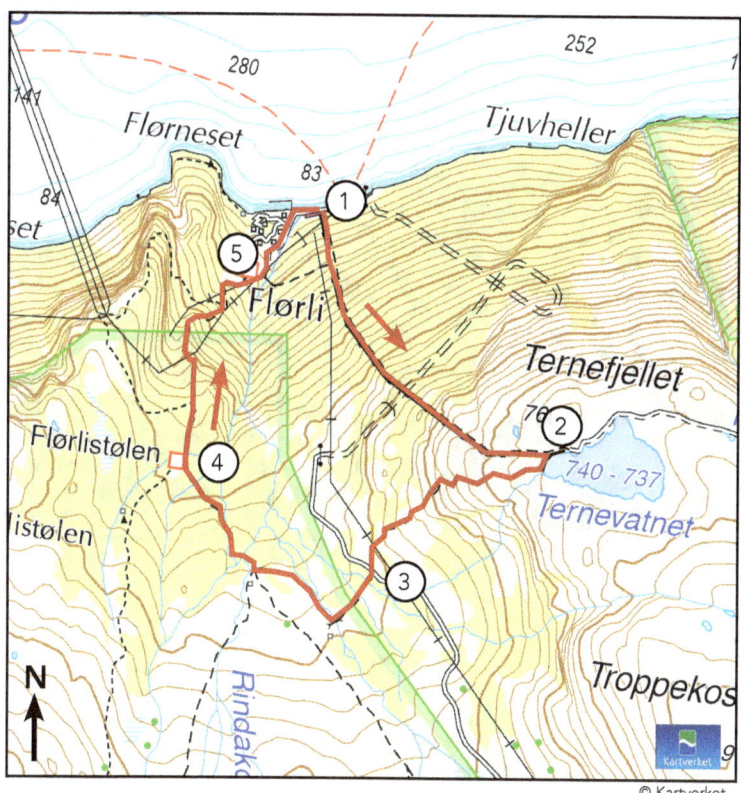

© Kartverket

hydroelectric plant. Turn right along the top of the dam, and follow the signs to Flørli and Rallarsti. The red markers show the route across the mountain top to a large cairn. This is a good place to appreciate the view before beginning the descent, which is signposted "Rallarsti" and marked with red T's. The trail leads down the mountain side, and crosses a gravel road (3) followed by a bridge over a river. Here you enter a forest and turn back towards the north again. Just after a second bridge is the hill farm at Flørlistølen (4).

Beyond Flørlistølen, the trail continues steeply down through the forest to the STF cabin at Flørli (5) and then returns to the side of the fjord.

At Flørli there is a cafe and, if you have time, a museum in the former hydroelectric building. The museum has old photos and plans from the

Around the Lysefjord

Hike 10.8 | The Flørli Steps

building of the hydroelectric plant, which surround the walls. Some of the machinery is still intact, as is the control room, which is open to visitors.

Flørlistølen
The old mountain cabin at Flørlistølen is a STF cabin that is available for private renting. The key has to be collected from the STF shop in Stavanger centre and all supplies have to be brought along. It does make for a very special adventure, giving everyone involved a taste of what life might have looked like in the mountains a few hundred years ago.

Hike 10.9: Kjerag

An exhilarating hike in the mountains to this spectacular natural feature

Kjeragbolten is a local icon seen on many a postcard from Rogaland. A boulder is lodged in a crevice hundreds of metres high above Lysefjord, deposited there by a glacier eons ago. The sight of it perched high above the cliffs of the fjord is stunning. Like its spectacular cousin Preikestolen (hike 10.1), Kjeragbolten draws crowds from near and afar. Don't be fooled though: it may be a tourist attraction, but this is a serious mountain hike over tough terrain.

Access 🚗 or 🚌 or 🚌 + ⛴	Grading 🚶
Terrain: mountain, boggy moorland	Length: 8.8km
Facilities: Tourist Information, toilets and cafe at the car park	Time: 5hrs+

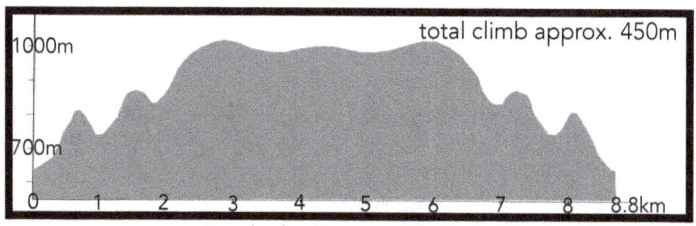

Data taken from Statens Kartverk, Geovekst and Kommunes, ©Kartverket

Hike 10.9 | Kjerag

To reach the start of the hike:

By car: From Stavanger take the E39 south towards Kristiansand. Just after leaving Ålgård, turn left along Fv450 towards Sirdal. Follow Fv450 for approximately 72km, until you reach a T-junction at Sinnes. Turn left here along Rv 975 (Sirdalsveien) towards Sirdal/Setesdal. After about 14 km, turn left along Rv 986 (Lyseveien, later Fv500) towards Lysefjord. The car park is approximately 25 km along this narrow, winding road, on the left hand side just before the series of hairpin bends down into Lysefjord begins.
Parking here is not free, and at the time of writing was 200NOK per car.

Other ways to reach the start of this hike: Although no scheduled bus services come to the start of this hike, during the summer season various tour operators offer bus or bus and ferry trips here, with enough time allowed to do the hike and possibly enjoy some refreshments at the cafe afterwards. At the time of writing, there were bus tours as well as trips that combine bus transport with a cruise along Lysefjord either before or after the hike. For details of tour operators, please see the Appendix.

Hike Description

This trail is very well marked with signposts and red T-markers

NB: This trail is well marked. However, there are literally hundreds of cairns along the trail, and also many side-trails created by people exploring the area. Care is needed to remain on the correct trail!

From the car park, follow the marked route up the slope. The trail crosses bare rock, which can be slippery when wet or if your boots are covered in mud. Use the chains that are bolted into the rock as necessary. This slope rises steeply, and soon there are views of the hamlet of Lysebotn far below.

The trail briefly descends **(1)**, and then continues steeply up again. From the top of this second rise, there may be more glimpses of the fjord so far beneath you, before descending a short, steep slope into a valley. At the bottom of the valley is a trail junction **(2)**: turn right (signposted Kjeragbolten) and continue up the slope.

Kjerag | Hike 10.9

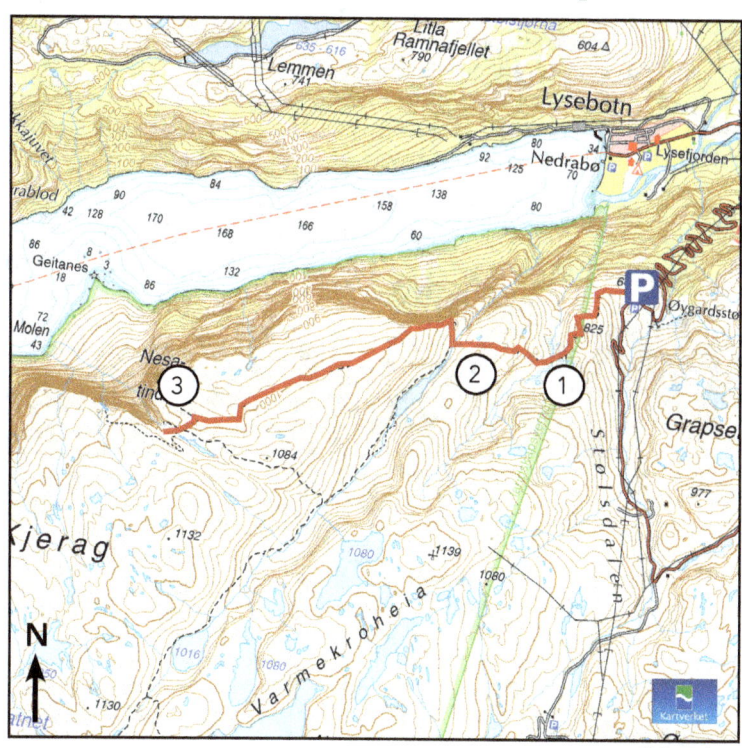

© Kartverket

The steep section gradually flattens out, and there is an almost level section before the trail turns to cross a gulley. It continues uphill for approximately half a kilometre to reach a large summit cairn with a number of signposts (3).

The trail to Kjeragbolten turns away from the edge of Lysefjord: it is almost a U-turn. Follow the T-markers to the edge of a gulley and turn right, joining a stream as the trail progresses down it. By now it is possible to see Kjeragbolten, stuck in the crevice as it has been for thousands of years. Take time here to appreciate the stunning surroundings.

When you are ready, return the way you came to the car park.

Longer trips are possible from Kjerag. From the path junction at (2), there is a marked trail to the STF cabin at Langavatn. From here,

Around the Lysefjord

Hike 10.9 | Kjerag

there are more possibilities, including trails to the STF cabin and other facilities at Flørli and from there to the STF cabin at Skåpet, by which time you have traversed the whole south side of Lysefjord. Many people complete this traverse in the other direction, beginning at Skåpet, taking in the Flørli Steps (hike 10.8) and finishing spectacularly with Kjerag, and then a cruise on the ferry from Lysefjord back to Stavanger.

The cafe at Øygardstøl
This cafe has to have one of the best views in Rogaland! Perched on the steep side of Lysefjord, the cafe has a viewing platform as well as tables with views. It is open all day during the summer season.

Appendix:
Useful Resources

General information on hiking/hillwalking can be found in many books, magazines and on the Internet. Therefore in this Appendix we will limit ourselves to provide hikers with information specific to hiking in the Stavanger region.

Weather information:
www.yr.no and www.storm.no are the best local websites. They have information in English too. When looking up places in Norway, bear in mind that the same place name can refer to many different places around the country. Reversely, spelling of a single location can vary as well, depending on locally spoken dialect.

Road information:

For information on roads, road closures or other relevant information related to road infrastructure: vegvesen.no and look for 'trafikkmeldinger'. You can even sign up to receive information via SMS to your phone (in Norwegian) for selected roads.

For information on public transport and ferry services in Rogaland consult:

www.kolumbus.no for bus and ferry information in the region and the city islands around Stavanger.
www.norled.no for ferry services. You will find some of the services operated by Norled (such as the Ryfylke and Finnøy ferries) listed on the Kolumbus website, but the Norled web page gives links to these and also information about the other cruises that they offer in the area.

www.rodne.no offers cruise & hike trips in the summer months for hikes 10.4 (Gryteknuten), 10.1 (Preikestolen), 10.3 (Moslifjellet), 10.9 (Kjerag) and 10.8 (the Flørli 4444 steps).

For information about the Lysefjord hikes:

The website www.preikestolenbasecamp.com gives a wealth of information about the facilities and activities in the Preikestolen area, including how to get there and the various accommodation options available. This will help you to get to (or from) hikes 10.1 (Preikestolen), 10.2 (Fantapytten), 10.3 (Moslifjellet), and 10.4 (Gryteknuten).

www.florli.no is a great resource for accommodation, recreational facilities and access to Flørli hamlet (hike 10.8, Flørli steps).

The Stavanger Basejumping club offers transfer services between Øygardstøl and Lysebotn in the summer season (hike 10.9, Kjerag). They also hire out recreational equipment. For information see www.sbkbase.com.

At the end of the Lysefjord you will find Lysefjordenlodge, the cabin of the Stavanger Hiking Association. For information see **www.lysefjordenlodge.dnt.no**, should you want to stay over after your adventure on the Kjeragbolten (hike 10.9) or venture into the mountains beyond.

If the Lysefjord chapter hikes leave you wanting more and longer routes, there is the option for hiking all the way around the Lysefjord. For more information consider the Cicerone guide '**Hiking in Norway - South, the 10 best multi-day treks**' by our author Ute Koninx. There you will find everything you need to plan a multi-day adventure around many areas in Southern Norway, including the Lysefjord.

For information on maps of Norway and hiking maps:

www.norgeskart.no as well as www.norgeskart.no/turkart; most mapping data in Norway can be used and downloaded free of charge and it is possible to create your own hiking map with the tools on this website. We strongly advise that you take a map along when hiking.

For information on even more hikes in Rogaland:

www.ut.no provides Norway-wide information on outdoor activities, grading and planning of hikes, maps etc.

www.stf.no, the local Stavanger Hiking Association, is constantly evolving its services and information to make it easier to go out and enjoy the outdoors for both its members and the general public. In the last couple of years there has been an increased focus on accessibility of the outdoors by public transport. The network is increasing every season, so it is worthwhile keeping an eye on their website. The information is currently only available in Norwegian (med buss og båt till fjells), but this might change in the future.

The Stavanger Hiking Association also offers guided walks and hikes, some of which are offered with English speaking guides. They also have a number of private cabins in their care, which are available for members to hire for overnight stays. The cabins are locked, and the keys are collected upon reservation from the Stavanger Hiking Association (Stavanger Turistforening, or STF in Norwegian) shop in Stavanger. This is at Olav V's Gate 18, telephone 51 84 0200. One of these cabins is Flørlistølen, a former hill farm. A stay here would combine very well with the Flørli Steps, Hike 10.8.

www.dnt.no is the Norwegian Hiking/Trekking Association's website with information about the 20,000 km of marked trails in the country and much, much more.

The Norwegian Mountain Cabins

In this book we present hikes to just a small number of the 500 mountain cabins that are maintained by the Norwegian Trekking Association (DNT) through their local affiliates. Many like Tomannsbu (Hike 9.10), Kvitlen (Hike 9.9), Viglesdalen (Hike 9.7), and Flørli (Hike 10.8) can be visited on a day trip, but would also invite for an overnight stay. Others, such as Flørlistølen (Hike 10.8), may be rented privately. Visitors to the Preikestolen area could choose to stay at Preikestolen BaseCamp and complete the hikes in the area (hikes 10.1 through 10.4) on consecutive days.

There are three types of cabins/huts. The cabins typically have a variety of sleeping facilities, from two- and four-bed bedrooms to attics where mattresses lie next to each other. Staffed cabins offer breakfast and dinner and may have indoor showers and toilets. The self-service cabins have everything a hiker needs to make their own food, including a pantry from which the guest can pick and pay as needed.

The no-service cabins still have all the kitchen equipment, but might be more basic in their sleeping quarters and have no pantry. This means you would have to bring all food along.

In addition there are a number of private cabins that can be rented separately by DNT members.

Members of the Trekking Association pay reduced fees on all services and get preferential treatment at busy times. For some cabins it is now also possible to reserve beds in specific rooms, provided you arrive early enough, preferably before 7pm. This is to encourage families to go out to cabins together knowing they will have a guaranteed place to sleep (everybody that comes to the cabin is able to stay, but is not guaranteed a bed or mattress - in very busy times hikers might have to sleep on the floor or in the living room).

The www.dnt.no English website has excellent information on all the details for planning a stay. To check out the various huts, **visit www.ut.no** where each cabin is featured on its own separate page.

Allemannsretten - The right to roam

In Norway everyone has unrestricted right of access to the countryside, including the national parks. This ancient custom has been set out by legislation since 1957, and ensures that everybody can enjoy nature on equal terms. The right is based on the consideration and respect for nature and allows anybody to put up a tent or sleep under the stars for one night anywhere in the countryside, near lakes, on beaches, in forest or in the mountains as long as one keeps out of cultivated fields or lay-bys and stays away at least 150m from the nearest house or cabin. One may pick berries, flowers and mushrooms for own consumption (with the exception of some parts in northern Norway where cloudberries are protected) as well as fish for saltwater fish for own use (though fishing in lakes or streams requires a permit!). For more information on this right see also: www.visitnorway.com

One of your most important responsibilities: outdoor toilet etiquette

If you enjoy many of the hikes in this book (and we hope that you will), sooner or later you will find yourself in the position of needing to go to the toilet when you are far, far away from any facilities. The Norwegians are very pragmatic about this: they expect you to do what you need to do, but *not in a way that makes life unpleasant for those who come after you!*

This means that you will need to step a good distance from the path, where nobody will easily see you. Anything that you wouldn't want to step in yourself must be well buried or removed from the hill. Don't leave toilet paper out in the wild. It will blow away into someone's path before it decomposes (if it ever decomposes in the high, wild, and fragile ecosystems of the mountains).

Where facilities do exist, please use them, and contribute to their maintenance via the local parking charges.

Car Park Locations via What3Words

What3words is a quick and simple way to find, share and save a location and increasingly works with other navigation systems, some of them even using voice recognition. There is also an app that can be downloaded for free. We use the English UK words.

While our descriptions should get you to the start of your hike by just using the book and without the need for phone connectivity or a navigation system, there could always be a reason for you to find a different way. This could be roadworks, road closures due to unforeseen circumstances or events, or if you are simply coming from a different direction than Stavanger city centre. Here we share the what3words of every parking lot for the hikes in our book.

Chapter 6: Urban Fresh Air and Sunday Waffles

Hike Number	Title	What 3 words (English UK)
Hike 6.1	Lille Stokkavatn and Byhaug Cafe	///remarks.precautions.secures
Hike 6.2	The Kvernevik Coast	///typhoon.nest.firelight
Hike 6.3	Madlasandnes	///volcano.damp.shins
Hike 6.4	Sørmarka and Ullandhaug Tarn	///snores.props.blossom
Hike 6.5	The Viste Coastline	///insurance.staging.communal
Hike 6.6	Mariero to Jåtta	///tweaked.fronted.cutaway
Hike 6.7	Store Stokkavatn	///waxing.buns.clay
Hike 6.8	Hålandsvatnet	///typhoon.nest.firelight
Hike 6.9	The Arboretum and Steinfjellet	///sleepless.detriment.flames
Hike 6.10	Orre Frilufshuset and Beach	///sling.jumbo.fancied
Hike 6.11	Hå Gamle Prestegard to Obrestad Havn	///warrior.utensil.movie

Chapter 7: Shorter Hikes, Stunning Scenery

Hike Number	Title	What 3 words (English UK)
Hike 7.1	The Lundesnes Tour	///keepers.safe.tunes
Hike 7.2	Around Vassøy	///honey.takeover.ashes
Hike 7.3	The Tungenes Peninsula	///housework.hint.beaten
Hike 7.4	Hellestø	///resembles.jams.missions
Hike 7.5	Reianes	///gifts.interviewer.juggler
Hike 7.6	Røssdalen	///strapping.wells.chief
Hike 7.7	Ogna to Brusand	///pinging.juggler.observe
Hike 7.8	Frøylandsvatnet	///bulge.flickers.noting
Hike 7.9	Synesvarden	///soft.starring.constants

Chapter 8: The Way to the Top: Local Hills and Fantastic Views

Hike Number	Title	What 3 words (English UK)
Hike 8.1	Dalsnuten	///toasters.sings.sanded
Hike 8.2	Vårlivarden	///windpipe.galaxy.scuba
Hike 8.3	Skjørestadfjellet	///landlady.ruling.footsteps
Hike 8.4	Lifjell	///landlady.ruling.footsteps
Hike 8.5	Bjørndalsfjellet	///toasters.sings.sanded
Hike 8.6	Storaberget	///relieves.powering.exhale
Hike 8.7	Eikefjellet	///aims.breached.pasting
Hike 8.8	Øykjafjellet	///satellite.changed.sailor
Hike 8.9	Undeknuten	///cracker.spit.revamping
Hike 8.10	Rennesøy Hodet	///frostbite.valve.latches
Hike 8.11	Vårlivarden (longer route)	///soonest.immune.solution

Chapter 9: Longer Days and Overnight Adventures

Hike Number	Title	What 3 words (English UK)
Hike 9.1	Reinaknuten	///accordion.relieves.friday
Hike 9.2	Storaberget (longer route)	///relieves.powering.exhale
Hike 9.3	Bynuten	///slung.anode.drop
Hike 9.4	Selvigstakken	///slung.anode.drop
Hike 9.5	Vådlandsknuten	////hardly.pollution.muted
Hike 9.6	Manåfossen and Månedalen	///girder.fires.intrigues
Hike 9.7	Viglesdalen	////blame.seriously.look
Hike 9.8	Vinjakula	///spit.delays.elated
Hike 9.9	Kvitlen	///jeeps.operating.talent
Hike 9.10	Tomannsbu	///bounding.nervy.riding

Chapter 10: Around the Lysefjord

Hike Number	Title	What 3 words (English UK)
Hike 10.1	Preikestolen	///paler.bulges.premiums
Hike 10.2	Fantapytten	///stint.brave.shudders
Hike 10.3	Moslifjellet	///paler.bulges.premiums
Hike 10.4	Gryteknuten	///paler.bulges.premiums
Hike 10.5	Sokkaknuten	///outnumber.yelled.relate
Hike 10.6	Uburen	///ranches.anchors.generally
Hike 10.7	Sollifjellet	///eggshell.snap.braced
Hike 10.8	The Flørli Steps	///surnames.ghost.shortens
Hike 10.9	Kjerag	///list.sunshine.loafing

About the authors

Ute Koninx

Ute fell in love with the Norwegian outdoors whilst living and working in Stavanger between 2009-2015. The idea for a hiking guide of this wonderful region grew out of her own experiences as well as conversations with visitors, travellers and fellow hikers. Whilst she currently does not live in Norway, she returns whenever she can to guide, hike, ski and kayak. Ute has also written a guidebook to long-distance treks, "Hiking in Norway - South", and hosts iventureout.com.

Rosslyn Nicholson

Ros lived in the Stavanger area for a total of seven years. An avid hiker and outdoor enthusiast for most of her life, she has climbed mountains in the Highlands of Scotland and the Pyrenees, hiked multi-day trails in England and Scotland and completed shorter hikes on three continents. She has toured the Scottish coast by bicycle and the Alaskan coast by kayak. She now lives in Aberdeen, where she has written a book of local city walks, "Exploring Aberdeen", and she often returns to the Stavanger region to hike.

Acknowledgements

This book was our brainchild, but it would not have appeared without the help and support of many others. We are immensely grateful to everyone who encouraged, helped and supported us along the way.

In the beginning, we were unsure how to distil our ideas into a coherent form. Many thanks to Per Gunnar Hettervik of NCE Tourism, Gunhild Vevik of Regionen Stavanger, and Finn Bakke (author), who shared their insights and knowledge. Inge Tone Ødegård and Randi Mannsåker from INN Rogaland, and Wenche Hansen from Guidecompaniet encouraged us from the start: we would like to thank them for their enthusiasm for the project and ideas.

Our families have helped us in so many ways. Thank you to Jean-Paul, Lisa, and Felix Koninx, and Hugh and Hazel Nicholson for coming on all those hikes, help, suggestions, proof-reading, endless patience and allowing us to use your photos. We couldn't have done it without you!

We were lucky to have friends who contributed wonderful ideas or companionship as we discussed the project. Thank you to Maureen Jones, Ida Pedersen, Lee McKenna, Glaemy Briceno, the Shulkin Family, the Eden Family, the Weiss Family, and the Minsaas Family in particular.

For this second edition, we would like to thank the company what3words for allowing the use of their unique geolocation system to refer to the starts of the hikes.

This edition would not have been possible without several visits to Stavanger; thank you once again to Wendy and Tor Minsaas for their generosity and hospitality.

www.ingramcontent.com/pod-product-compliance
Lightning Source LLC
Chambersburg PA
CBHW070644120526
44590CB00013BA/838